ENTREPRENEURSHIP
AND ECONOMIC GROWTH IN
CHINA

editors

Ting Zhang
University of Baltimore, USA

Roger R Stough
George Mason University, USA

ENTREPRENEURSHIP
AND ECONOMIC GROWTH IN
CHINA

 World Scientific

NEW JERSEY • LONDON • SINGAPORE • BEIJING • SHANGHAI • HONG KONG • TAIPEI • CHENNAI

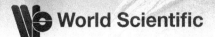

Published by

World Scientific Publishing Co. Pte. Ltd.
5 Toh Tuck Link, Singapore 596224
USA office: 27 Warren Street, Suite 401-402, Hackensack, NJ 07601
UK office: 57 Shelton Street, Covent Garden, London WC2H 9HE

British Library Cataloguing-in-Publication Data
A catalogue record for this book is available from the British Library.

ENTREPRENEURSHIP AND ECONOMIC GROWTH IN CHINA

ISBN 978-981-4273-36-7

In-house Editors: Sandhya Venkatesh/Divya Srikanth

Typeset by Stallion Press
Email: enquiries@stallionpress.com

Printed in Singapore.

Contents

Editors' Note

This book is dedicated to Prof. Kingsley Haynes, who has been a constant inspirational force behind the writing of several chapters of this book and who is now on sick leave. We wish him a smooth recovery. This book is offered to readers who are interested in growth, development and future of entrepreneurship in China. We would like to express our deepest gratitude to the contributing authors of this book. We also express our gratitude to the book's reviewers, who have immensely contributed to the high quality of the content. Last, but not the least, special thanks are due to the faculty members of the George Mason University School of Public Policy, who have guided and motivated the research behind several chapters of this book.

Ting Zhang
Roger R. Stough
September 2012

About the Editors

Ting Zhang

Ting Zhang is a Research Assistant Professor at Jacob France Institute, Merrick School of Business, University of Baltimore. Her research specializations include labor, entrepreneurship, regional economy, and aging. She is currently a principal investigator in several national and local labor economic research projects involving the use of administrative records. She has been a winner of the Kauffman Dissertation Fellowship Award and was a finalist at the Charles Tiebout Prize for Regional Science, the US Department of Labor Employment & Training Administration Research Fellowship Award, Public Policy Paper Competition by Virginia Department of Transportation, and other awards, grants, and fellowships. She is a published author of books and academic journal articles. One of her books, *Elderly Entrepreneurship in an Aging US Economy* (World Scientific, 2008) was recently reviewed by *The Gerontologist*. Dr. Zhang conducts research at The Jacob France Institute and teaches at the Merrick School of Business. She previously taught at University of Maryland, Baltimore County and conducted research at George Mason University, the World Bank, the Urban Institute, and the Council of Graduate Schools.

Roger R. Stough

Roger R. Stough is the Vice President for Research & Economic Development; President, George Mason Intellectual Properties (GMIP); and University Professor and Eminent Scholar at George Mason University. His research specializations include leadership and entrepreneurship in regional economic development, regional economic modeling, and transport analysis and planning. During the past decade, Dr. Stough was heavily involved in the development of research entrepreneurship training and education programs, including advising enterprise development and incubation centers in China and India. His publication record includes many scholarly and professional publications and more than 30 books, with sponsored research and matching awards totaling more than $80 million from a variety of sources in the US and abroad. He has supervised and/or participated in numerous Ph.D. dissertation committees and his students hold various positions around the world, including professorial and leadership posts in universities, government agencies, corporations, think tanks, and in international donor agencies. Dr. Stough served as President of the Regional Science Association International (RSAI) (2007–2008) and has been the Joint Editor-in-Chief of the *Annals of Regional Science* (1984–2010). He also holds a variety of other editorial positions. He is also the President of the Technopolicy Network (TPN), a global membership organization that promotes the use of science and technology in the development process. He is a Fellow of the Western Regional Science Association and a Fellow of the Regional Science Association International, the highest professional recognitions of these organizations. He also directed the Mason Enterprise Center, the National Center for ITS Deployment Research (until 2007) and the National Center for Transport and Regional Economic Development.

List of Contributors

Zoltán J. Ács
Center for Entrepreneurship and Public Policy
School of Public Policy
George Mason University
3351 Fairfax Drive
MS 3B1 Arlington, VA 22201, USA
zacs@gmu.edu

Shaoming Cheng
Department of Public Administration
Florida International University
11200 SW 8th Street, Miami, FL 33199, USA
scheng@fiu.edu

Jian Gao
Department of Innovation and Entrepreneurship
School of Economics and Management
Tsinghua University, Beijing 100084, China
gaoj@sem.tsinghua.edu.cn

Mark Leipnik
Department of Geography and Geology
Sam Houston State University, TX 77340, USA
geo_mrl@shsu.edu

Huaqun Li
Regional Economic Models, Inc.
433 West Street, Amherst MA 01002, USA
huaqunli@gmail.com

Yanchun Liu
International Trade Section
Georgetown Economic Services LLC
3050 K Street Northwest, Washington, DC 20007, USA
yliu@georgetowneconomics.com

Haifeng Qian
Maxine Goodman Levin College of Urban Affairs
Cleveland State University
2121 Euclid Avenue
Cleveland, OH 44115, USA
h.qian@csuohio.edu

Shi Shude
Department of Innovation and Entrepreneurship
School of Economics and Management
Tsinghua University, Beijing 100084, China
shishd.04@sem.tsinghua.edu.cn

Chunpu Song
Milliman
71 S. Wacker Drive, 31st Floor
Chicago, IL 60606, USA
schunpu@gmail.com

Roger R. Stough
George Mason University
4400 University Drive, MS 6D5
Fairfax, VA 22030, USA
rstough@gmu.edu

Jiamin Wang
School of Public Policy
George Mason University
3351 Fairfax Drive, Arlington VA 22201, USA
jwangd@masonlive.gmu.edu

Emily Xiaoxia Wang
Global Manufacturing, Agribusiness and Services
International Finance Corporation
2121 Pennsylvania Avenue NW, Washington, DC 20433, USA
xwang7@ifc.org

Xinyue Ye
Center for Regional Development & School of Earth
   Environment, and Society
Bowling Green State University
Bowling Green, OH 43403-0187, USA
xye@bgsu.edu

Junbo Yu
School of Administration
Jilin University
2699 Qianjin Street, Changchun City
Jilin Province 130012, China
junbo_yu@jlu.edu.cn

Junyang Yuan
School of Public Policy
George Mason University
3351 Fairfax Drive
Arlington, VA 22201, USA
yjunyang@gmu.edu

Ting Zhang
Jacob France Institute
Merrick School of Business
University of Baltimore
1420 N Charles Street, Baltimore, MD 21201, USA
tingzhangphd@gmail.com; tzhang@ubalt.edu

List of Figures and Tables

Entrepreneurship and Economic Growth in China

Table 4.3.   Results of unit root test and co-integration test for variables in production function   91

Table 4.4.   Results of DGMM and SGMM estimation to dynamic multi-input production model   93

Figure 4.2.   Roadmap of Malmquist TFP index decomposition   94

Figure 4.3.   Regional efficiency distribution of China in 1979   95

Figure 4.4.   Regional efficiency distribution of China in 2001   96

Figure 4.5.   Regional entrepreneurship capital distribution of China in 2001   97

Table 4.5.   Summarization of technical efficiency (TE) and Entrepreneurship capital (Entrecap) at provincial level in China, 1996–2004   98

Table 4.6.   Results of canonical correlation analysis for technical efficiency and entrepreneurship capital at provincial level in China, 1996–2004   98

Table 5.1.   Nominal and real GDP in China   107

Figure 5.1.   Real GDP of China: 1978–2006   110

Figure 5.2.   Real GDP growth rate: 1978–2006   110

Figure 5.3.   Real GDP growth rate: 1991–2006   111

Figure 5.4.   Regional outputs in China (1985)   112

Table 5.2.   Top 10 countries with highest GDP in 2002   112

Figure 5.5.   Regional outputs in China (1995)   113

Figure 5.6.   Regional output in China (2006)   113

Figure 5.7.   Regional output of top and bottom three provinces   114

Figure 5.8.   Percentages of regional output of top and bottom three provinces to national output   115

Figure 5.9.   Distribution of regional output in 1985   115

Entrepreneurship and Economic Growth in China

Part I
Introduction and Historical Background

Chapter 1

Introduction

Ting Zhang*, Roger R. Stough[†], and Chunpu Song[‡]

*University of Baltimore,
†George Mason University
‡Milliman

1.1. Introduction

China's emerging economy is drawing increasing world attention. China, as an outstanding representative in the world of transitional economies, has been intensively studied for its remarkable economic success as well as its institutional development and its resulting inadequacies. With overwhelming world attention focused on China's market, entrepreneurship in China is often questioned, simultaneously evoking widespread curiosity. Foreigners interested in investing and doing business in China wonder about China's business and entrepreneurial environment. For China and the Chinese, further development of entrepreneurship is required to improve China's long-term economic prosperity by building sustainable core competencies. In the meantime, globalization and marketization in China make private ownership increasingly cherished. Ownership of businesses and creation of something new therefore have become the dream of many Chinese people.

The concept of entrepreneurship has many connotations. However, the basic notion is most often related to channeling a business idea into the market. The market is naturally the "invisible" dominating hand.

However, in a transitional economy like China, where government control has significant influence in economic activities, the market often functions differently when compared to more fully developed countries. This situation raises many questions, such as: does entrepreneurship actually exist in China? If so, is entrepreneurship in China different from that in the Western world? Does entrepreneurship in China drive economic growth? What are the factors that affect entrepreneurship and business performance in China? What are the policy implications of developing entrepreneurship and business in China? These questions are routinely posed by those intrigued about the concept of entrepreneurship in China.

This book interprets entrepreneurship in China particularly from the perspectives of economic growth and related theories, hence the title "*Entrepreneurship and Economic Growth in China*." The book first introduces the history of entrepreneurship and entrepreneurship policy development in modern China in Part I. Then, drawing upon economic growth theories, the book presents the theoretical framework in Part II. Part III examines the role of entrepreneurship in China's economic growth. Part IV showcases and examines China's entrepreneur financing, followed by Part V, which investigates several key factors that are thought to drive entrepreneurship development in China. In Part VI, two entrepreneurship development case studies are presented. In summary, the book encompasses history in Part I; theory in Part II; three broad areas of entrepreneurship measurement, i.e., the impact of entrepreneurship, in Part III; entrepreneurial performance in Part IV; the determinants of entrepreneurship in Part V; and finally a case study in Part VI.

Entrepreneurship in China has several unique characteristics. First, its market condition allows for a relatively strong non-market dimension of entrepreneurship. Second, its political environment created town-and-village enterprises (TVEs), which was an early form of non-market entrepreneurship in modern China from 1978 to 1992. TVEs are viewed as collective enterprises that enjoy much clearer and articulated support from the state than private-owned enterprises because their identities are conceptually more related to non-private ideology (Che and Qian, 1998). Third,

China's high degree of institutional uncertainty resulted in the creation of entrepreneurs with a "red hat".[1] This "red hat" helped to ensure similar treatment that the state and collective enterprises enjoyed, thus offsetting the potential risks and costs that might result from the unstable trajectory of state policy toward the private sector (Yang, 2007).

Strong government influence penetrates every aspect of entrepreneurship in China, similar to many other transitional economies, particularly those which were formerly centrally planned economies. In China, the legacy of socialism, combined with a long centrally controlled yet multiethnic history, resulted in a culture that values strong family ties , a strong communal concept, and the virtue of prioritizing collective interests and benefits. The Chinese Government often embodies authority, trust, and accumulation of resources. Consequently, public universities and schools hire the best teachers, require higher entrance scores, issue official credentials, and are generally believed to offer better quality education. Furthermore, public hospitals are staffed with the best doctors and are the preferred medical institutions of the Chinese because of their trusted services. Market orientation and globalization is slowly changing this culture; however, culture always occur over a period of time.

Despite the presence of a strong government, China's economy is not under absolute government control. The market plays an increasingly important role, even more important than is realized outside of China. The "red hat" enterprise strategy has a true private identity yet is registered under public shelter. Even China's largest public venture capital program does not appear to have crowded out private sources (see Chapter 6).

Entrepreneurship in China also exhibits significant regional disparities, as illustrated in Chapters 2 and 8. These disparities are usually found in wealth, stage of development and access, and advanced education. At the same time, the national policy is designed to reduce these differences.

---

[1]The "red hat" enterprises allowed businesses to register as public-owned organizations, thus concealing their intrinsic private ownership.

1.2. Structure of the Book and Content Summaries of the Chapters

Part I of the book begins with this introductory chapter and concludes with a historical review of entrepreneurship development in modern China in Chapter 2. This review is presented in three parts:

1. 1978–1992, the emergence of private enterprise
2. 1992–2000, rapid growth of the non-public sector and the decrease of the relative importance of state-owned enterprises (SOEs)
3. 2000–present, increasingly supportive and encouraging policies designed and implemented to channel and focus private investment.

Some entrepreneurial characteristics specific to China are also revealed and discussed in this chapter.

Part II consists of Chapter 3, which examines the theoretical landscape, thus reviewing the entrepreneurship and regional economic growth literature. It then applies the relevant theories and common global entrepreneurial activity measures to China, which are in turn used to benchmark China's entrepreneurship development. Starting from the importance of small businesses, the chapter adds other elements from the entrepreneurship and economic growth literature. This analysis begins with the examination of the intellectual path from agglomeration theory to the new growth theory and then incorporates concepts from the Jaffe–Feldman–Varga model and Knowledge Spillover Theory of Entrepreneurship (i.e., the theory of endogenous entrepreneurship). These theoretical components are used to build the conceptual foundation of the book. The new growth theory and the new economics of innovation are used to explain how entrepreneurship facilitates the spillover of knowledge and then in turn propels endogenous economic growth. Moreover, the chapter also uses the Global Entrepreneurship Index to measure the general level of productive entrepreneurship in China, with the main conclusion that China functions significantly above the entrepreneurial inspirational sub-index but below the activity sub-index.

Part III consists of Chapters 4 and 5 and focuses on the impact of entrepreneurship and innovation on economic development. Chapter 4 examines two major interpretations of the relationship between entrepreneurship and economic growth, interpreting entrepreneurship either as an endogenous production factor, like capital and labor, or as a factor for exogenous technical conditions. These approaches are used to incorporate entrepreneurship into the production process and to propose revisions to current approaches based on China's provincial data. In particular, this chapter suggests that international empirical study on the contribution of entrepreneurship to economic growth is far from satisfactory. The empirical analysis built on the growth theories outlined in this chapter uses a dynamic panel data approach to address stationarity concerns, which demonstrates that feasible models investigating the connection between entrepreneurship and economic growth tend to be country-specific. It is then concluded that the analysis demonstrates the uniqueness of China's entrepreneurship and economic growth. This is the first chapter in Part III that explains the role of entrepreneurship in China's economic growth.

Different from most other countries, SOEs play key roles in China's economy and serve as technology innovation hubs. In Part III, Chapter 5 examines the role SOEs play in China's economic growth. China's GDP and the telecommunication sector developed rapidly in the recent past. In Chapter 5, GDP and telecommunication infrastructure (particularly teledensity) development are argued to be related due to similar development trends and regional spatial patterns. The analysis demonstrates that together they have contributed to China's fast economic growth, thus providing support for a conclusion. The chapter illustrates the regional disparity in economic growth as well as in SOEs and the contribution of the private sector to output.

In Part V, both Chapters 6 and 7 introduce China's entrepreneurship financing through public or government venture capital and through the private financial market. Chapter 6 is an evaluation of China's largest public venture investment program, Innofund. Chapter 7 examines the private financing market.

Innofund stimulates innovative SME development and induces less market speculation behavior such as rent seeking due to strong government control and evaluation. Based on Chapter 6, China's Innofund does not appear to have crowded out private sources of investment financing but, at the same time, it has not fully achieved its expected catalytic effect at the local level. Further, it has had a stronger effect than local governments in encouraging awardees to contribute more of their own capital and has demonstrated this to be an important source of support for many innovative technology- and science-driven small- and medium-sized enterprises. Based on the findings and experience from other countries that have a more mature market economy, the author suggests that the Innofund should strengthen enforcement of the matching ratio requirement for local governments, further fine-tune the relative proportions of the funds operations and local government funding for different technology-based small- and medium-sized enterprises, and shift reliance from bureaucratic oversight to market infrastructure and related mechanisms.

From the perspective of private enterprise financing, corporate governance can enhance investor protection by increasing information symmetry and thus improve firm performance. In Chapter 7, this point is tested and demonstrated through stock market data. China's corporate governance format and stock market development are also reviewed and critiqued. Furthermore, the importance of the financial market in developing and fostering entrepreneurship development in China is discussed. In particular, sound corporate governance is viewed as essential for such an entrepreneurial financing mechanism to work properly in China. This research identifies a positive relationship between firm performance and corporate governance when controlling for firm size. It also notes regional disparities in corporate governance from the east to the west of China. Public companies whose controlling shareholder held state-owned legal person shares were found to have the poorest corporate governance. The chapter points out the need for stronger corporate governance policy in order for China to achieve better entrepreneurial activities and firm performance.

In a sense, Innofund actually serves as a role model for corporate governance by offering a referral service to connect funding needs of current awardees and future funding from possible private venture capital sources. Innofund also helps to catalyze the venture capital and financial institutional environment in China's entrepreneurship development.

Part VI contains four chapters that examine the driving factors to develop China's entrepreneurship. Chapter 8 empirically tests for possible factors that explain firm formation rates in China. As part of this examination, disparities between developed and lesser developed regions and disparities between two economic cycles in which the new firm formation rates differ are considered. The authors find that private wealth level, entrepreneurial culture, and human capital are all positively related to new firm formation in China. The data also show that unemployment rates are consistently and positively associated with new firm formation rates across regions and within regions.

In Chapter 9, the literature regarding diversity and innovation is discussed. A diversity index based on the *Hukou* concept is created to measure diversity in China and empirically test the impact of diversity and other factors on innovation and entrepreneurship. This study analyzes whether social diversity may influence regional entrepreneurship in China. The official residences of most Chinese are assigned to their city of birth. When a person moves to another place in China, his/her official residence stays with the original residence and is called that person's *Hukou*. Although no clear relationship is found between diversity as measured by the *Hukou* Index and entrepreneurship, the level of regional entrepreneurship is found to be highly dependent on patents per capital and human capital levels in a region. Regional innovation in China, according to this study, relies primarily on stocks of human capital and R&D and the university. The university, together with the wage level and service amenities, is also found to be indirectly associated with innovation and entrepreneurship through its effects on human capital. The effectiveness of the *Hukou* index is discussed, though this is bounded by data and measurement limitations that may have impacted the findings.

The policy, culture and institutional background, and history of China's entrepreneurship development, particularly in the private sector (i.e., non-state-owned sectors) are analyzed in Chapter 10. The author argues that China's private-sector entrepreneurs must possess skills to be institutionally and politically nimble, careful to avoid economic exploitation, and culturally sensitive in the pursuit of interpersonal harmony. They need to be highly networked to pursue both profitability and legitimacy required to maximize economic profits while at the same time minimizing political and institutional risks.

Through a comparison of cultural and entrepreneurship policy differences between the U.S. and China, Chapter 11 analyzes the cultural impacts on entrepreneurship policy. For China, the high power distance results in the dominance of governments in business and entrepreneurship policy initiatives from the national leader. Hofstede (1994) defines power distance as the extent to which less-powerful parties expect and accept the inequity of power distribution. China's high-context culture brings about the relatively insufficient explicitly written laws for entrepreneurship development and lack of a credible and accessible capital market system in the market economy. Hall (1981) describe a high-context culture as situations where most of the communication is either in the physical context or internalized in the person, and very little is in the coded, explicit, or transmitted part of the message. The collectiveness of Chinese culture results in the policy focus on large businesses, not the small businesses. These scenarios are opposite to that in the U.S., where the low power distance and the reliance on market results in the smaller role of the government or national leader for promoting entrepreneurship and the immigrant culture makes the U.S. a low-context culture and requires detailed written laws to regulate economic activities. With increasing globalization, the advent of the information age, and the nature of the market economy, the author argues that the further development of China's market economy calls for the entrepreneurship policy to integrate Western-style entrepreneurial attributes with China's unique culture perspectives.

Part V presents two case studies for entrepreneurship development in China. Chapter 12 analyzes the development path of the well-known private sector small business hub — Wenzhou, Zhejiang Province, while Chapter 13 uses a public resource approach to showcase entrepreneurship development. Wenzhou's entrepreneurship has achieved great development and success in the past three decades. This region has been driven primarily by private-owned small businesses fostered by local government, owned by local families with personal connections of a local diaspora of immigrants who serve as a nexus to the global economy and source of investment capital, trade outlets, and expertise.

Both location and non-SOEs play significant roles in the uneven regional development observed in Zhejiang. The development of private enterprises is the major reason for the rise and uneven development in Zhejiang as well as across China, particularly between the coastal periphery and interior regions of China. It is noted that a rising coastal–interior income and opportunity divide within the municipality has occurred. The authors therefore interestingly point out that this divide mirrors the larger divide between the haves and the have-nots, which is perhaps the biggest social and economic challenge in the 21st century China.

Chapter 13 reveals the rationale of initiating entrepreneurship via government expense through surveying the operation of the U.S. Mason Enterprise Center and its Virginia Procurement & Technical Assistance Program. It also summarizes the experience of the U.S. in improving long-term government performance by systematic improvements in government procurement. This study suggests a solution for Chinese government to refine their current procurement system by exploiting the already widespread business incubators to channel the distribution of government procurement contracts in a more productive way.

1.3. Policy Implications

Policy implications are proposed throughout the chapters. The findings from several chapters call for improved institutional support and changes in the policy milieu for entrepreneurship growth in China. In general, for policy makers, more streamlined and efficient flows from financial markets, creating more supportive yet well-monitored financial institutions, and allowing for more private ownership and market orientation are seen as helpful initiatives for business owners and potential entrepreneurs.

Furthermore, understanding the unique Chinese culture, economic environment, and regional disparities are viewed as the first steps for expanding the entrepreneurial arena in China. Flexibility and an understanding of the various public and private stakeholders' perspectives and goals are crucial to business success. The uniqueness of the China case not only shows the potential challenges for entrepreneurial opportunities but also reveals abundant opportunities. The dynamics between entrepreneurship and economic growth in China provides insights that can be extended to the developed world and serve as a showcase for many developing countries.

References

Che, J., and Y. Qian. (1998). Insecure property rights and government ownership of firms. *Quarterly Journal of Economics* **113**: 467–496.

Hall, E. T. (1981). *Beyond Culture*. New York: Doubleday.

Hofstede, G. (1994). *Cultures and Organizations — Intercultural Cooperation and its Importance for Survival*. London: HarperCollins Business.

Yang, K. (2007). *Entrepreneurship in China*. Hampshire: Ashgate Publishing.

Chapter 2

History and Development of Entrepreneurship in China

Huaqun Li

Regional Economic Models, Inc.

2.1. Introduction

Entrepreneurship is nearly always defined in terms of who an entrepreneur is and what the entrepreneur does (Venkataraman, 1997). Entrepreneurs have no unambiguous identities in reality but are defined by their behavior, i.e., entrepreneurial activities. Entrepreneurial activities are usually defined as creating "new combinations" in the market (Schumpeter, 1961), such as new ventures or organizations and new means–ends relationship that are believed to be able to yield a profit (Amit, Glosten, and Muller, 1993; Shane and Venkataraman, 2000). The difficulty in operationalizing the theoretical definition of entrepreneurship in reality has produced different definitions of entrepreneurship used in the literature. In this chapter, we rely on the existing literature focusing on China's entrepreneurship (Yang, 2007; Yang and Li, 2008) and refer to entrepreneurship in China as those that are new established businesses, including private start-ups and town-and-village enterprises (TVEs). Privately owned businesses include the firms held by individual households (*getihu*), with the total number of employees less than seven, and private enterprises that employ more than eight employees. Yang and Li (2008) also treat transformed state-owned enterprises (SOEs) as entrepreneurship. In this chapter, we ignore the discussion on SOEs in order to focus on the start-up concept of entrepreneurial activities.

The rapid economic growth in China after the implementation of its "Open-Door Policy" in 1978 has been witnessed by the rest of the world. This economic boom has been accompanied by the decrease of state-owned businesses and the dramatic growth of private businesses. It was reported in 2006 that the private sector accounted for about half of China's GDP (*China Statistical Yearbook*, 2007). After 30 years of sustained market-oriented deregulation and decentralization policies, domestic entrepreneurship and private business have been identified as "one of the most important driving forces behind China's rapid economic development" (Yang and Li, 2007). According to the 2007 report of Global Entrepreneurship Monitor (GEM), the Chinese government has become very supportive for new incubators and new science parks. Although some improvements are still needed, the entrepreneurial environment has become more and more friendly and accommodating. About 70% of the Chinese who were surveyed think entrepreneurship is a good career choice (GEM, 2007). It should be noted that, as a transition economy, China has spent a fair amount of time in making changes and allowing entrepreneurship to take root.

The Chinese evolutionary approach of economic transition is different from the "Big Bang" approach undertaken by Eastern Europe and former Soviet Union. China's transition from being a command-and-control economy to an economy that allows marketization and privatization has been a gradual, incremental, and experimental process. The legitimacy of private enterprises was not accepted at the beginning of the introduction of reform and openness policy. As a result, the implementation of China's reform policy created an environment where the emergence of market mechanism was accompanied by price controls and central planning, and a dominant role was played by the state and collective sector, especially in the early years of market reform. The pragmatic and experimental approach of reforming has resulted in a less-than-smooth process and the gradual realization of marketization and privatization. The observation of China's entrepreneurship development in the background of phased institutional transition provides an excellent opportunity to examine how the evolution of China's entrepreneurship responds to socio-economic factors and institutional environments. Yang and Li (2007) point out that the temporal dimension of entrepreneurship development has been largely ignored in the literature. Entrepreneurship research for the mature market economies has focused on explaining how entrepreneurial opportunities are identified in the market and what the determinants of entrepreneurship are, not only from the macro socio-economic level but also from the individual level, while entrepreneurship research in the context of transitional economies has treated the interaction between entrepreneurship and institutional evolution as an important research topic (Chang and MacMillan, 1991).

This chapter is meant to examine the history and development of entrepreneurship in China in the reform period and to clarify the stages of entrepreneurship evolution from the perspective of institutional transition. Based on the review of the history of entrepreneurship, the characteristics of China's entrepreneurship in terms of strategic choice, distribution, and dynamic change are identified.

This chapter is organized as follows, starting from the demonstration of the historical trend of entrepreneurship development using official statistics. Section 2.2 provides the basic temporal picture for private businesses. We then divide the historical development of China's entrepreneurship into four phases. The entrepreneurship trend related to the institutional environment is individually identified for each stage. Section 2.3 describes the unique characteristics of entrepreneurship in China and how they are shaped. Section 2.4 concludes the chapter.

2.2. The Stage of Market Transitions: Opportunities and Challenges for Entrepreneurship

The discussion of the history on entrepreneurship takes us to the year 1949, when the new People's Republic of China was established. However, the period from 1949 to 1978 has a negligible position in the history of entrepreneurship development. The goal of the Chinese Communist Party (CCP) was to turn China into a socialist economy. Following the ideology of collective ownership and identity, the government asserted the legitimacy of central control over the national economy. Private ownership was regarded to be incompatible with a socialist regime. By 1956, the private sectors had been transformed into SOEs in different ways during the process of eliminating capitalism. However, private entrepreneurial activities that generated personal income were never completely eliminated from the practical life during the years of socialist construction period from 1956 to 1966 (Liao and Sohmen, 2001; Tsai, 2007). During the disastrous years of Cultural Revolution (1966–1976), all private businesses were attached to a stigma of "the capitalist tails". The private sector was extremely suppressed due to the political turmoil for the rest of the Mao era.

Modern entrepreneurship in China was not unleashed until the beginning of the reform era. Table 2.1 presents data showing the growth of registered private businesses, including individual businesses with less than eight employees and private enterprises with more than eight employees in terms of the numbers of private businesses. Table 2.2 presents the growth of employees in the private sector. As indicated in Table 2.1, starting from 1979, there was a dramatic growth in individual household businesses because of the originally small base. The existing political turmoil contributed to the economic downturn of private businesses in 1989–1992. Renewed and speedy growth occurred after Deng Xiaoping's widely acclaimed speech in 1992, which centered on creating a more progressive future for China.

2.2.1. *From 1978 to 1992*

2.2.1.1. *The emergence and rise of TVEs*

The Third Plenary Session of the CCP's 11th Central Committee in 1978 marked the inception of China's reform and "opening up policy". The first step of the reform policy was the decentralization of agriculture. The command-style commune system was replaced by the household contract responsibility system, and the peasants were granted the rights to use the land and profit from it. Thus, peasants were allowed to decide what to grow and furthermore, the stipulations from this crucial new policy direction on agriculture provided for individual household business (*getihu*) to operate. The implementation of the responsibility system in rural areas had facilitated a dramatic increase in China's agricultural output, which

Table 2.1. Growth of registered private businesses, 1978–2005 (number of businesses)

Year	Individual Household (millions)	Individual Household Growth (%)	Private Enterprises (millions)	Private Enterprise Growth (%)
1978	0.3	n.a.	n.a.	n.a.
1979	0.56	86.7	n.a.	n.a.
1980	0.9	60.2	n.a.	n.a.
1981	1.83	103.8	n.a.	n.a.
1982	2.61	43	n.a.	n.a.
1983	5.9	125.7	n.a.	n.a.
1984	9.33	58.1	n.a.	n.a.
1985	11.71	25.5	n.a.	n.a.
1986	12.11	3.4	n.a.	n.a.
1987	13.73	13.3	n.a.	n.a.
1988	14.53	5.8	n.a.	n.a.
1989	12.47	−14.1	0.09	n.a.
1990	13.28	6.5	0.1	8.3
1991	14.15	6.5	0.11	9.9
1992	15.34	8.4	0.14	29.5
1993	17.67	15.2	0.24	70.4
1994	21.87	23.8	0.43	81.7
1995	25.28	15.6	0.65	51.4
1996	27.04	7	0.82	25.2
1997	28.51	5.4	0.96	17.3
1998	31.2	9.4	1.2	25
1999	31.6	1.3	1.51	25.6
2000	26.71	−18.3	1.76	17
2001	24.33	−5.8	2.03	15
2002	23.77	−2.3	2.44	20
2003	23.53	−10	3.01	23.4
2004	23.51	−0.1	3.65	21.5
2005	24.64	4.8	4.3	17.8

Source: Zhang, H., L. Ming and Z. Liang, eds., *Siying qiye lanpi shu: Zhongguo siying qiye fazhan baogao* [*Blue Book of Private Enterprises: A Report on the Development of China's Private Enterprises*], various years, Beijing: Social Sciences Academic Press.

has been confirmed by many official reports. The success in the reform initiated in the rural areas also promoted the extension of reform policies to the urban areas.

Table 2.2.   Number employed in the private sector, 1978–2005

Year	Individual Household (millions)	Individual Household Growth (%)	Private Enterprises (millions)	Private Enterprise Growth (%)
1978	0.33	n.a.	n.a.	n.a.
1979	0.68	102.4	n.a.	n.a.
1980	1.66	145.3	n.a.	n.a.
1981	2.27	37.2	n.a.	n.a.
1982	3.2	40.7	n.a.	n.a.
1983	7.46	133.3	n.a.	n.a.
1984	13.51	81	n.a.	n.a.
1985	18.32	35.6	n.a.	n.a.
1986	19.21	4.9	n.a.	n.a.
1987	21.48	11.8	n.a.	n.a.
1988	23.05	7.3	n.a.	n.a.
1989	19.41	−15.8	n.a.	n.a.
1990	20.93	7.8	1.7	n.a.
1991	22.58	7.9	1.84	8.2
1992	24.68	9.3	2.32	26.1
1993	29.39	19.1	3.73	60.8
1994	37.76	28.5	6.48	73.7
1995	46.14	22.2	9.56	47.5
1996	50.17	8.7	11.71	22.5
1997	54.42	8.5	13.5	15.3
1998	61.14	12.3	17.1	26.7
1999	62.41	2.1	20.22	18.2
2000	50.7	−18.8	24.06	19
2001	47.6	−6.1	27.14	12.8
2002	47.43	−0.4	34.09	25.6
2003	46.37	−2.2	35.96	5.5
2004	45.87	−1.1	40.69	13.1
2005	49.01	6.8	47.14	15.9

Source: Zhang, H., L. Ming and Z. Liang, eds., *Siying qiye lanpi shu: Zhongguo siying qiye fazhan baogao* [*Blue Book of Private Enterprises: A Report on the Development of China's Private Enterprises*], various years.

The direct effect of agricultural reform on entrepreneurship development in China was the rise of TVEs. The economic liberation in rural areas significantly improved labor productivity and resulted in a shortage of arable land and a surplus of labor. A wide range of unemployment problems were avoided when a large number of peasants chose not to be constrained by crop farming and began to follow other methods of farming or farming-related manufacturing. TVEs have been extolled as one of the great creations by Chinese peasants and in keeping with Chinese cultural characteristics. It has played a decisive role in rural industrialization and improving the living standard in rural areas (Chen, 2006). The success and prosperity of TVEs contributed significantly to the country's economic growth in the 1980s. By the end of the 1980s, TVEs accounted for about 20% of China's gross output (Liao and Sohmen, 2001). The annual output from TVEs grew by 28% between 1979 and 1987 (Chang and MacMillan, 1991). In the meantime, TVEs have also contributed to the national economy by creating competition with the SOEs. It can be concluded that the first generation of Chinese modern entrepreneurs emerged from the development of TVEs.

TVEs are defined as "all those rural non-state enterprise subordinate to the townships or village governments and owned and operated collectively" (Luo, Tan, and Shenkar, 1998: p. 33). Although always located in rural areas or of rural origins, TVEs can take several different forms. "From the ownership point of view, they are set up by townships, villages, several households (or partnerships), individual household (or private), or jointly by Chinese and foreign partners through shareholding mechanisms or shareholding cooperative systems" (Liang, 2006: p 235). TVEs are usually referred to as collective enterprises and thus enjoy much clearer and articulated support from the state than private-owned enterprises since it belonged to the range of non-private ideology (Che and Qian, 1998). For example, until 1981, there was a restriction for private enterprises of less than eight employees but not for TVEs at that time (Che and Qian, 1998). However, as a matter of fact, most of the TVEs were privately owned were marked as public entitles (Liang, 2006; Peng and Heath, 1996).

Although the managers of TVEs were different from authentic entrepreneurs because most of them were contractors and did not own these enterprises, many entrepreneurial characteristics were demonstrated in the development of TVEs. First, TVEs established an alliance with the local government in the form of collective enterprises to seek institutional legitimacy at the beginning stage of economic reform characterized by weak market structures (Luo, Tan, and Shenkar, 1998). The entrepreneurial spirit of local government officials in public sectors was reflected in the process of contracting out government responsibility role and was even referred to as "local government entrepreneurship" (Hubbard, 1995). Second, although local governments provided TVEs with part of the capital, markets, and land, the TVE entrepreneurs had to adapt to the market prices and costs in the pursuit of profits. On the other hand, the TVE entrepreneurs took the initiative to form an alliance with local government officials and their agents. Krug and Mehta (2004) identified this kind of ability to "form an alliance with those economic agents who possess or control the financial assets, physical assets, or specific human capital need for brokering market entry..." as the key factor in successful entrepreneurship in China. From these two viewpoints, TVEs can be regarded as the beginning of contemporary Chinese entrepreneurship. TVE entrepreneurship was the dominant form of Chinese entrepreneurship throughout the 1980s (Li and Matlay, 2006). The success of TVEs in promoting rural economic growth accelerated the transition from a centrally planned economic system to a more market-oriented economy and the concept of entrepreneurship then diffused into urban areas.

2.2.1.2. *The emergence of private enterprise*

The counterpart of the TVE entrepreneurs in urban areas is a second group of Chinese entrepreneurs who are self-employed individual business-owners. During the late 1970s, the movement of "up to mountains and down to villages"[1] in the Cultural Revolution came to an end, and hundreds of thousands of young people went back to urban areas. The huge young population could not find jobs immediately after return and expanded the number of "unoccupied idle labor" in urban areas. It was estimated that there were about 15 million unemployed people in cities

---

[1]This movement refers to a program where urban youths were sent to rural areas to be trained and educated by farmers which were viewed to be an ideologically purer class).

and towns (Yang, 2007). The party leaders perceived this high unemployment rate as a serious social problem threatening the nation's stability and solidarity. Thus, a series of government policies, which were in fact beneficial to the previously firmly constrained private businesses, were brought about to cope with the unemployment crisis. In dealing with this crisis, the central government encouraged unemployed people to undertake individual businesses in "repair, service, and handicraft industries", as illustrated by the policy of the State Administration for Industry and Commerce (Wu, 2005: p. 181). However, the release of constraints on private business was not completed in one step. At first, private businesses were limited to some specific businesses, and opening a new business required the approval of relevant government departments. In addition, hiring labor was not allowed except family members when the policy was first released. After the hot debate on "employment and exploitation" during the early 1980s (Yang, 2007), the business owners were allowed to employ seven or less employees to ensure that they were not accused of capitalist exploitation. However, the development of originally small-scale individual businesses would never remain truly individual or household. Given the situation of the economic shortage right after the Cultural Revolution, the individual businesses experienced rapid growth under the government's cautious supporting policies. The gradual expansion of household businesses from individual to privately owned enterprises served as a warning to the political leaders to maintain a balance between developing the economy and maintaining political correctness, since at that time, private businesses were not regarded as ideologically consistent with the principles of socialist nations. It was the luck of the newly booming private entrepreneurs that a tacit consent stance was adopted, as represented by Deng Xiaoping's "wait and see" approach was taken to deal with the issues regarding the nature of private businesses. In 1983, a "Three-No" policy of no promotion, no public propaganda and no crackdown was proposed to regulate the development of private enterprises (Chen, 2007: p. 6).

The tacit and ambiguous attitude toward privates business was replaced by a clearer and friendlier posture in 1987. In the 13th Party Congress, the CCP admitted that private enterprises played an important role in developing the national economy and improving people's quality of life. In 1988, as the "supplementary component of China's socialist economy", the legitimate status of private enterprises was formally established in a constitutional amendment. A more specific regulation, *The Interim Stipulations on Private Enterprises*, was released by the State Council and gave a clear definition for "private enterprises" (a for-profit organization that is owned by an individual and employs more than eight people) and provided the legal basis for private enterprises to operate. However, it was also stated that the private sector should be subject to state supervision, guidance, and control. The direct result from these encouraging policies was that, from 1988 to 1989, the number of private firms doubled (Schönleber, 2000). However, the development of private businesses was shaken by the political turmoil of 1989. It was reported that the growth rate of private enterprises dropped suddenly in the period 1989–1990 by about 50% (Schönleber, 2000). The negative perception of governments attitude toward private enterprises also came from periodic political movements, such as the campaign against spiritual pollution (1983–1984) and the "anti-bourgeois liberalization campaign" of 1987. The security of private rights was not securely guaranteed for private entrepreneurs, although there was existing written legislation. Facing such an unstable institutional environment, private enterprises were worried about policy changes in the future and reacted by taking flexible strategy choices, which are discussed in the next section.

2.2.2. From 1992 to 2000

This period witnessed the rapid growth of non-public sectors and the decrease of the relative importance of SOEs. Output from SOEs declined dramatically, from 77% in 1978 to about 28% in 1999. In the meantime, there was a rapid increase in the contribution of privately owned enterprises from zero in 1978 to over 18% in 1999. (Anderson *et al.*, 2003).

In 1992, Deng Xiaoping, who was the general architect of Chinese reform, called for deepening the transition to a socialist market economy in the famous "South Tour". Deng's southern tour assumed significant meaning because it sought out to assauge people's doubts on whether to support the development of private-owned enterprises. In the following year after his speech, the growth rate of private enterprises recorded remarkable increases (Anderson *et al.*, 2003). It seems that the signals of political acceptance sent out by the speeches of party leaders were associated with the surge of individual entrepreneurship.

Although the market mechanism as an invisible hand in economic system was emphasized relative to the economic regulation approach of command and control, according to the report of the Third Plenary Session of the 14th Party Congress, the mainstay status of the public sector should still be maintained at the national level. This meant that private businesses still did not enjoy the same treatment as those in the public sector, although private sector was already a legitimate element of the national economy at that time. The 15th Party Congress Meeting recognized the legal status of private enterprises as one of parity with the public sector in 1997, and a 1999 constitutional amendment acknowledged that non-public enterprises are an important part of a socialist market economy.

After introducing the concept of a socialist market economy, the government carried out a series of reform policies that came to effect and provided the necessary foundations for the development of both SOEs and private firms such as fiscal and tax reform, company law, and foreign exchange reform (Anderson *et al.*, 2003)

2.2.3. *From 2000 to Present*

The year 2000 was the beginning of the third stage of China's entrepreneurship development. Increasingly supportive and encouraging policies have been issued to channel private investment. In 2002, Zeng Peiyan, Minister of the State Development Planning Commission, asserted in a public speech that the government will "eliminate all restrictive and discriminatory regulations that are not friendly towards private investment and private economic development in taxes, land use, business start-ups, and imports and exports". This statement meant that the government was ready to treat public and private business equally.

Chen (2007) pointed out that the small- and medium-sized enterprises (SMEs) promotion law promulgated in 2002 marked the start of a new era for the development of SMEs. Most of the SMEs in China are non-public entrepreneurial activities. Furthermore, China's accession to WTO in November 2001 symbolized that entrepreneurship in China would be more influenced by global competition. Since the 1990s, more than 75% of the added value in industrial output came from SMEs, and the private sector was reported to account for over two-thirds of industrial output (Chen, 2007; Tsai, 2007). On the whole, this period is characterized by a rapid growth of modern entrepreneurship in China. The role of entrepreneurship in promoting economic growth, expanding employment, and stimulating technology innovation had become less bounded by the constraints from institutional ambiguities.

Entrepreneurship was once interpreted as an occupation for idle people who could not find other jobs and for those with criminal records (Nair, 1996). The social status of entrepreneurs has improved significantly in light of an altered policy orientation, exposure to the global market and Western values, and also the success stories of a large number of entrepreneurs. Private entrepreneurs were even invited to enter the Party to participate in the management of state affairs by the Party leader Jiang Zemin in a speech celebrating the Party's 79th anniversary (Chen, 2007). The National People's Congress amended the constitution to protect "the lawful rights and interest of the private sector of the economy". This new legislation indicates that Chinese government policy characterized by volatile attitudes toward private business is changing. However, it would be expected that the actual implementation of private property protection will lag due to its systemic implications for China's political and judicial situation (Tsai, 2007). While considerable progress and improvements continue in today's China, it is important to note that entrepreneurial activities remain subject to infant legislation and unpublished regulations.

2.3. Chinese Characteristics in Entrepreneurship

2.3.1. *Disguised Entrepreneurship: Red Hat Strategy*

The earlier review about the different stages of entrepreneurship development reveals that private businesses founded in the early stages of the market transition suffered from a more unstable and hostile environment than those established later. The legal status of private enterprises with more than eight employees was not admitted until 1988. Before 1988, the registered private business only included individual household businesses. In reality, there were many private enterprises with more than eight employees running disguised as collective enterprises or public businesses. The literature on TVEs revealed that a considerable portion of the TVEs and urban collective-owned enterprises were in fact privately owned (He, 2000; Naughton, 1994). In the early years of market transition, the private firms took the popular "red hat" strategy, whereby they registered themselves as public-owned organizations and concealed their intrinsic private ownership. A private firm can obtain a legitimate non-private ownership in a variety of ways such as by running a private business branch within a state or collective enterprises or cooperating with the public sector in operating a joint-venture and exchange benefits, e.g., by submitting a certain amount of profit to the local government in order to be recognized as public owned (Yang, 2007). These approaches of realizing a "red hat" label were was a way to achieve legitimacy through different disguises but it was not legally prohibited. Thus, it can also be regarded as one form of entrepreneurial opportunity that comes from exploiting the changing institutional rules. As pointed out in Yang's discussion (2007), in the case of China, entrepreneurial opportunities arise not only in the market but also from institutional transition. The strategy of wearing a "red hat" can be considered as a kind of entrepreneurial activity to fill in the gaps between market demands and opaque institutional rules.

The adaptive strategy of wearing a "red hat" can be explained by the tacit and discriminating rules for private businesses. Before the declaration of explicit policies toward individual entrepreneurs in 1988, there had been a long-established "wait and see" policy since the initiation of the

reform policy. The pragmatic experimental approach of this Chinese market transition determined the business environment characterized by the
coexistence of the public-owned and free private enterprise sectors for a
relatively long period. The public sector has been coordinated by state
central planning, with the features of controlled prices and no competition, while the private sectors were subject to the price mechanism (Krug
and Mehta, 2004). The chronological public policies regarding how to
cultivate and maintain balance between the two sectors have created an
uncertain institutional environment and poorly functioning markets for
entrepreneurship development, especially in the first stage of market transition. The Chinese government held an ambivalent attitude toward the
private sector. On one hand, it was necessary to keep private businesses as
the vehicles to generate employment opportunities, eliminate poverty
problems, and promote economic growth. On the other hand, the party
leaders spared no effort to maintain the dominant position of the public
sector in the national economy. Thus, even after the legitimate status of
private enterprises with more than eight employees was acknowledged in
1988, a lot of implicitly and explicitly discriminating and inequitable rules
and policies toward private businesses still existed. For example, private
enterprises faced restrictions in entering into several sectors, which
remained open only to state enterprises. The prohibited sectors include
financial services, tobacco, telecommunications, automobiles production
and rail and air civil transportation (Tsai, 2007: p. 56). The institutional
ambiguity could also be shown in the determination of the administrative
organization in charge of private business affairs. There has been no
administrative body directly responsible for private enterprises while
every government department has the right to supervise and guide
private businesses (Yang, 2007). Another discriminating rule came in the
Chinese taxation system. In the 1980s, the private sector was subject to
higher rates of taxation than state and collective enterprises and also many
arbitrary charges from local government agencies (Yang, 2007). Although
the market transition reform has provided the foundation for exploiting
entrepreneurial opportunities, the entrepreneurial activities have been
intensively constrained by institutional discrimination. The ultimate reason for discrimination is based on the status of private ownership. The red
hat strategy is a form of fuzzy property rights arrangement and has the

advantage of disguising the true underlying private ownership while maintaining legitimate and more adaptive ownership.

The main advantage of "wearing a red hat" is that private entrepreneurs can worry less about the instability of state policy toward the private sector. The identity of public ownership obtained by "wearing a red hat" can ensure similar treatment as that of state and collective enterprises. For example, "red hat" entrepreneurs have easier access to bank loans, enjoy lower tax rates, and are no longer subject to arbitrary charges from local governments. The "red hat" strategy has become a common and standardized operating practice for private entrepreneurs in China (Tsai, 2007). The popularity of the "red hat" strategy is also due to the alliance between private entrepreneurs and government officials. While entrepreneurs benefit from this adaptive strategy, government officials also have a vested interest in accepting the "red hat" strategy and promoting the expansion and development of private enterprises as a way to expand local revenues (Tsai, 2007). Private entrepreneurs try actively to establish an alliance with government officials who have the actual power of designating labor, land, and capital to exploit the identified entrepreneurial opportunities in the market. The alliance between entrepreneurs and government officials has been identified as an important mechanism to explain the rapid growth of private enterprises (Peng and Luo, 2000).

Entrepreneurship in China is dubbed as double entrepreneurship in the literature (Yang, 2007). The "red hat" strategy popular among Chinese entrepreneurs is the non-market dimension of double entrepreneurship that enables the manipulation of institutional rules in an underdeveloped market economy. This is one of the distinct characteristics of entrepreneurship in China.

2.3.2. *Regional Variation of China's Entrepreneurship*

Apart from institutional transition at national level, the local characteristics of the political, social, and economic situation have also exerted their effects on entrepreneurship development. The regional difference in entrepreneurship can be indicated by regional variation in the magnitude of private businesses. In 2003, 69.3% of the registered private enterprises were located in coastal China, 17.1% were in central provinces, and 13.5% were in the west. In the case of total registered individual businesses, 48.3%, 31%, and 20.7% were concentrated in East, Central, and West China, respectively.[2] These statistics show that there is a notable regional disparity in terms of entrepreneurship distribution.

The concentration of entrepreneurial activities in East China can be explained by the existence of a coastal-biased reform policy. The special economic zones located in coastal provinces were first selected as the frontier of implementing opening-up policy. The preferential policies in terms of launching international trade and accommodating foreign investment were granted to these special economic zones. Afterward, these preferential policies were expanded to other coastal cities. The advantage of coastal areas in developing entrepreneurship also comes from their innate geographical endowments. Southern coastal China has geographical proximity and tight cultural and linguistic links with overseas Chinese communities, such as Hong Kong, Macau, and Taiwan, which were once primary sources of FDI in China. Chen (2007) argued that private firms in the coastal region are less likely to adopt the "red hat" strategy than their inland counterparts inland since polices in coastal provinces have been more market oriented.

Another source of regional variation in entrepreneurship derives from the fact that local interpretation and implementation of reform polices depends on the actual situation of local jurisdictions. It is widely admitted that the central policy may look very different by the time it reaches particular localities (Tsai, 2007). There is a wide range of opportunities for private entrepreneurs and local officials to exploit and realize their entrepreneurial activities and in the meantime take action within the confines of the government regulations. Tsai (2007) proposed five regional development models related to the development of the private sector. These models are the Wenzhou model, the Sunan model, the Zhujiang model, the

---

[2]United Front for Industry and Commerce (UFIC, 2005), cited by Tsai (2007).

state-dominated model, and the pattern of limited development model. The variability of entrepreneurship development in terms of legitimacy and viability in these five typical regions is regarded as due to the "combination of differential national policies and local responses to those polices" (Tsai, 2007: p. 153).

2.3.3. *Changing Entrepreneurship: From Network-Based to Innovation-Based*

Peng (2003) argues that there is a decline in the importance of informal connections *vis-à-vis* competitiveness and capabilities in the process of institutional transition toward a market-oriented economy. Since the end of the 1970s, characterized by a seller's economy, China's market was filled with opportunities for entrepreneurs due to a lack of demand for consumption and productive goods across the board. However, those people who could identify the existence of entrepreneurial opportunities were not all able to realize practical entrepreneurial activities due to a lack of access to market resources, such as labor, capital, some factor inputs, land, and other market information. When private enterprises had not been granted legal status and were excluded from the state's universal distribution system, they always relied on government agencies or state-owned enterprises to access input or output markets (Zhang *et al.*, 2006). Thus, those individual entrepreneurs who could acquire access to market factors and establish business relations were more able to succeed. Constrained by the poor property rights and institutional uncertainty, the first generation of Chinese entrepreneurs had to make use of their personal networks (*guanxi*) among family members, relatives, and friends to form alliances with local government officials (Yang, 2007). Tsang (1998) argues the *guanxi*-based social capital became a necessary and popular way for private businesses to obtain favors from resourceful agents. Carlisle and Flynn (2005) point out that *guanxi* served as a means for accumulating social capital that private enterprises needed to achieve sufficient legitimacy in the imperfect market. Entrepreneurs also tried to establish political connections with the CCP to acquire desirable resources and legitimacy. After Deng Xiaoping's southern tour in 1992, an increasing number of party members in government agencies and managers of SOEs quit their stable jobs and started their own businesses. Apart from the more relaxed environment for private businesses, one important factor related to this part of thriving entrepreneurship is the work experience gained by these entrepreneurs in the government and SOEs allowed them to form advantageous networks with key party members and government officials (Li *et al.*, 2008).

Since the 1978 reform, there have been numerous changes in the policies, regulations, and laws as well as in the Party's attitude toward private businesses in China. Present-day China differs dramatically with regard to both "formal and informal rules" related to entrepreneurship (Kshetri, 2007: p. 416). In the meantime, the private sector is playing an increasingly important role in promoting economic growth since the adoption of the opening-up policy. An entrepreneurship-friendly environment is emerging in China due to the adoption of a number of favorable policies. Yang and Li (2008) define the current stage of market transition as the "early stage of market transition"(p. 351), which is the stage before the completion of market transition. The significance attached to personal network–related social capital is not at the same level as that in the beginning of the reform. Facing intensified competition from transformed SOEs, foreign investment enterprises, and multinationals, private enterprises have to shift their attention from establishing personal networks to corporate entrepreneurship based on innovation. Scholars have noted that corporate entrepreneurial activities are necessary conditions for Chinese domestic firms to successfully compete in international markets (Yiu, Lau, and Bruton, 2007). However, the current situation in China is that domestic entrepreneurs are working on strengthening their capabilities in innovation, while their competitiveness is still based on low prices and large volumes (Yang and Li, 2007). Thus, the transition from network-based entrepreneurship toward innovation-based entrepreneurship is an important task for domestic entrepreneurs and for Chinese public policy makers.

2.4. Conclusion

This chapter provides a historical review of the development of domestic entrepreneurship in China since 1949, especially during the reform period. The socialist political system has been perceived as the most influential determinant of entrepreneurship development (Yu and Stough, 2006). Thus, from the perspective of institutional transition, entrepreneurship development has been divided into three stages: 1978–1992, 1992–2000, and 2000-present. Chinese modern entrepreneurship originated from TVEs in rural areas. The speedy growth of township enterprises disseminated entrepreneurial activities to urban areas. These ambiguous policies toward private businesses in this period, on one hand, provide institutional opportunities for the emergence of entrepreneurship. On the other hand, the vulnerability of private businesses to local government due to its unequal status to state-owned sector shaped an institutional obstacle for entrepreneurship. The stages after 1992 witnessed a more matured institutional environment, since the legitimacy of private businesses was granted and the constitution was amended to protect private property rights. The social status of entrepreneurs has also been admitted and respected. Although the government is trying to create favorable market conditions for private firms by providing equal regulations and rules, there is still a long waiting time for the arrival of perfect market conditions. Thus, compared to the entrepreneurship development in western economies, entrepreneurship development in China is still in its infancy due to the imperfect institutional environment.

The historical review reveals some Chinese-specific characteristics in entrepreneurship. First, China's highly institutional uncertainty has created entrepreneurs with a "red hat". Private firms took the fuzzy property rights arrangement to evade discrimination in obtaining market attributes. Another Chinese characteristic is the significant regional variation in entrepreneurship development. Regional disparity in entrepreneurship is due to a variety of local socio-economic factors and local implementation of central policies. Last but not the least, China is now in the transition from network-based entrepreneurship toward innovation-based entrepreneurship. The extensive efforts made by Chinese entrepreneurs in establishing personal relationships need to be shifted to technology improvement in order to win in the face of higher levels of competition in the international market. The Chinese government should be very cautious in its provision of a favorable policy environment to encourage entrepreneurship development since its ambivalent attitude toward entrepreneurship due to the ideological controversy cannot be resolved in a short time. At the same time, the government should deepen its reform policy to provide a healthy venture capital market and technology transfer mechanism to encourage entrepreneurship based on independent innovation.

References

Amit, R., L. Glosten and E. Muller (1993). Challenges to theory development in entrepreneurship research. *Journal of Management Studies* **30**(5): 815–834.

Anderson, A. R., J. -H. Li, R. T. Harrison and P. J. A. Robson (2003). The increasing role of small business in the Chinese economy. *Journal of Small Business Management* **41**(3): 310–316.

Bosma, N., K., Jones, E., Autio and J. Levie (2008). Global Entrepreneurship Monitor 2007 Executive Report. London: Global Entrepreneurship Research Association

Carlisle, E., and D. Flynn (2005). Small business survival in China: Guanxi, legitimacy, and social capital. *Journal of Developmental Entrepreneurship* **10**(1): 79–96.

Chang, W., and I. C. MacMillan (1991). A review of entrepreneurial development in the People's Republic of China. *Journal of Business Venturing* **6**(6): 375–379.

Che, J., and Y. Qian (1998). Insecure property rights and government ownership of firms. *Quarterly Journal of Economics* **113**: 467–496.

Chen, J. (2006). Development of Chinese small and medium-sized enterprises. *Journal of Small Business and Enterprise Development* **13**(2): 140–147.

Chen, W. (2007). Does the colour of the cat matter? The red hat strategy in China's private enterprises. *Management and Organization Review* **3**(1): 55–80.

Dana, L. P. (1999). Small business as a supplement in the People's Republic of China (PRC). *Journal of Small Business Management* **37**(3): 76–80.

He, Q. (2000). Symbiosis of mandarins and businessmen: The Chinese foreordination? *Viewpoint* **3**.

Hubbard, P. J. (1995). Urban design in local economic development: A case study of Birmingham. *Cities* **12**: 243–253

Krug, B., and J. Mehta (2004). Entrepreneurship by alliance. In B. Krug (Ed.) *China's Rational Entrepreneurs: The Development of the New Private Business Sector*, London: Routledge Curzon.

Kshetri, N. (2007). Institutional changes affecting entrepreneurship in China. *Journal of Developmental Entrepreneurship* **12**(4): 415.

Li, H., L. Meng, Q. Wang and L. -A. Zhou (2008). Political connections, financing and firm performance: Evidence from Chinese private firms. *Journal of Development Economics* **87**(2): 283–299.

Li, J., and H. Matlay (2006). Chinese entrepreneurship and small business development: An overview and research agenda. *Journal of Small Business and Enterprise Development* **13**(2): 248.

Liang, X. (2006). The evolution of township and village enterprises (TVEs) in China. *Journal of Small Business and Enterprise Development* **13**(2): 235.

Liao, D., and P. Sohen (2001). The development of modern entrepreneurship in China. *Stanford Journal of East Asian Affairs* **1**: 27–31.

Luo, Y., J. J. Tan and O. Shenkar (1998). Strategic responses to competitive pressure: The case of township and village enterprises in China. *Asia Pacific Journal of Management* **15**(1): 33.

Nair, S. R. (1996). Doing business in China: It's far from easy. *USA Today,* **124**: 27–29.

Naughton, B. (1994). Chinese institutional innovation and privatization from below. *The American Economic Review* **84**(2): 266–270.

Peng, M. W. (2003). Institutional transitions and strategic choices. *Academy of Management Review* **28**(2): 275–296.

Peng, M. W. (2005). How network strategies and institutional transitions evolve in Asia. *Asia Pacific Journal of Management* **22**(4): 321–336.

Peng, M. W., and Y. Luo (2000) Managerial ties and firm performance in a transition economy: The nature of a micro-macro link. *Academy of Management Journal,* **43** (3): 486–501.

Peng, M. W., and P. S. Heath (1996). The growth of the firm in planned economies in transition: Institutions, organizations, and strategic choice. *Academy of Management Review* **21**: 492–528.

Pistrui, D. W. Huang, D. Oksoy, Oksoy, Z. Oksoy and H. Welsch (2001). Entrepreneurship in China: Characteristics, attributes, and family forces shaping the emerging private sector. *Family Business Review* **14**(2): 141–152.

Schönleber, H. (2000). *Development of China's Private Economy (Die Entwicklung der chinesischen Privatwirtschaft).* Beijing: DIHK-ACFIC Partnership Project.

Schumpeter, J. A. (1961). *The Theory of Economic Development.* New York: Oxford University Press.

Shane, S. A., and S. Venkataraman (2000). The promise of entrepreneurship as a field of research. *Academy of Management Review* **25**(1): 217–226.

Tsai, K. S. (2007). *Capitalism without Democracy.* Ithaca and London: Cornell University Press.

Tsang, E. W. K. (1998). Can *guanxi* be a source of sustained competitive advantage for doing business in China? *Academy of Management Executive* **12**(2): 64–73.

Venkataraman S. (1997). The distinctive domain of entrepreneurship research. Advances in entrepreneurship. *Firm Emergence and Growth* **3**: 119–138.

Wu, J. (2005). *Understanding and Interpreting Chinese Economic Reform.* Singapore: Thomson/South-Western.

Yang, J. Y., and J. T. Li (2008). The development of entrepreneurship in China. *Asia Pacific Journal of Management* **25**(2): 335–359.

Yang, K. (2007). *Entrepreneurship in China.* Hampshire: Ashgate Publishing.

Yiu, D. W., and C. M. Lau (2008). Corporate entrepreneurship as resource capital configuration in emerging market firms. *Entrepreneurship: Theory and Practice* **32**(1): 37–57.

Yiu, D. W., C. M. Lau and G. D. Bruton (2007). International venturing by emerging economy firms: The effects of firm capabilities, home country networks and corporate entrepreneurship. *Journal of International Business Studies* **38**: 519–540.

Yu, J., and R. Stough (2006). The determinants of entrepreneurship development in China. *International Journal of Enterprise Development* **3**(1/2): 30–52.

Zapalska, A. M., and W. Edwards (2001). Chinese entrepreneurship in a cultural and economic perspective. *Journal of Small Business Management* **39**(3): 286–292.

Zhang, J., L. Zhang, S. Rozelle and S. Boucher (2006). Self-employment with Chinese Characteristics: The forgotten engine of rural China's growth. *Contempory Economic Policy* **24**(3): 446–458.

Part II
Theoretical Framework

Chapter 3

Jaffe–Feldman–Varga: The Search for Knowledge Spillovers

Zoltán J. Ács
George Mason University

3.1. Introduction

In *The Structure of Scientific Revolutions,* Kuhn (1962) argued that "normal science" shares two essential characteristics: (1) their achievement was sufficiently unprecedented to attract an enduring group of adherents away from competing modes of scientific activity; (2) it was sufficiently open-ended to leave all sorts of problems for the redefined group of practitioners to solve (Kuhn, 1962: p. 10). The shift between from the old growth theory to new growth theory represented one such transformation. In the words of Romer (1986: p. 204), this revolution "...removes the dead end in neoclassical theory and links microeconomic observations on routines, machine designs and the like with macroeconomic discussions of technology." In the new growth theory, a fundamental anomaly that remains unresolved is the identification and measurement of R&D spillovers, or the extent to which a start-up is able to economically exploit the investment in R&D made by another organization (Griliches, 1979).

Audretsch and Ács were attracted to the economics of technological change by innovative prowls of new technology-based firms in the 1980s. While the conventional wisdom was that large firms had an innovative advantage over small firms, in a 1988 article in the *American Economic*

Review, they discovered an anomaly instead of solving a problem. "A perhaps somewhat surprising result is that not only is the coefficient of the large-firm employment share positive and significant for small-firm innovations, but it is actually greater in magnitude than for large firms. This suggests that, *ceteris paribus*, the greater the extent to which an industry is composed of large firms, the greater will be the innovative activity, but that increased innovative activity will tend to emanate more from the small firms than from the large firms" (Ács and Audretsch, 1988: p. 686). The anomaly of where new technology-based start-ups acquire knowledge was unresolved.

Building on the work of Griliches (1979), Adam Jaffe (1989) was the first to identify the extent to which university research spills over into the generation of commercial activity. Building on Jaffe's work, Maryann Feldman at Carnegie Mellon University expanded the knowledge production function to innovative activity and incorporated aspects of the regional knowledge infrastructure. Attila Varga at West Virginia University extended the Jaffe–Feldman approach by focusing on a more precise measure of local geographic spillovers. Varga approached the issue of knowledge spillovers from an explicit spatial econometric perspective. The Jaffe–Feldman–Varga (JFV) spillovers take us a long way toward understanding the role of knowledge spillovers in technological change. Building on this foundation, the model has been recently extended to identify entrepreneurship as a conduit through which knowledge spillovers take place (Ács *et al.*, 2006). Finally, the role of agglomerations in knowledge spillovers represents the final frontier in this scientific revolution (Clark, Feldman, and Gertler, 2000). The purpose of this chapter is to catalog the contribution of JFV (two of them students of mine) that simultaneously and independently sparked a search for the mechanism of knowledge spillovers. Section 3.2 outlines the main contributions of Jaffe, Feldman, and Varga. Section 3.3 examines extensions of the model by Jaffe, Trajtenberg, and Henderson as well as recent criticisms of the model by Thomson and Fox-Kean. Section 3.4 examines spatialized explanations of economic growth by Ács and Varga; Fujita, Krugman, and Venables; and Romer. Section 3.5 presents work on a knowledge spillover theory of entrepreneurship. Section 3.6 discusses China and entrepreneurship.

Section 3.7 discusses the policy questions. Conclusions are arrived at in the final section.

3.2. Jaffe–Feldman–Varga

In a 1989 paper in the *American Economic Review*, Adam Jaffe extended his pathbreaking 1986 study measuring the total R&D pool available for spillovers to identify the contribution of spillovers from university research to commercial innovation. Jaffe's findings were the first to identify the extent to which university research spills over into the generation of inventions and innovations by private firms. In order to relate the response of this measure to R&D spillovers from universities, Jaffe modifies the "knowledge production function" introduced by Zvi Griliches (1979) for two inputs: private corporate expenditures on R&D and research expenditures undertaken at universities.

In essence, this is a two-factor Cobb–Douglas production function that relates an output measure for "knowledge" to two input measures: research and development performed by industry and research performed by universities. Formally, this is expressed as:

$$\log(K) = \beta_{K1} \log(R) + \beta_{K2} \log(U) + \varepsilon_K \qquad (3.1)$$

where K is a proxy for knowledge measured by patent counts, R is industry R&D, and U is university research, with ε_K as a stochastic error term. The analysis is carried out for U.S. states for several points in time and disaggregated by sector. The potential interaction between university and industry research is captured by extending the model with two additional equations that allow for simultaneity between these two variables:

$$\log(R) = \beta_{R1} \log(U) + \beta_{R2} Z_2 + \varepsilon_R \qquad (3.2)$$

and

$$\log(U) = \beta_{U1} \log(R) + \beta_{U2} Z_1 + \varepsilon_U \qquad (3.3)$$

where U and R are as before, Z_1 and Z_2 are sets of exogenous local characteristics, and ε_R and ε_U are stochastic error terms.

Jaffe's statistical results provide evidence that corporate patent activity responds positively to commercial spillovers from university research. The lack of evidence that geographic proximity within the state matters as well, however, clouds results concerning the role of geographic proximity in spillovers from university research. According to Jaffe (1989: p. 968), "there is only weak evidence that spillovers are facilitated by geographic coincidence of universities and research labs within the state". In other words, we know very little where knowledge spillovers go.

Maryann Feldman expanded on the work of Jaffe in two ways (Feldman, 1994; Feldman and Florida, 1994; Ács, Audretsch, and Feldman, 1992, 1994). First, she used a new data source — a literature-based innovation output indicator developed by the U.S. Small Business Administration that directly measures innovative activity (Ács and Audretsch, 1988) and extended the knowledge production function (Jaffe, 1989) to account for tacit knowledge and commercialization linkages.

Grilliches (1979) introduced a model of technological innovation, which views innovative output as the product of knowledge-generating inputs. Jaffe (1989) modified this production function approach to consider spatial and technical area dimensions. However, Jaffe's model only considers what were previously defined as the elements of the formal knowledge base. Such a formulation does not consider other types of knowledge inputs, which contribute to the realization of innovative output. This is important since innovation requires both technical and business knowledge if profitability is to be the guide for making investments in research and development. Following the innovation knowledge base conceptual model, a more complete specification of innovative inputs would include

$$\log(K) = \beta_{K1} \log(R) + \beta_{K2} \log(U) + \beta_{K3} \log(BSERV) \\ + \beta_{K4} \log(VA) + \varepsilon_K \qquad (3.4)$$

where K is measured by counts of innovations, and R and U are as before. *VA* is the tacit knowledge embodied by the industry's presence in an area and *BSERV* stands for the presence of business services that represents a link to commercialization.

The last input in the knowledge base model is the most evasive. There are a variety of producer services that provide knowledge to the market and the commercialization process. For example, the services of patent attorneys are a critical input to the innovation process. Similarly, marketing information plays an important role in the commercialization process.

Substitution of the direct measure of innovative activity for the patent measure in the knowledge-production function generally strengthens Jaffe's (1989) arguments and reinforces his findings. Most importantly, use of the innovation data provides even greater support than was found by Jaffe: as he predicted, spillovers are facilitated by the geographic coincidence of universities and research labs within the state. In addition, there is at least some evidence that, because the patent and innovation measures capture different aspects of the process of technological change, results for specific sectors may be, at least to some extent, influenced by the technological regime. Thus, it is found that the importance of university spillovers relative to private-company R&D spending is considerably greater in the electronics sector when the direct measure of innovative activity is substituted for the patent measure.

However, the relative importance of industry R&D and university research as inputs in generating innovative output clearly varies between large and small firms (Ács, Audretsch, and Feldman, 1994). That is, for large firms, not only is the elasticity of innovative activity with respect to industry R&D expenditures more than two times greater than the elasticity with respect to expenditures on research by universities, but it is nearly twice as large as the elasticity of small-firm innovative activity with respect to industry R&D. In contrast, for small firms the elasticity of innovative output with respect to expenditures on research by universities is about one-fifth greater than the elasticity with respect to industry R&D.

Moreover, the elasticity of innovative activity with respect to university research is about 50% greater for small enterprises than for large corporations.

These results support the hypothesis that private corporation R&D plays a relatively more important role in generating innovative activity in large corporations than in small firms. In contrast, spillovers from the research activities of universities play a more decisive role in the innovative activity of small firms. Geographic proximity between university and corporate laboratories within a state clearly serves as a catalyst for innovative activity for firms of all sizes. However, the impact is apparently greater on small firms than large firms.

There were two limitations of the Jaffe–Feldman research. First, the unit of analysis at the state level highly aggregate was, requiring a geographical coincidence index to control for colocation. Second, the research did not take into consideration the potential influence of spatial dependence that may invalidate the interpretation of econometric analyses based on contiguous cross-sectional data. Attila Varga extended this research by examining both the state and the metropolitan statistical area (MSA) levels and using spatial econometric techniques[1] (Varga, 1998, 2000; Anselin, Varga, and Ács, 1997, 2000a, 2000b; Ács, Anselin, and Varga, 2002).

These extensions yielded a more precise insight into the range of spatial externalities between innovation and R&D in the Metropolitan Statistical Area (MSA) and university research both within the MSA and in surrounding counties. Attila Varga was able to shed some initial light on this issue for high-technology innovations measured as an aggregate across 5 two-digit SIC industries and also at a more detailed industrial

---

[1] When models are estimated for cross-sectional data on neighboring spatial units, the lack of independence across these units (or, the presence of spatial autocorrelation) can cause serious problems of model misspecification when ignored (Anselin, 1988). The methodology of spatial econometrics consists of testing for the potential presence of these misspecifications and of using the proper estimators for models that incorporate the spatial dependence explicitly (for a recent review, see Anselin, 2001).

sector level. He found a positive and highly significant relationship between MSA innovations and university research, indicating the presence of localized university research spillovers in innovation. In comparison to the effect of industrial knowledge spillovers (i.e., knowledge flows among industrial research laboratories) the size of the university effect is considerably smaller as it is one-third of the size of the industrial research coefficient. University knowledge spillovers follow a definite distance decay pattern as shown by the statistically significant albeit smaller size university research coefficient for adjoining counties within a 50-mile distance range from the MSA center.

There are notable differences among sectors with respect to the localized university effect as studied at the MSA level. Specifically for the four high-technology sectors such as machinery, chemicals, electronics, and instruments, significant localized university spillover impact was found only for electronics and instruments while for the other two industries the university research coefficient remains consistently insignificant.

Ács, Anselin, and Varga (2002) tested whether the patent data developed by the U.S. Patent and Trademark Office is in fact a reliable proxy measure of innovative activity at the regional level as compared to the literature-based innovation output indicator developed by the U.S. Small Business Administration. This is important, since the patent data are readily available over time and can be used to study the dynamics of localized knowledge flows within regional innovation systems. Before this study, there were some evidence that patents provide a reliable measure of innovative activity at the industry level (Ács and Audretsch, 1989) and some evidence that patents and innovations behave similarly at the state level (Ács, Audretsch, and Feldman, 1992). However, this has not been tested at the sub-state level.

The correlation between the PTO patent and SBA innovation counts at the MSA level is reasonably high (0.79) and this could be taken as a first indication that patents might be a reliable measure of innovation at the regional level. However, this correlation coefficient value is not high enough to guarantee that the role of different regional actors in knowledge creation would turn out similar with both measures if applied in the same empirical model. Varga proceeded by replacing innovation counts with the patent measure in the same model as in Anselin, Varga, and Ács (1997) to be able to directly compare the results of the two measures of new technological knowledge and assess the extent to which patents may be used as a reliable proxy.

The sizes of all the parameters in the estimated knowledge production function are smaller for innovation than for patents, suggesting that firms in the product development stage rely on localized interactions (with universities as well as with other actors) less intensively than in earlier stages of the innovation process. The other important finding of this comparative study is that the importance of university knowledge spillovers (measured by the size of the university research parameter) compared to that of R&D spillovers among private firms is substantially less pronounced for patents than for innovations. Since patenting reflects more on the earlier stages of innovation whereas the direct innovation measure accounts for the concluding stage of the innovation process, the relatively higher weight of local universities in innovation than in patenting appears to reflect the different spatial patterns of basic and applied research collaboration. To collaborate with universities in applied research, firms tend to choose local academic institutions whereas basic research collaboration can be carried out over larger distances.

3.3. Extensions of the JFV Model

Jaffe, Trajtenberg, and Henderson (1993, 2005) expand on the above work to answer the question if knowledge externalities are localized. This is important since growth theory assumed that knowledge spills over to agents within the country but not to other countries. This implicit assumption begs the question to what extent knowledge externalities are localized. Jaffe, Trajtenberg, and Henderson extend the search for knowledge spillovers by using a matching method that found that knowledge spillovers are strongly localized. Their method matches each citing patent to a non-citing patent intended to control for the pre-existing geographic concentration of production. Using patent data, they came to two conclusions: (1) spillovers are particularly significant at the local level and (2) localization fades only slowly over time. These results and the large research issue are reproduced in Jaffe and Trajtenberg (2002).

Audretsch and Feldman (1996) explore the question of the geography of innovation and production. They provide evidence concerning the spatial dimension of knowledge spillovers. Their findings suggest that knowledge spillovers are geographically bounded and localized within spatial proximity to the knowledge source. Feldman and Audretsch (1999) further examine the question of knowledge spillovers by looking into the question of specialization versus diversity in cities. Their research supports the ideas that diversity leads to more innovation.

Recently, Thompson and Fox-Kean (2005a, 2005b) have challenged the findings of Jaffe, Trajtenberg, and Henderson. They suggest that the Jaffe, Trajtenberg, and Henderson method matched case control methodology included a serious spurious component. Controlling for unobservables using matching methods is invariably a dangerous exercise because one can rarely be confident that the controls are doing their job. In some cases, imperfect matching may simply introduce noise and a corresponding loss of efficiency. Thompson and Fox-Kean (2005a, 2005b) therefore suggest at least two reasons why the matching method may not adequately control for existing patent activity. First, the level of aggregation might not be fine enough. Second, patents typically contain many distinct claims to which a technological classification is assigned. These two features of the control selection process mean that there is no guarantee that the control patent has any industrial similarity with the citing or to the originating patent. Of course, one of their conclusions that spillovers stop at the country level also needs explanation.

Empirical research done within the JFV framework and the extensions introduced so far were established and originally carried out in the U.S. with the use of state-, MSA- and county-level data sets. However, the issue of the geographic extent of knowledge spillovers has a definite international validity. Within the last decade, the JFV model has been replicated and continuously refined to search for the geographical boundaries of knowledge flows in Europe, South America, and Asia. Varga (2006) provides an assessment of the size of this international literature.

3.4. The "Spatialized" Explanation of Economic Growth

Building on the JFV model of knowledge spillovers, Ács and Varga (2002) suggest a "spatialized" theoretical framework of technology-led economic growth that needs to reflect three fundamental issues. First, it should provide an explanation of why knowledge-related economic activities concentrate in certain regions, leaving others relatively underdeveloped. Second, it needs to answer the questions of how technological advance occur and what are the key processes and institutions involved, with a particular focus on the geographic dimension. Third, it has to present an analytical framework where the role of technological change in regional and national economic growth is clearly explained. In order to answer these three questions, Ács and Varga examine three separate and distinct literatures: the new economic geography, the new growth theory, and the new economics of innovation.

The three approaches focus on different aspects but at the same time are also complements of each other. The "new" theories of growth endogenize technological change and as such interlink technological change with macroeconomic growth. However, the way technological change is described is strongly simplistic and the economy investigated is formulated in an aspatial model. On the other hand, systems of innovation frameworks are very detailed with respect to the innovation process but say nothing about macroeconomic growth. However, the spatial dimension has been introduced into the framework in the recently developed "regional innovation systems" studies (Braczyk, Cooke, and Hedenreich, 1998).

The idea behind the innovation systems approach is quite simple but extremely appealing. According to this approach, in most cases, innovation is a result of a collective process and this process is shaped in a systemic manner. The elements of the system are innovating firms and firms in related and connected industries (suppliers, buyers), private and public research laboratories, universities, supporting business services (like legal or technical services), financial institutions (especially venture capital), and the government. These elements are interconnected by innovation-related linkages, where these linkages represent knowledge flows among them. Linkages can be informal in nature (occasional meetings in conferences, social events, etc.) or they can also be definitely formal (contracted research, collaborative product development, etc.). The effectiveness (i.e., productivity in terms of number of innovations) of the system is determined by both the knowledge already accumulated by the actors and the level of their interconnectedness (i.e., the intensity of knowledge flows). Ability and motivations for interactions are shaped largely by traditions, social norms, values, and the countries' legal systems.

New economic geography models investigate general equilibrium in a spatial setting (Krugman, 1991). This means that they provide explanations not only for the determination of equilibrium prices, incomes, and quantities in each market but also for the development of the particular geographical structure of the economy. In other words, new economic geography derives economic and spatial equilibrium simultaneously (Fujita, Krugman, and Venables, 1999; Fujita and Thisse, 2002). Spatial equilibrium arises as an outcome of the balance between centripetal forces working toward agglomeration (such as increasing returns to scale, industrial demand, localized knowledge spillovers) and centrifugal forces promoting dispersion (such as transportation costs). Until the latest developments in recent years, the new economic geography models did not consider the spatial aspects of economic growth. However, even the recent models of technological change follow the same pattern as endogenous growth models and fail to reach the complexity inherent in innovation systems studies.

As emphasized by Ács and Varga (2002), each one of the above three approaches has its strengths and weaknesses but they could serve to create the building blocks of an explanatory framework of technology-led economic growth. They suggest that a specific combination of the Krugmanian theory of initial conditions for spatial concentration of economic activities with the Romerian theory of endogenous economic growth complemented with a systematic representation of interactions among the actors of Nelson's innovation system could be a way of developing an appropriate model of technology-led regional economic development.

Following Ács and Varga (2002), Varga (2006) developed an empirical modeling framework of geographical growth explanation. This framework is the spatial extension of the endogenous growth model in Romer (1990) and it integrates elements of the innovation systems and the new economic geography literature. For a more formal treatment, Varga (2006) applied the generalized version of the Romer (1990) equation of macroeconomic level knowledge production developed by Jones (1995)[2]:

$$dA = \delta H_A^\lambda A^\varphi \tag{3.5}$$

where H_A stands for human capital in the research sector working on knowledge production (operationalized by the number of researchers), A is the total stock of technological knowledge available at a certain point in time, and dA is the change in technological knowledge resulted from private efforts to invest in research and development. δ, λ, and φ are various parameters, explained below.

Technological change is generated by research and its extent depends on the number of researchers involved in knowledge creation (H_A). However, their efficiency is directly related to the total stock of already available knowledge (A). Knowledge spillovers are central to the growth process: the higher A is, the larger the change in technology produced by the same number of researchers. Thus, macroeconomic growth is strongly related to knowledge spillovers.

Parameters in the Romer knowledge production function play a decisive role in the effectiveness of macrolevel knowledge production. The same number of researchers with a similar value of A can raise the level of already existing technological knowledge with significant differences

---

[2] The functional form corresponds to the Jones (1995) version, however, the interpretation of λ and φ is different in Varga (2006).

depending on the size of the parameters. First, consider δ $(0<\delta<1)$, which is the research productivity parameter. The larger the δ value, the more efficient H_A is in producing economically useful new knowledge.

The size of φ reflects the extent to which the total stock of already established knowledge impacts knowledge production. Given that A stands for the level of codified knowledge (available in books, scientific papers, or patent documentations), I call φ as the parameter of codified knowledge spillovers. The size of φ reflects the portion of A that spills over and, as such, its value largely influences the effectiveness of research in generating new technologies.

λ is the research spillover parameter. The larger the λ value, the stronger the impact and the role of the same number of researchers in technological change. In contrast to φ and δ that are determined primarily in the research sector and as such their values are exogenous to the economy, λ is endogenous. Its value reflects the diffusion of (codified and tacit) knowledge accumulated by researchers. Technological diffusion depends on three interactions: First, the intensity of interactions among researchers (H_A); second, the quality of public research and the extent to which the private research sector is connected to it (especially to universities) by formal and informal linkages; and third, the development level of supporting/connected industries and business services and the integration of innovating firms into the system. The extensive innovation systems literature evidences that the same number of researchers contribute to different efficiencies depending on the development of the system. In the Romer equation, this is reflected in the size of λ.

Within the JFV framework, a series of papers demonstrate that a significant fraction of knowledge spillovers is bounded spatially. These findings imply that the geographic structure of R&D is a determinant of technological change and ultimately economic growth. *Ceteris paribus* in an economy where R&D institutions are well-concentrated intensive knowledge spillovers result in a higher level of innovation than in a system where research is more evenly distributed over space. Thus λ is also sensitive to the spatial structure of H_A. Even with the same number of researchers, λ can have different values depending on the extent to which research and development is concentrated in space.

3.5. A Knowledge Spillover Theory of Entrepreneurship

In this section, the JFV model of knowledge spillovers is extended by Ács and Audretsch, who develop a Knowledge Spillover Theory of Entrepreneurship in order to answer the question, "What is the conduit by which knowledge spillovers occur?" As a first step in this direction, the theory incorporates two of the above literatures, new growth theory (Romer) and the new economics of innovation (Nelson, 1991) to explain how entrepreneurship facilitates the spillover of knowledge.

A modern synthesis of the entrepreneur is someone who specializes in taking judgmental decisions about the coordination of scarce resources (Lazear, 2005). In this definition, the term "someone" emphasizes that the entrepreneur is an individual. Judgmental decisions are decisions for which no obvious correct procedure exists — a judgmental decision cannot be made simply by plugging available numbers into a scientific formula and acting based on the number that comes out. In this framework, entrepreneurial activity depends upon the interaction between the characteristics of opportunity and the characteristics of the people who exploit them. Since discovery is a cognitive process, it can take place only at the individual level. Individuals, whether they are working in an existing organization or unemployed at the time of their discovery, are the entities that discover opportunities. The organizations that employ people are inanimate and cannot engage in *discovery*. Therefore, any explanation for the mode of opportunity discovery must be based on choices made by individuals about how they would like to exploit the opportunity that they have discovered (Hayek, 1937).

So where do opportunities come from? Today we know that the technology opportunity set is endogenously created by investments in new knowledge. The new growth theory, formalized by Romer (1986), assumes that firms exist exogenously and then engage in the pursuit of new economic knowledge as input into the process of generating endogenous growth. Technological change plays a central role in the explanation of economic growth, since on the steady state growth path the rate of per capita GDP growth equals the rate of technological change.

However, not only does new knowledge contribute to technological change, it also creates opportunities for use by third-party firms, often entrepreneurial start-ups (Shane, 2001). The creation of new knowledge gives rise to new opportunities through knowledge spillovers, therefore, entrepreneurial activity does not involve simply the arbitrage of opportunities (Kirzner, 1973) but also the exploitation of new opportunities created but not appropriated by incumbent organizations (Hellmann, 2007). Thus, while the entrepreneurship literature considers opportunity to exist exogenously, in the new economic growth literature, opportunities are endogenously created through the purposeful investment in new knowledge. The theory as suggested by Audretsch (1995: p. 48) "...proposes shifting the unit of observation away from exogenously assumed firms to individual agents confronted with new knowledge and the decision whether and how to act upon that new knowledge."

The theory relaxes two central (and unrealistic) assumptions of the endogenous growth model to develop a theory that improves the microeconomic foundations of endogenous growth theory (Ács *et al.*, 2006). The first is that knowledge is automatically equated with economic knowledge. In fact, as Arrow (1962) emphasized, knowledge is inherently different from the traditional factors of production, resulting in a gap between knowledge (K) and what he called economic knowledge (K^c). The second involves the assumed spillover of knowledge. The existence of the factor of knowledge is equated with its automatic spillover, yielding endogenous growth. In the Knowledge Spillover Theory of Entrepreneurship, *institutions* impose a gap between new knowledge and economic knowledge ($0 < K^c / K < 1$) and results in a lower level of knowledge spillovers.

The model is one where new product innovations can come either from incumbent organizations or from entrepreneurial start-ups (Schumpeter, 1934). According to Baumol (2004: p. 9), "the bulk of private R&D

spending is shown to come from a tiny number of very large firms. Yet, the revolutionary breakthroughs continue to come predominantly from small entrepreneurial enterprises, with large industry providing streams of incremental improvements that also add up to major contributions." We can think of incumbent firms that rely on the *flow* of knowledge to innovate focusing on incremental innovation, i.e., product improvements (Ács and Audretsch, 1988). Entrepreneurial start-ups that have access to knowledge spillovers from the *stock* of knowledge and entrepreneurial talent are more likely to be engaged in radical innovation that leads to new industries or completely replace existing products (Ács, Audretsch, and Feldman, 1994). Start-ups played a major role in radical innovations such as software, semiconductors, biotechnology (Zucker, Darby, and Brewer, 1998), and the information and communications technologies (Jorgenson, 2001). The presence of these activities is especially important at the early stages of the life cycle when technology is still fluid.

Equation (3.6) suggests that entrepreneurial start-ups (E) will be a function of the difference between expected profits (π^*) minus wages (w). Expected profits are conditioned by the knowledge stock (K) that positively affects start-ups and is negatively conditioned by knowledge commercialized by incumbent firms. Yet a rich literature suggests that there is a compelling array of financial, institutional, and individual barriers to entrepreneurship, which results in a modification of the entrepreneurial choice equation:

$$E = \gamma (\pi^* (K^{\xi}) - w)/\beta \tag{3.6}$$

where β represents those institutional and individual barriers to entrepreneurship, spanning factors such as risk aversion, financial constraints, and legal and regulatory restrictions (Acemoglu, Simon, and Robinson, 2004). The existence of such barriers explains why economic agents might choose not to enter into entrepreneurship, even when confronted with knowledge that would otherwise generate a potentially profitable opportunity. Thus, this mode shows how local differences in knowledge stocks, the presence of large firms as deterrents to knowledge exploitation, and an entrepreneurial culture might explain regional variations in the rates of entrepreneurial activity. The primary theoretical predictions of the model are:

- An increase in the stock of knowledge has a positive effect on the level of entrepreneurship.
- The more efficient incumbents are at exploiting knowledge flows, the smaller the effect of new knowledge on entrepreneurship.
- Entrepreneurial activities are decreasing in the face of higher regulations, administrative barriers, and governmental market intervention.

Thus, entrepreneurship becomes central to generating economic growth by serving as a conduit, albeit not the sole conduit, by which knowledge created by incumbent organizations spills over to agents who endogenously create new firms. The theory is actually a theory of *endogenous entrepreneurship*, where entrepreneurship is a response to opportunities created by investments in new knowledge that was not commercialized by incumbent firms. The theory suggests that, *ceteris paribus*, entrepreneurial activity will tend to be greater in contexts where investments in new knowledge are relatively high, since the start-ups will benefit from knowledge that has spilled over from the source actually producing that new knowledge. In a low-knowledge context, the lack of new ideas will not generate entrepreneurial opportunities based on potential knowledge spillovers. In a recent series of studies, Ács and Armington (2006), Audretsch, Keilbach, and Lehmann (2006) link entrepreneurship and economic growth at the regional level and Ács *et al.* (2006) at the national level find that entrepreneurship does in fact offer an explanation for how knowledge spillovers occur.

Ács and Varga (2005) empirically test the theory within the JFV framework. They build their modeling approach on the interpretation of the Romerian equation (Equation 3.5) provided in Section 3.4. They start with the assumption that the value of λ bears the influence of the level of entrepreneurship because the value of new economic knowledge is uncertain. While most R&D is carried out in large firms and universities, it does not mean that the same individuals that discover the opportunity will carry out the exploitation. An implication of the theory of firm selection is that new firms may enter an industry in large numbers to exploit knowledge spillovers. The higher the rate of startups the greater should be the value of λ because of knowledge spillovers.

The empirical model in which the parameter λ in Equation (3.5) is endogenized has the following form:

$$\log(NK) = \delta + \lambda\log(H) + \varphi\log(A) + \varepsilon \tag{3.7}$$

$$\lambda = (\beta_1 + \beta_2\log(\text{ENTR}) + \beta_3\log(\text{AGGL}) \tag{3.8}$$

where NK stands for new knowledge (i.e., the change in A or dA), ENTR is entrepreneurship, AGGL is agglomeration, A is the set of publicly available scientific-technological knowledge, and ε is stochastic error term. Implementation of (3.7) into (3.8) results in the following estimated equation:

$$\log(NK) = \delta + \beta_1\log(H) + \beta_2\log(\text{ENTR})\log(H) + \beta_3\log(\text{AGGL})\log(H) + \varphi\log(A) + \varepsilon \tag{3.9}$$

In Equation (3.9), the estimated value of the parameter β_2 measures the extent to which research interacted with entrepreneurship contributes to knowledge spillovers. Applying to European data, Ács and Varga (2005) found a statistically significant value of β_2 that is taken as a supporting evidence of the knowledge spillover theory of entrepreneurship.

All countries in the global economy now face a period of transition from a more or less planned economy to a market economy. In other words, all countries need to worry about the level of their technology and the quality of their institutions. Again it is worthwhile to go back in time to get a better handle on this. In his classic text, Rostow (1960) suggested that countries go through five stages of economic growth: (1) the traditional society, (2) the preconditions for take-off, (3) the take-off, (4) the drive to maturity, and (5) the age of high mass-consumption. While these stages are a simplified way of measuring the development of modern economies, they identify critical events. When the Soviet Union did not develop into a mass-consumption society (in part due to a lack of total factor productivity), the stages approach to economic growth went out of fashion.

However, growth is not an end in itself as Rostow thought. The beginning and the end of growth is opportunity. A generation's worth of work on the determinants of growth has put the cart before the horse, focusing on the factors that result in growth rather than on the dynamics of the societies within which growth occurs. As a consequence, for a generation, political leaders and policy-makers alike have systematically neglected the vital role of entrepreneurship in capitalist development. As Schumpeter described over a century ago, entrepreneurs are vital to economic development not because they take risks (as we have seen recently in financial markets, risk-taking does in itself not correlate with the creation of social value) but rather because they create "new combinations" of economic activity.

Influenced by recent developments in economics, Porter (2002) has provided a modern rendition of this approach by identifying three stages of development as opposed to growth: (1) a factor-driven stage, (2) an efficiency-driven stage, and (3) an innovation-driven stage and two transitions. While Rostow focused on the *age of high mass-consumption*, Porter following recent developments in the economics of innovation focuses on the *innovation-driven stage*. Historically, an elite entrepreneurial class appears to have played a leading role in economic development. Today we believe that they are also crucial for the *innovation-driven stage*.

The factor-driven stage is marked by high rates of agricultural self-employment. Countries in this stage compete through low-cost efficiencies in the production of commodities or low value-added products. Sole proprietorships — i.e., the self-employed — probably account for most small manufacturing firms and service firms. Almost all economies experience this stage of economic development. These countries neither create knowledge for innovation nor use knowledge for exporting. To move into the second stage, the efficiency-driven stage, countries must increase their production efficiency and educate the workforce to be able to adapt in the subsequent technological development phase: the preconditions for take-off plays a crucial role. The drive to efficiency describes the first transition that is predominantly institutional in nature.

To compete in the efficiency-driven stage, countries must have efficient productive practices in large markets, which allow companies to exploit economies of scale. Industries in this stage are manufacturers that provide basic services. The efficiency-driven stage is marked by decreasing rates of self-employment. When capital and labor are substitutes, an increase in the capital stock increases returns from working and lowers returns from managing.[3] For over a century, there has been a trend in economic activity — exhibited in virtually every developing country — toward larger firms. The transition to the innovation-driven stage is characterized by increased activity by individual agents.

The innovation-driven stage is marked by an increase in knowledge-intensive activities (Romer, 1990). In the efficiency-driven economy, capital and labor play a crucial role in productivity; the firm is exogenous to our analysis and the focus is on technology in the decision-making process. In the innovation-driven stage, knowledge provides the key input. In this stage, the focus shifts from firms to agents in possession of new knowledge (Ács *et al.*, 2009). The agent decides to start a new firm based on expected net returns from a new product. The innovation-driven stage is biased toward high-value-added industries in which entrepreneurial activity is important (Jorgenson, 2001). Aquilina, Klump, and Pietrobelli (2004) suggest that the easier it is to substitute capital for labor, the easier it is to become an entrepreneur.

---

[3] There are other more simplistic explanations for why self-employment may decline as economies develop. Improvements in the economy's infrastructure such as transportation, telecommunications, and credit markets probably increase the advantages of larger firms over smaller firms. Improvements in transportation and telecommunications make it cheaper to distribute goods and services over larger areas. Assuming there are scale economies up to a point, better distribution systems enable firms to operate larger production units that can serve larger markets.

According to Sala-I-Martin *et al.* (2007), the first two stages of development are dominated by institutions. In fact, innovation accounts for only about 5% of economic activity in factor-driven economies and rises to 10% in the efficiency-driven stage. However, in the innovation-driven stage, when opportunities have been exhausted in factors and efficiency, innovation accounts for 30% of economic activity in the innovation-driven stage. We see an S-shaped relationship between entrepreneurship and economic development because in the first transition stage, entrepreneurship plays a role but it increases at a decreasing rate as the efficiency stage takes over. However, as we move from the efficiency-driven stage to the innovation-driven stage (the knowledge-driven stage) entrepreneurship plays a more important role increasing at an increasing rate.

3.6. Agglomeration: The Case of China

This section examines China in some detail to demonstrate the use of the Global Entrepreneurship Index for policy purposes. While the index is not at the city or regional level, the idea of knowledge spillovers are behind the methodology. Total Early-Stage Entrepreneurial Activity (TEA) is a combined measure of the proportion of working-age adults who are starting or running a new business. This activity-based measure is one way of measuring entrepreneurship in a country, but Global Entrepreneurship Monitor (GEM) generates many other measures as well, including measures of aspiration, such as the proportion of TEA that is innovative and technology-based and has high growth. GEM also collects a wide range of data on attitudes to entrepreneurship. Entrepreneurship has greater impact on economic development if it takes place in a favorable environment.

The Global Entrepreneurship Index (GEINDEX) harnesses the information in GEM measures to create a wider measure of productive entrepreneurship in general in a nation. The GEINDEX combines measures of activity, aspiration, and attitudes with relevant measures of the favorability of the environment for entrepreneurship. The GEINDEX is simply the average of three sub-indices, one for attitudes, one for activity, and one for aspiration. Similarly, each sub-index is the average of four or five normalized indicator scores, after adjustment for "bottlenecks," or the weakest indicator in a country (see Ács and Azerb, 2009).

The GEINDEX correlates strongly with economic development, and so it can be used to highlight strong and weak aspects of entrepreneurship in a nation by showing how its nation ranks on the overall index and its three sub-indices (attitudes, activity, and aspiration). Moreover, it is easy to demonstrate where the nation stands on the indicators of each of the sub-indices. Finally, the tool is helpful to identify whether the weak performance of a certain indicator is due to the low institutional development of the nation or the unsatisfactory level of aggregated individual factors.

We now illustrate the practical application of GEINDEX, its 3 sub-indices, the 14 indicators, and the 28 variables with the example of 3 countries in different stages of their economic development. The following charts and tables can serve as visual aids to capture the attention of policymakers, GEM team members, the public, or the media. One can investigate which components are relatively good or bad in relation to other nations by examining the tables below the charts. By showing how each component contributes to the overall link between entrepreneurship, environment, and economic growth, nations can demonstrate the relevance of policies designed to change the weak component.

The investigation is conducted in three levels, (1) the sub-indexes, (2) the indicators, and (3) the variables (individual and institutional) see Tables A1–A3.

(1) On the *sub-indicator level*, we present the relative position of the particular nation in comparison to other nations. The associated trend line of the attitudes, activity, and aspiration sub-indexes makes possible to see if the nation sits above or below the associated trend line.

(2) On the *indicator level*, we display the normalized measures of each indicators within the sub-indexes and three shades of gray are used to show the relative position of a country on each indicators, ranked from highest to lowest and split into top (lightest gray, favorable), middle (to light gray, neutral), and bottom (dark gray, unfavorable).

(3) On the *variable level*, we demonstrate how the normalized values of the institutional and the individual variables contribute to the performance of the indicators. Similar to the previous cases, we apply different shades of gray but in this case not on the indicator but on the variable level. By comparing the shades of the individual and the institutional variables to the indicators, one can quickly figure out how these variables contribute to the overall level of the indicator.

China is a middle-income country with per capita GDP close to $10,000. It is an efficiency-driven economy with a large manufacturing sector and ranks 39th on the GEINDEX and has a moderate level of entrepreneurship. As shown in Figure 3.1, China is above the trend line. While China is below the entrepreneurial activity sub-index, it is significantly above

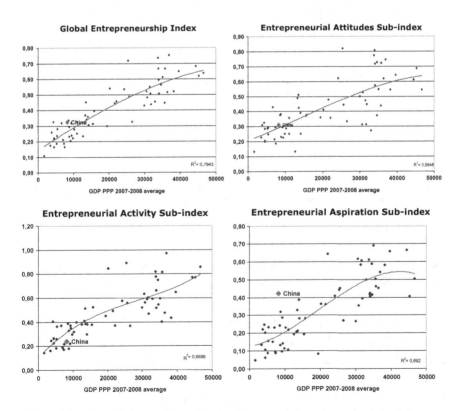

Figure 3.1. The relative position of China in terms of the entrepreneurial sub-indexes and the GEINDEX.

Table 3.1.   The relative position of China in the indicator level

Components of Entrepreneurial Attitudes Sub-index (normalized scores)

	Opportunity Perception	Start-up Skills	Nonfear of Failure	Networking	Cultural Support
China	0.70	0.13	0.63	0.11	0.23
33%	0.34	0.41	0.35	0.17	0.28
67%	0.60	0.64	0.68	0.40	0.57

Components of Entrepreneurial Activity Sub-index (normalized scores)

	Opportunity Start-up	Tech Sector	Quality of Human Resource	Competition
China	0.33	0.31	0.23	0.12
33%	0.40	0.26	0.33	0.42
67%	0.72	0.46	0.60	0.60

Components of Entrepreneurial Aspirations Sub-index (normalized scores)

	New Product	New Techology	High Growth	Internationa-lization	Risk Capital
China	0.50	0.54	0.63	0.28	0.27
33%	0.09	0.26	0.33	0.27	0.10
67%	0.32	0.48	0.53	0.51	0.31

Note: lightest gray: country score lies in top third of all countries by rank; lighter gray: second third; Dark gray: last third

the inspirational sub-index. This drives entrepreneurial activity in China. China could increase its activity sub-index to boost economic development.

Table 3.1 shows the components of the sub-indexes. In the case of aspiration (ASP), that is the highest value out of the three sub-indexes, China appears to have a particular problem with the component RISK CAPITAL, meaning that risk capital investment is too low in China. This can be deduced from the table because the cell for RISK CAPITAL is amber in color, and the number in the cell is considerably below the 67th percentile (the point at which the middle third of nations ranked on this component meet the top third). Moreover, RISK CAPITAL is the lowest value out of the four ASP indicators. According to the PFB methodology, China should improve its performance in aspirations by raising the value of RISK CAPITAL. This would have positive effects on all the other four indicators in the ASP sub-index.

The next step would be to check whether the issue is the low level of the informal investment or the institutional part in this component by analyzing the two variables of the indicator in Table 3.2. In this case, the institutional VENTCAP variable representing the availability of formal venture capital is relatively low (normalized score of VETCAP = 0.25) as opposed to the informal investment value (INFINV = 0.40), hence RISK CAPITAL should be raised by improving the availability of venture capital.

The results here suggest that China is in fact following a knowledge-intensive path to economic development. Knowledge spillovers appear to play an important role in the technology development of the country.

Table 3.2.   The relative position of China in the variable level

Institutional variables		Individual variables		Indicators	
Market size	0.99	Opportunity	0.35	Opportunity Perception	0.70
EDUC	0.19	Skill	0.32	Start-up Skills	0.13
CRR	0.67	Nonfear	0.86	Nonfear of Failure	0.63
Internet usage	0.09	Knowent	0.67	Networking	0.11
CPI	0.20	Carstat	0.59	Cultural Support	0.23
DB	0.52	Teaopport	0.28	Opportunity Start-up	0.33
Tech available	0.30	Techsect	0.45	Tech Sector	0.31
HDI	0.59	HIGHEDUC	0.25	Quality of Human Resource	0.22
Freedom	0.04	COMPET	0.00	Competition	0.12
GERD	0.31	NEWP	0.66	New Product	0.50
Innovcat	0.34	NEWT	0.56	New Techology	0.54
BSS	0.32	Gazelle	0.52	High Growth	0.63
GLOB	0.52	Export	0.314	Internationalization	0.28
VENTCAP	0.25	INFINV	0.40	Risk Capital	0.27
Institutions	0.38	Individual	0.44	GEI	0.32

Note: lightest gray: country lies in top third of all countries by rank; lighter gray: second third; Dark gray: last third.

3.7. Public Policy

Policy makers are interested in promoting economic growth at the national and the regional level. Politicians look to academia to help them understand the process of economic development and inform their decisions. Academics long ago identified technical change through innovation as a key process for generating long-term stable economic growth. However, it begs the question, "What causes innovation in a region or economy?"(Ács and Sanders, 2007).

In accordance with the evidence, the entrepreneur is the agent with whom the buck stops. The creation of the knowledge he/she commercializes is not (necessarily) motivated by the rents that the entrepreneur receives for commercialization. Rents reward the act of commercialization, and as such should not be destroyed, to enhance static efficiency. However, the claim to these rents should also not be transferred to the generators of knowledge that may have had no intent of commercializing and/or require no incentive to create such knowledge in the first place.[4] It is not the generation but the implementation of new knowledge that is valuable to society at large and generates economic growth. Knowledge creation, of course, is a necessary but insufficient condition for innovation and growth, and creation without implementation is clearly a waste of resources. We argue, therefore, that policy makers should stop and think about where the bottlenecks in the innovative process are, before committing large amounts of public money and/or entitlements to profits and rent to the (formal) knowledge generation process.

These results also carry over to the regional level if we consider the impact of limited geographical labor mobility, transport costs, and communication costs. As the knowledge spillovers that drive economic growth are likely to be regionalized, regional policies should aim to smoothen the spillover. A first requirement is that sufficient resources are available for both knowledge creation and knowledge commercialization.

---

[4] As argued in Ács and Sanders (2008), it may well be the effect of stronger patent and IPR-protection.

And as entrepreneurial talent is a key resource in the innovation chain, regional policies should aim to develop it. Moreover, the impediments to knowledge spillovers from creators to commercializers deserve attention. Legal impediments such as non-competition clauses in labor contracts can easily be abandoned. But by investing in physical and communication infrastructures and by stimulating or enabling the exchange of knowledge, local and regional governments can support the entire innovation chain. Direct support to new entrants or R&D should be given only as long as that does not reduce the incentives to create or commercialize new knowledge.

The model outlined in this chapter has important policy implications at the aggregate and regional level but also raises important questions to be addressed. The presence of knowledge spillovers is well documented in the literature. But the exact channels through which such spillovers arise are a challenging area for further research. Our three propositions predicting regional clustering are empirically indistinguishable in most studies, due to data availability issues. The detailed case studies by Klepper (2008) provide support for the first channel that was identified with evidence on importance of physical support infrastructure. Florida presents evidence in support of the third channel we have discussed, but to our knowledge, studies that try to distinguish between them have not yet been done. In addition, at the aggregate level, our theory and its underlying assumptions require further empirical scrutiny. We feel the available evidence supports our claim that knowledge spillovers are important for (regional) economic growth but a lot more can be done to test the model predictions. This empirical research agenda will hopefully inspire other researchers to join us in pursuing it.

3.8. Conclusions

In this review, we introduced the JFV model and made an assessment as to its relevance for economics research. It is highlighted that this approach has become a widely applied tool for testing the spatial extent of knowledge spillovers in different countries, different sectors, and at different spatial scales. In addition, this model became a workhorse of empirical studies of entrepreneurship, agglomeration, and growth. The JFV approach has also proven to become a crucial element in "new generation development policy modeling". Thus the JFV model of knowledge spillovers and its extensions offer an avenue to re-explain the mechanism by which knowledge spillovers operate and open the door for a new understanding of regional and macroeconomic development. If this indeed happens, we would have experienced a paradigm shift in economic science.

References

Acemoglu, D., S. Johnson, and J. Robinson (2004). Institutions as the Fundamental Cause of Long-Run Growth, Chapter 6 in P. Aghion and S. Durlauf (Eds.), *Handbook of Economic Growth*, Vol. 1, New York, NY: Elsevier North Holland, pp. 405–472.

Ács, Z. J., and C. Armington (2006). *Entrepreneurship, Geography and American Economic Growth*. Cambridge, UK: Cambridge University Press.

Ács, Z. J., and D. B. Audretsch (1988). Innovation in large and small firms: An empirical analysis. *The American Economic Review* **78**(4): 678–689.

Ács, Z. J., and D. B. Audretsch, (1989). Patents as a measure of innovative activity. *Kyklos* **42**: 171–180.

Ács, Z. J., and M. Sanders (2008). *Intellectual Property and the Knowledge Spillover Theory of Entrepreneurship*. Jena: Max Planck Institute of Economics.

Ács, Z. J., and A. Varga (2002). Geography, endogenous growth and innovation. *International Regional Science Review* **25**: 132–148.

Ács, Z. J., and A. Varga (2005). Entrepreneurship, agglomeration and technological change. *Small Business Economics* **24**(3): 323–334.

Ács, Z. J., L. Anselin and A. Varga (2002). Patents and innovation counts as measures of regional production of new knowledge. *Research Policy* **31**: 1069–1085.

Ács, Z. J., D. Audretsch and M. P. Feldman (1992). Real effects of academic research: Comment, *American Economic Review* **82**: 363–367.

Ács, Z. J., D. Audretsch and M. P. Feldman (1994). R&D spillovers and recipient firm size. *Review of Economic Statistics* **99**: 336–340.

Ács, Z. J., D. Audretsch, P. Braunerhjelm and B. Carsson (2006). *The Knowledge Spillover Theory of Entrepreneurship*. London: Center for Economic Policy Research.

Anselin, L. (1988). *Spatial Econometrics: Methods and Models*. Boston, MA: Kluwer Academic Publishers.

Anselin, L. (2001). Spatial Econometrics, in B. Baltagi (Ed.), *A Companion to Theoretical Econometrics*. Oxford: Basil Blackwell, pp. 310–330.

Anselin, L., A. Varga and Z. J. Ács (1997). Local geographic spillovers between university research and high technology innovation. *Journal of Urban Economics* **42**: 422–448.

Anselin, L., A. Varga and Z. J. Ács (2000a). Geographic and sectoral characteristics of academic knowledge spillovers. *Papers in Regional Science* **79**: 435–445.

Anselin, L., A. Varga and Z. J. Ács (2000b). Geographic spillovers and university research: A spatial econometric approach. *Growth and Change* **31**: 501–515.

Audretsch, D. (1995). *Innovation and Industry Evolution.* Cambridge, MA: MIT Press.

Audretsch, D., and M. P. Feldman (1996). R&D spillovers and the geography of innovation and production. *American Economic Review* **86**: 630–640.

Audretsch, D., M. C. Keilbach and E. E. Lehmann (2006). *Entrepreneurship and Economic Growth.* Oxford, UK: Oxford University Press.

Baldwin, R. E., and R. Forslid (2000). The core–periphery model and endogenous growth: Stabilising and de-stabilizing integration. *Economica* **67**: 307–324.

Baldwin, R., R. Forslid, Martin Ph., G. Ottaviano and F. Robert-Nicoud (2003). *Economic Geography and Public Policy.* Princeton, NJ: Princeton University Press.

Baumol, W. (2004). Entrepreneurial enterprises, large established firms and other components of the free-market growth machine. *Small Business Economics* **23**(1), 9–21.

Braczyk, H., P. Cooke and M. Heidenreich (1998). *Regional Innovation Systems: The Role of Governances in a Globalized World.* London, UK: UCL Press.

Clark, G. L., M. P. Feldman and M. S. Gertler (2000). *The Oxford Handbook of Economic Geography.* Oxford, UK: Oxford University Press.

Feldman, M. P. (1994). *The Geography of Innovation.* New York, NY: Kluwer Academic Publishers.

Feldman, M. P., and R. Florida (1994). The geographic sources of innovation: Technological infrastructure and product innovation in the United States. *Annals of the Association of American Geographers* **84**: 210–229.

Feldman, M. P., and D. B. Audretsch (1999). Innovation in cities: Science-based diversity, specialization and localized competition. *European Economic Review* **43**: 409–429.

Fujita, M., P. Krugman and A. Venables (1999). *The Spatial Economy.* Cambridge, MA: MIT Press.

Fujita, M., and J. Thisse (2002). *Economics of Agglomeration. Cities, Industrial Location, and Regional Growth.* Cambridge, MA and London, UK: Cambridge University Press.

Griliches, Z. (1979). Issues in assessing the contributions of research and development to productivity growth. *The Bell Journal of Economics* **10**: 92–116.

Hayek, F., A. von (1937). Economics and knowledge. *Economica* (New Series), **4**: 33–54.

Hellmann, T. (2007). When do employees become entrepreneurs? *Management Science* **53**(6).

Jaffe, A. (1989). The real effects of academic research. *American Economic Review* **79**: 957–970.

Jaffe, A., M. Trajtenberg and R. Henderson (1993). Geography, location of knowledge spillovers as evidence of patent citations. *Quarterly Journal of Economics* **108**: 483–499.

Jaffe, A., and M. Trajtenberg (2002). *Patents, Citations and Innovations: A Window on the Knowledge Economy.* Cambridge, MA: MIT Press.

Jaffe, A., M. Trajtenberg and R. Henderson (2005). Patent citations and the geography of knowledge spillovers: A reassessment: Comment. *American Economic Review* **95**(1) 461–465.

Jones, C. (1995). R&D based models of economic growth. *Journal of Political Economy* **103**: 759–784.

66   *Entrepreneurship and Economic Growth in China*

Jorgenson, D. W. (2001). Information Technology and the U.S. Economy, *American Economic Review* **91**: 1–32.

Kirzner, I. M. (1973). *Competition and Entrepreneurship.* Chicago, IL: University of Chicago Press.

Krugman, P. (1991). Increasing returns and economic geography. *Journal of Political Economy* **99**: 483–499.

Kuhn, T. (1962). *The Structure of Scientific Revolutions.* Chicago, IL: The University of Chicago Press.

Lazear, E. P. (2005). Entrepreneurship. *Journal of Labor Economics* **23**(4): 649–680.

Nelson, J. R. (1991.) *National Innovation Systems.* Cambridge, MA: Harvard University Press.

Romer, P. (1986). Increasing returns and economic growth. *Journal of Political Economy* **94**: 1002–1037.

Romer, P. (1990). Endogenous technological change. *Journal of Political Economy* **98**, S71–S102.

Rostow, W. W. (1960). The five stages of growth, Chapter 2 in *The Stages of Economic Growth: A Non-Communist Manifesto.* Cambridge: Cambridge University Press, pp. 416.

Schumpeter, J. A. (1911) [1934]. *The Theory of Economic Development*, Cambridge, MA: Harvard University Press.

Shane, S. (2001). Technological opportunity and new firm creation. *Management Science* **47**(2): 205–220.

Thissen, M. (2003). RAEM 2.0 *A Regional Applied General Equilibrium Model for the Netherlands.* Manuscript, pp. 19.

Thompson, P., and M. Fox-Kean. (2005a). Patent citations and the geography of knowledge spillovers: A reassessment. *American Economic Review* **95**(1): 450–461.

Thompson, P., and M. Fox-Kean. (2005b). Patent citations and the geography of knowledge spillovers: A reassessment: Reply. *American Economic Review* **95**(1), 465–467.

Varga, A. (1998). *University Research and Regional Innovation: A Spatial Econometric Analysis of Academic Technology Transfers.* Boston, MA: Kluwer Academic Publishers.

Varga, A. (2000). Local academic knowledge spillovers and the concentration of economic activity. *Journal of Regional Science* **40**: 289–309.

Varga, A. (2001). Universities and regional economic development: Does agglomeration matter? in B. Johansson, C. Karlsson and R. Stough (Eds.) *Theories of Endogenous Regional Growth — Lessons for Regional Policies*, Berlin: Springer, pp. 345–367.

Varga, A., and H. J. Schalk (2004). Knowledge spillovers, agglomeration and macroeconomic growth: An empirical approach. *Regional Studies* **38**: 977–989.

Varga, A. (2006). The spatial dimension of innovation and growth: Empirical research methodology and policy analysis. *European Planning Studies* **9**: 1171–1186.

Varga, A. (2007). GMR-HUNGARY: A complex macro-regional model for the analysis of development policy impacts on the Hungarian economy. Final Report, Project No. NFH 370/2005.

Varga, A. (2008). From the geography of innovation to development policy analysis: The GMR-approach. *Annals of Economics and Statistics* **87–88**, 83–102.

Zucker, L. G., M. R. Darby and M. B. Brewer (1998). Intellectual human capital and the birth of U.S. biotechnology enterprises. *American Economic Review* **88**(1), 290–306.

APPENDIX

Table A1. The description of the applied variables and indicators of the Entrepreneurial Attitude (ATT) sub-index

Individual Variable	Institutional Variable	Source	Calculation	Indicator
OPPORTUNITY is defined as the percentage of the 18–64 population identifying good opportunity in the area they live.	MARKETSIZE is defined as the size of the market on a seven-point Likert scale.	World Economic Forum	OPPORTUNITY × MARKET SIZE	OPPORTUNITY PERCEPTION
SKILL is defined as the percentage of the 18–64 population possessing adequate start-up skills	EDUC is the percentage of the population enrolled in post-secondary education.	World Bank	SKILL × EDUC	STARTUP SKILLS
NONFEAR is defined as the percentage of the 18–64 population who do not fear failure starting a business.	CRR is the Country Risk Rate that refers to the financial, macroeconomic, and business climate. The alphabetical rating is turned to a seven-point Likert scale to fit to our data set.	Coface	NONFEAR × CRR	NONFEAR OF FAILURE
KNOWENT is defined as the percentage of the 18–64 population who knows an entrepreneur personally who started a business in two years.	INTERNETUSAGE is the Internet users per 100 inhabitants.	International Telecommunication Union	KNOWENT × INTERNET-USAGE	NETWORKING
CARSTAT is the average of the percentages of the 18–64 population who say that entrepreneurship is a good career choice and has social high status.	CPI is the perceived levels of corruption, as determined by expert assessments and opinion surveys on a seven-point Likert scale.	Transparency International	CARSTAT × CPI	CULTURAL SUPPORT

Table A2. The description of the applied variables and indicators of the Entrepreneurial Activity (ACT) sub-index

Individual Variable	Institutional Variable	Source	Calculation	Indicator
TEAOPPORT is the percentage of the 18–64 population who are nascent entrepreneurs or who own and manage a business aged less than 3 to 5 years and started the business because of opportunity motivation divided by the TEA	DB is the normalized value of the ease of doing business, reflecting how the regulatory environment is conducive to the operation of business.	World Bank	TEAOPPORT × DB	OPPORTUNITY STARTUP
TECHSECT is the percentages of TEA that are in the medium- or high-tech sector	TECHAVAILABLE is the availability of the latest technology on a seven-point Likert scale.	World Economic Forum,	TECHSECT × TECHAVAIL-ABLE	TECHNOLOGY SECTOR
HIGHEDUC is the percentage of TEA entrepreneurs having at least a post-secondary education.	HDI is a measure of the quality of human resource combining life expectancy, educational attainment, and income.	United Nations	HIGHEDUC × HDI	QUALITY OF HUMAN RESOURCES
COMPET is the percentage of TEA where few competitors offer the same product.	FREEDOM is the freedom of the economy is one sub-index of the overall economic freedom score for each country, where 100 represents the maximum freedom	Heritage Foundation	COMPET × FREEDOM	COMPETITION

Table A3. The description of the applied variables and indicators of the Entrepreneurial Aspiration (ASP) sub-index

Individual Variable	Institutional Variable	Source	Calculation	Indicator
NEWP is the percentage of TEA business where entrepreneurs think that the product is new to at least some customers	GERD is the R&D percentage of GDP	OECD	NEWPROD × GERD	NEW PRODUCT
NEWT is defined as the percentage of TEA business where the technology is less than 5 years old	INNOVCAT is a measure of whether a business environment allows cutting edge innovations	World Economic Forum (GCI)	NEWT × INNOVCAT	NEW TECH
GAZELLE is defined as the percentage of high-growth TEA business (employing 10 plus persons and over 50% growth in 5 years)	BSS refers to the ability of companies to pursue distinctive strategies, which involves differentiated positioning and innovative means of production and service delivery	World Economic Forum GCI	GAZELLE × BSS	HIGH GROWTH

(Continued)

Table A3. (*Continued*)

Individual Variable	Institutional Variable	Source	Calculation	Indicator
EXPORT is the percentage of TEA business exporting at least 1% of product	GLOB is the Index of Globalization measuring the economic, social, and political dimensions of globalization.	KOF Swiss Economic Institute	EXPORT × GLOB	INTERNATION ALIZATION
INFINV is defined as the percentage of informal investors in the 18–64 aged population multiplied by the average amount of informal investment.	VENTCAP is a measure of the venture capital availability on a seven-point Likert scale	World Economic Forum	INFINV × VENTCAP	RISK CAPITAL

Part III

Economic Impact of Entrepreneurship, Innovation, and Technology

Chapter 4

Factor Accumulation or TFP: How does Entrepreneurship Empirically Account for Economic Growth?

Junbo Yu

Jilin University

For a long time, unsettled controversies have existed in explaining the source of growth. Although many development practitioners and researchers continue to target capital (physical capital, human capital, and other supplements suggested by endogenous economic growth literatures) accumulation as the driving force in economic growth, "something else" besides capital accumulation is critical for understanding differences in economic growth and income across countries (Easterly and Levine, 2001). Economists typically refer to the "something else" as *total factor productivity* (TFP).

Earlier, entrepreneurship has been touted as the generating factor for "creative destruction", thus for continuous technology change and long-term economic growth ever since the publishing of Schumpeter's economic development theory. However, not until the advent of the post-industrialization age and the prevalence of the "endogenous economic growth theory", could entrepreneurship theory be integrated into mainstream economic analysis and thus be able to exploit its adjunctive empirical research methods. Urged by expressions such as "the long-term imprint of any growth theory must ultimately depend on the extent to which it generates a productive empirical literature" (Pack, 1994), positive research literatures are pouring out at an increasing rate in the entrepreneurship field, aiming to substantiate Schumpeter with econometric facts. As a consequence, entrepreneurship is incrementally involved with the debate on the source of growth: capital accumulation versus TFP.

This chapter documents important attempts to incorporate entrepreneurship into growth empirics. It does not argue which attempt is more successful, since countries at specific junctures usually do not share the same explanation for their growth. On the contrary, this study encourages analogous works, nevertheless, it corrects concept misinterpretations among them and proposes revised techniques to reproduce more delicate facts. Its proposition has also been preliminarily demonstrated by growth empirics from China.

4.1. Rationale of the Debate: Capital Accumulation versus TFP

We begin by briefly exploring the rationale of the debate so that when entrepreneurship enters in subsequent sections, the conceptual thread will remain clear.

Basically, the controversy on the source of long-term growth reflects the economist's suspicion on the prediction made by Solow growth model. Divergent results generated by standard growth accounting principle stimulate such suspicion:

Starting from a conventional Cobb–Douglas neoclassical production function

$$Y = AK^{\alpha}(L^{1-\alpha}) \qquad (4.1)$$

where Y is national output, A is an index of the level of technology,[1] K is the physical capital stock, L is the number of units of labor input (reflecting work patterns, human capital, and the like), and α is a production

---

[1]To simplify the algebra, we assume that technology is Hicks neutral rather than Harrod neutral.

function parameter (equal to the share of capital income in national output under perfect competition).

Under the assumption of constant return to scale, the capital share and the labor share add to 1. Output growth is then divided into components attributable to changes in the factors of production. Rewriting Equation (4.1) in growth rates:

$$(\Delta Y/Y) = (\Delta A/A) + \alpha(\Delta K/K) + (1-\alpha)(\Delta L/L) \qquad (4.2)$$

In other words, the growth rate of aggregate output equals $\Delta A/A$, the growth rate of TFP, plus a weighted average of the growth rate of the two inputs, where the weights are the corresponding input shares.

In such a model, increases in saving and the investment on human capital will substantially spark growth, since they are assumed to be the key inputs for production while A is postulated to be exogenous and comparatively constant in the short term. However, despite cases in which factor accumulation is closely tied to economic success, more growth accounting examinations suggest that TFP growth frequently account for the bulk of growth in output per worker and many countries failed to obtain desired prosperity through their outlays on the expansion of capital stock (Easterly and Levine, 2001). As a response to the challenge from reality, succeeding literatures sought to find supplemental theories to account for growth empirics more accurately.

Following along the path pioneered by Romer (1986) and Lucas (1988), endogenous growth theory argues that there are additional variables evidently encouraging growth, yet left unidentified in the Solow model. These so-called "ancillary variables" (Baumol, 1993) varied from widely acknowledged human capital to investment on equipment (DeLong and Summers, 1990), the measurement of political stability (Barro and Sala-i-Martin, 1990), and the openness of the economy to foreign trade (Dollar and Wolff, 1993). In these studies, the statistic results are considerably enriched by the addition of one (or several) variable(s) to the regressions used earlier to test whether countries are growing similar in terms of the level of GDP. Calculations using the added variable show that the forces of "conditional convergence" do exist and tend to encompass far more countries, extend over longer time than that indicated by earlier simpler studies.

However, growth accounting by incorporating such additional variables remains controversial: Changes in factor accumulation still do not closely track changes in economic growth. This finding is consistent across very different frequencies of data no matter what additional variable(s) we take into account as a new input factor. Therefore, Pack (1994) argued that most empirical research rooted from endogenous growth theory merely construct a refined approach to test Solow model's inferences, e.g., convergence, rather than providing substantial evidence for their own hypotheses.

In contrast, an alternative approach focused on dissecting A, the TFP, and identifying the policies and institutions most conducive to its growth. Literatures along this route concentrate on one-hedged hypothesis employed by the Solow model while it is trying to simplify the determinants for growth: the growth rate of technology A (conventionally represented by g) is not only exogenous but also constant across countries. Such an assumption directly leads us to the prediction of Solow model where more light has been shed on saving rate and population growth. The outcome of growth accounting we mentioned previously, however, rejected this hypothesis evidently and presented that the intertemporal and cross-country differences of technology growth rates are rather more significant than the variances of saving and population growth rate. The acknowledgement to this violation can also have further implications stemming from the fact that convergence or conditional convergence did not occur: Solow model need not necessarily be invalidated since it was not designed and constructed to predict growth while the production function and its rate of shift (i.e., the technological constant A and its rate of increase g) vary.

The above interpretation results in a consensus among certain group of economists that sustainable economic development and growth should be understood as the process by which an economy continuously increases its capacity of creating and absorbing technology. From their perspectives, "ancillary variables", e.g., human capital, institution quality, and policy properness, identified by endogenous growth theory, should be testified as the determinants of TFP instead of as any direct input in the production function while more determinants are still left to be discovered in this regard (Easterly and Levine, 2001).

Despite the absence of an agreement, the disputes between factor accumulation and TFP nevertheless force every researcher to scrutinize those empirics and associated explanations contained in his work, in case they could be applied within the alternative approach to reach a more tenable result. Namely, factor accumulation and TFP have become two standard yet somewhat mutually exclusive tunnels to connect a growth element with the empirical research framework. The way in which entrepreneurship surfaced in empirical growth literatures will demonstrate this pattern for us in subsequent sections.

4.2. Entrepreneurship in the Capital Accumulation Approach

The notion of considering entrepreneurship as a crucial yet ignored input originates from Marshall's *Principles of Economics* (1890), where he stressed that entrepreneurship is another type of necessary input for economic growth besides labor, money, and land. Some recent literatures are fascinated by this idea since the authors believe that entrepreneurship deserves more than the residual item, i.e., TFP. Theories such as "entrepreneurship capital" (Audretsch and Keilbach, 2005) and "the missing link" (Ács *et al.*, 2004) explicitly demonstrated that entrepreneurship has played an irreplaceable role in the endogenous economic growth theory and neither conventional inputs like physical capital and labor nor human capital or R&D expenditure could substitute it with respect to the commercialization of inventions or the application of imported technology. Furthermore, related empirical studies have surfaced subsequently, where the authors' measurements of entrepreneurship input, mostly quasi self-employment rate indicators, were regressed with other determinants of economic growth (Ács *et al.*, 2005). Their conclusions, as we can expect, uniformly confirmed that the accumulation of "entrepreneurship capital" significantly improved the growth performance among OECD countries.

Theoretically, this capital accumulation approach is more straightforward than the TFP approach in terms of building a direct connection between entrepreneurship and economic growth. However, this does not relieve criticism to its associated empirical works. Challenges apart from the measurement deficiency[2] include econometric skills to deal with the endogeneity of entrepreneurship; concerns on the violation of production theory when regressions chose the Cobb–Douglas form, especially the assumption that the substitution elasticity among entrepreneurship and other inputs is 1; and heterogeneity of entrepreneurship, e.g., the difference between entrepreneurship for survival and entrepreneurship for achievements may violate the homogenous assumption in production theory as well. Any of the above critiques can become a fatal disease to the empirical results of those listed literatures, thus urgently requiring further improvements.

An additional drawback of testifying entrepreneurship's contribution to economic growth as an extra capital was found to be the incapability to distinguish its own uniqueness from other "ancillary variables" (Baumol, 1993). Despite the fact that all these ancillary variables, including the entrepreneurship capital, were identified as accelerators for output increase, a remarkable feature is that all of these analyses reach qualitative conclusions that are essentially the same, regardless of the set of statistics they have employed as ancillary variables. A plausible explanation of this rather implausible result is that many, if not all, of the ancillary variables selected for inclusion in the analysis have behavior patterns that are exceedingly similar. Were it so, then any of them can, in a statistical sense, serve as a proxy for the others. The similarity in their intertemporal

---

[2]Namely the distortion of the concept of entrepreneurship and the proper estimation of entrepreneurship capital stock. Actually, it is more depressing to see that extant theories have not been able to explain or estimate the investment rate and depreciation rate of "entrepreneurship capital".

trajectories means that as far as a regression analysis is concerned they are all virtually the same variable. Such inferences actually produce an annoying paradox: the empirics we discovered are supporting entrepreneurship's contribution while implying the falsification of its irreplaceable role in the growth process.

This paradox may be tentatively ascribed to the failure of confronting endogeneity, particularly the causality among entrepreneurship and other ancillary variables. Extant empirical entrepreneurship studies along the capital accumulation approach are overeager to prove the superiority of their concern over any other variable. They skip the process to explore and define a reasonable path to relate entrepreneurship with human capital, R&D investment, political stability, and the openness of an economy before treating them equally in a regression based on the augmented production function. In contrast, it has been recognized for a long time in theoretical literatures that, in terms of the standard list of the variables affecting economic growth, entrepreneurship enters only indirectly. For instance, innovation and technology transfer were assumed to be encouraged by the work of the entrepreneurs (Baumol, 1993; Schumpeter and Opie, 1934) while they would act upon economic output more straightforward. Causalities have also been distinguished among given ancillary variables and entrepreneurship, e.g., globalization and political regime were found to be crucially influential to the supply of entrepreneurs (Audretsch, 2002; North, 1981; Rosenberg and Birdzell, 1986). An overlook to these literatures in the name of simplicity will, no surprisingly, end with the ambiguous result that appeared previously.

4.3. Entrepreneurship in the TFP Approach

Ignited by Solow's breakthrough in 1957, a growing body of research suggests that, even after physical capital accumulation is accounted for, TFP accounts for the bulk intertemporal and cross-country differences in the level and growth rate of gross domestic product (GDP). The subsequent failure of employing ancillary variables as omitted inputs to reduce TFP's importance in growth accounting, suggested by endogenous growth theory, further encouraged economists to develop conceptual models of

TFP, concentrating on the disparity of technology level A and the growth rate of technology g across countries.

Different theories offer very different conceptions of TFP. These range from changes in technology to the role of externalities, changes in the sector composition of production, and the adoption of lower-cost production methods. Evidence that confidently assesses how well these conceptions of TFP explain economic growth is lacking. Even with this flaw, it is noticeable that entrepreneurship finally managed to participate, aiming to explain the source of TFP.

Aghion and Howitt (1992) offered the most well-known piece to accommodate Schumpeterian entrepreneurship in a dynamic general equilibrium system for addressing technology innovation process. They exploited the term "creative destruction", so as to stress that their growth model, which is rooted on vivid display of entrepreneurial activities, should be taken as the descendent of Schumpeterian development theory. Its inherent logic was that entrepreneurship contributes to competition, innovation, technology progress, and hence to economic growth. This does fairly reflect the Schumpeterian entrepreneurship theory. However, the above authors were apparently more interested in formulating the mechanism bridging technology progress and continuous growth. As a result, TFP was not explicitly mentioned as the empirical counterparts for technology progress, which in reverse suppresses the information that this paper could provide for later empirical studies. In a nutshell, the authors were successful in terms of modeling the linkage between entrepreneurship and g, yet still one step away from regarding g as TFP growth rate empirically, thus could not combine entrepreneurship and TFP growth.

In contrast, Harberger (1998) clearly pointed out that:

> The pioneer writings of the recent endogenous growth literature can, I think, be said to reflect a kind of annoyance at something like R or R' (TFP) being considered exogenous. There was an urge to surmount that inelegance by somehow making the residual endogenous. [p. 3].

(Contents in the parentheses are added by the author).

Such an expression concisely clarifies that TFP as the outcome of empirical growth accounting not only provides the stylized facts stimulating endogenous economic growth theory but also naturally provides an approach to testify the validity of associated theories, i.e., any new variable or factor incorporated in an endogenous model should be a significant determinant of TFP after its magnitude has been empirically captured.

Right from this recognition, Harberger proposed to treat TFP as the real cost reduction in production process and convert TFP to the number of dollars saved by real cost reduction, making itself a tangible and measurable quantity. Moreover, he took his concept as:

> It gives the residual a name (real cost reduction), an address (the firm), and a face (the face of the entrepreneur, the CEO, the production manager, etc.). And, finally, we shall see that there can be vastly different expressions on that face, even as we move from firm to firm in a given industry, as the TFP experience of period moves from sharply positive to devastatingly negative. [p. 4]

(Contents in the last parentheses are added by the author).

Explicitly, Harberger ascribed TFP growth to entrepreneurship, which presented us a vision to empirically examine entrepreneurship's contribution to growth.

The reason Harberger recommended "real cost reduction" as an entrepreneurship-driven TFP explanation can be chiefly traced back to the common characteristics shared by entrepreneurship and TFP. Known to most of the entrepreneurship economists, in terms of macroeconomics, entrepreneurship has been defined as the function of carrying out the innovations, risk taking, and management, which includes both supervision and coordinating ability or even changing the production function or applying a new production function (Chang, 1969); in terms of microeconomics, it has been interpreted as a mental attitude dominated by the principles of acquisition, competition, and economic rationality

(Sombart, 1929); in terms of institutional economics, entrepreneurship represents the culture and legislation system encouraging enterprising actions (Baumol, 1990). In short, entrepreneurship shadows most of the factors listed by economists to explain TFP increase. As a consequence, making TFP a face of the entrepreneurs is rather logical in a conceptual sense.

Inspired by Harberger, High (2004) published a paper which entirely transferred the conceptual consistency between entrepreneurship and TFP into an empirical practice. Choosing the term "entrepreneurial value added" instead of real cost reduction, High calculated the sectoral TFP in the U.S. economy and considered them as entrepreneurship's contribution to economic growth. Earlier, Lu (2000) had also conducted similar estimation and concluded that 40% of the GDP growth in China from 1979 to 1998 should be attributed to entrepreneurship, an alias of TFP, among which management innovation accounted for about 20%.

4.4. Problematic Methodology

Is it appropriate to exploit Harberger's theory in this way? Let us shortly reconsider the China case: Before the social reform, from 1952 to 1978, China ran a typical central by planned economy while its ideology was strongly hostile to entrepreneurs. Given such adverse circumstances, we can hardly believe the existence of a productive entrepreneurship in China during that period. Meanwhile, TFP did exist and oscillated (Chow, 1993; Chow and Li, 2002). If we admit that TFP represents the contribution of entrepreneurship, how can we explain the phenomenon that there was little entrepreneurship in pre-reform China while its contribution to economic growth is evident?

The above puzzling question forces us to interrogate Harberger's theory and his followers' practice further. First of all, we suspect that Harberger did not distinguish three concepts precisely: the magnitude of entrepreneurship (ME), the magnitude of entrepreneurship's contribution (MEC) to economic growth, which is assumed by theories, and TFP. In a positive study attempting to testify entrepreneurship theory, the backbone should be those solid empirics could reveal the causal or at least positive correlation between ME and MEC. With respect to MEC, it is normally inferred from the coefficient of ME in a regression of growth/production function as previous literatures did from the capital accumulation approach. Otherwise, were researchers able to find an acceptable "equal" for MEC in growth accounting, e.g., TFP, ME should be tested as a determinant of MEC or its equal to justify the original hypothesis. Harberger and his adherents, however, never construct an indicator of ME to prove that entrepreneurship contributes to growth in the way they predicted. In other words, calculating TFP as MEC can become a job in vain since there are no empirics confirming the connection between MEC and ME, which is merely assumed to be existed by theories.

The unidentified connection between ME and MEC, unfortunately, often makes the calculation of TFP as MEC untenable. As is known to all, ME is subject to institutional constraints while TFP is basically a surplus that universally existed after growth accounting, regardless of the institution uniqueness. They may become separable in a global context, since only countries with favorable institutions could foster ME and generate MEC as a part of TFP while other countries with TFP growth do not necessarily count on, at least in a short term, the prosperity of ME. As a consequence, measuring ME turns out to be very important for addressing the connection between entrepreneurship and TFP growth more properly: for countries with little ME, TFP growth should be ascribed to other factors, for instance, the accumulation of human capital and the economy of scale; for countries with a varied ME, the trajectory of ME and TFP should be compared for identifying a possible causal relationship and MEC.

Second, deficiencies in TFP theory will sometimes weaken the conceptual connection between entrepreneurship and TFP. Two most commonly used methodologies in productivity growth literatures have been growth accounting and econometric estimation of production functions (Felipe, 1997). The appropriateness of these two methods hinges on how well the assumption of perfectly competitive markets approximates the real economy at the aggregate level. The application of such skills to developing countries or transitional countries like China will certainly violate their imposed assumptions, thus making the subsequent estimation of TFP problematic. How can we still empirically testify the correlation between entrepreneurship and TFP with dubious TFP calculation results? Additionally, Jorgenson (1995), Chen (1997), and Felipe (1997) have respectively criticized that the disembodied and Hicks-neutral technical progress assumption in traditional TFP calculation often resulted in the failure of the accountants to consider capital-embodied and labor-embodied technology progress, this would assign these improvements to TFP growth. Labor-embodied technology progress in most of the countries is due to improved education and health, while the source of capital-embodied technology varies from the renewal of capital in developed world to the import of advanced technology in developing countries. After they have been improperly assigned to TFP, we may further reject the hypothesis that TFP mostly comes from the contribution of entrepreneurship.

4.5. An Attempt to Revise along the TFP Approach

The revisions to preceding problems that we shall propose accordingly consist of the measuring of entrepreneurship and the decomposition of TFP. The former serves to empirically capture ME while the latter aims to construct and redefine a more appropriate counterpart as MEC in TFP.

Before undertaking these revisions, the rationale for empirical studies along TFP approach, which we displayed in the first section, should be reminded: TFP studies focus on the differences in terms of initial technology level and technology growth rate across regions, attempting to offer general and persuasive explanations. Therefore, calculating TFP simply generates the facts we are supposed to interpret, rather than the terminal for further exploration. Previous entrepreneurship studies along the TFP approach, however, appeared to disregard the principle of TFP research while they were more obsessed by presumably calculating TFP as MEC. This chapter, as a response, will try to demonstrate the connection between entrepreneurship and TFP with solid empirics, where the establishment of an indicator to measure MEC becomes necessary.

Meanwhile, since both entrepreneurship and TFP are well perceived to be intertemporal and cross-country phenomena, our research method including the case design, the selection of indicators, and adjunct econometric techniques, have to be comparatively flexible and robust when they are imposed with some strong country-specific constraints. Consequently, the appropriateness of indicator selection and TFP decomposition serving to distinguish ME from other TFP determinants, deserve sufficient consideration to satisfy countries' individual characteristics.

The way to measure entrepreneurship in current literatures includes Total Entrepreneurial Activity (TEA) index compiled by Global Entrepreneurship Monitor (GEM), which is a yearly updated cross-country survey database, and some other statistics analogous to self-employment, e.g., start-up rate. (Audretsch and Keilbach, 2005; Carree *et al.*, 2002; Reynolds *et al.*, 2005). GEM data appeared since 1999 and its time series for current 43 members are not balanced, hence its alternative, the quasi self-employment measurements, more available and somewhat comparable, are widely adopted. However, such measurements like the "start-up rate" only partially capture the multi-dimensioned content of entrepreneurship: seizing and acting upon opportunities, intensifying competition, fostering the culture of enterprising, and so on (Audretsch, 2002).

The loss of integrity during the process of abstracting and quantifying a multi-dimensioned concept is not unusual to economists. The justice of the loss mostly relies on whether the remaining parts can still describe the reality properly. And the answer, as what we will show later, is normally a country-specific issue. Meanwhile, such distorted measurements do require more delicate decomposition to their empirical regress and, otherwise, a test on the connection will suffer from mismatch and identify no correlation at all. Upon that, TFP decomposition skills are needed.

The methodology related to TFP decomposition is still rare and has been exclusively based on frontier production function estimations, in which TFP is broken down into technical progress and technical efficiency change (Fare *et al.*, 1994). Technical progress is associated with changes in the best-practice production frontier, and technical efficiency change with other productivity changes, such as learning by doing, improved managerial practices, and change in the efficiency with which a known technology is applied. Though not delicate enough, the combination of such methods and reasonable ME measurement is promising to produce some preliminary empirics confirming entrepreneurship's contribution to TFP growth from a whole new perspective.

4.6. An Empirical Test with the Case of China (1996–2004)

Empirical work that investigates the direct link between entrepreneurship and economic growth at a transitional economy level is quite scarce to our knowledge. This vacancy may lead to fragile hypothesis partially based on the experiences of developed countries, given the country-specific character of entrepreneurship. In contrast, the arguments developed in the preceding three sections will be applied in an empirical study consisting of 27 Chinese provinces over a nine-year period, covering the years from 1996 to 2004. The purpose of exploiting China's story is twofold: discovering some noticeable and unique pattern for entrepreneurship and TFP in a transitional economy scenario; illustrating that entrepreneurship contributes to China's post-reform economic growth via assumed channels. The channels to choose in between are those two approaches (capital accumulation and TFP) being evaluated in previous sections and are assumed to bridge our theoretical hypothesis and empirical results properly.

It is also noteworthy that the following empirical study is abstracted from two chapters in the authors' doctoral dissertation (Yu, 2007). Details on how we described the mechanism linking entrepreneurship and economic growth in an endogenous growth model, on the derivation of hypothesis to be tested for the empirical methodologies' mathematic expression, and the sources of the data, can be found in the dissertations accordingly. For this chapter particularly, we skip those details after a brief to the stories that the reader's must know, and then, start right from the empirical results and their implications.

4.7. Crucial Facts and Hypotheses

The following facts are crucial to understand the subsequent research design and empirical outcomes:

Fact I: 30 years to kill, 30 years to cure. A central planned economy used to dominate China before the economic and social reforms initiated from 1978. This means that since the completion of the so-called "Socialism Transformation" (*She Hui Zhu Yi Gai Zao*) in 1952, entrepreneurship had been ruled out of China economically as well as politically for nearly 30 years. The revival of entrepreneurship actually occurred gradually with the reconstruction of market economy and the boom of non-state sector in China, merely within the last 30 years (Li and Zhang, 2000).

Fact II: The myth behind miracles. Since 1978, China has been experiencing a nearly double-digit annual growth rate in the subsequent decades. However, when people review the myth of China's miracle, they could find that China has been exploiting an outstanding high investment rate to sustain its GDP growth (see Figure 4.1 and Table 4.1), e.g., over 40% of its GDP was annually invested in recent years (Bai, Hsieh, and Qian, 2006). Meanwhile, technology progress in China was mostly obtained from state-owned enterprises' (SOEs) purchase from advanced countries, such as the U.S. and Japan. Domestic private enterprises tend to replicate or imitate technologies due to their lack of R&D fund while the SOEs would not innovate either, which could be attributed to their advantages of administrative monopoly (Gilboy, 2004). Severe dependence on physical investment and the backwardness in technology innovation capability irritated widespread criticism and concerns on the prospect of China's economic growth (Zheng and Hu, 2006). As a response, the Chinese government announced a new development strategy recently titled as "Independent Innovation" and gradually intensified financial and currency policies to slowdown its infrastructure investment.

The combination of Facts I and II may yield a very interesting question: how does entrepreneurship account for the achievements and problems in China's reform period? Preliminary answers were offered in the author's

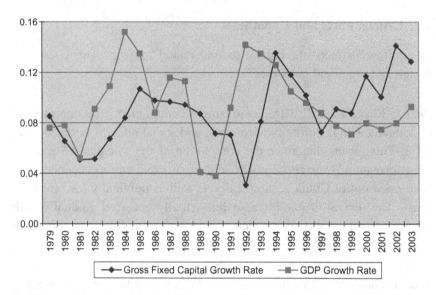

Figure 4.1. Growth rate of China's gross fixed capital and GDP, 1979–2003.

Source: National Bureau of Statistics of China and author's calculations.

Table 4.1. The comparison of capital formation rate between China and other sampled regions (%)

	1999	2002	2003
China	37.1	39.2	42.3
Low-Income Countries	21.3	21.3	21.7
Mid-Income Countries	22.4	23.2	24.5
Europe and Mid-East	19.9	21.7	21
South Asia	22.5	21.6	22.7
OECD	22	19	—

Source: http://www.worldbank.org.

dissertation while here we only present those hypotheses, methodologies, and results directly associated with the theme of this Chapter.

Hypothesis I: *Fact I* implies that entrepreneurship in China, just recovering and fledgling within a transitional economy, tends to promote economic performance in China mainly through a Kirzner-style arbitraging process, which is in accord with its primary development stage. Compared to the popular Schumpeterian entrepreneurship encouraged by most economists, starting up a business timely to seize a market share and profit ("arbitrage"), by applying or imitating proper technologies instead of inventing them individually, was more favored by Chinese entrepreneurs. Upon that, neoclassical assumptions such as free market with perfect competition and full information for decision-maker will overlap the importance of arbitraging consequently. Since endogenous growth models hold the same assumptions, "entrepreneurship capital" standing for arbitraging factor is expected to have small output elasticity, as long as it is tested along the capital accumulation approach.

Hypothesis II : Were *Hypothesis I* true, additional knowledge from *Fact II* further agrees that Chinese entrepreneurs are reluctant to innovate due to financial constraints, lack of demand or support from powerful SOEs due to their reliance on foreign technology, and the attraction of a still-wide arbitraging sphere created by transitional economy. Evidently, China's TFP growth obtained from large-scale technology import and application by SOEs or joint ventures should not be assigned to entrepreneurship development, which primarily occurred in the private sector. Meanwhile, Kirzner-style entrepreneurship also matters from a technology change perspective: competition for arbitrage sphere among private enterprises will greatly stimulate improvements in domestic regions' technology absorptive capacity and managerial skills and accelerate imitations to approach best practices (Pack, 1994). As we noted in the third section, if TFP can be reasonably broken down into technical progress, i.e., the shift of technology frontier, and technical efficiency change, i.e., the movement to or away from the technology frontier, we assume that the correlation between entrepreneurship and technical efficiency change in China would display entrepreneurship's contribution to economic growth more accurately.

4.8. Methodologies and Empirical Results

Our methodology will execute the two specific approaches that we have been discussing and adopt associated revisions being proposed to compare their refined output. First, it requires a measurement of the

Kirzner-style entrepreneurship in China. In this study, we selected the annual provincial start-up rate in private sector to represent the magnitude of entrepreneurship in terms of competition, imitation by expanding knowledge spillover, and arbitrage. Furthermore, ignited by Audretsch and Keibach (2005), we take this measurement as a proxy for the stock of "entrepreneurship capital" and estimate its contribution to output growth in a Cobb–Douglas production function. In a way of factor accumulation, we expect to test *Hypothesis I*.

This study also applied reasonable specifications and econometric techniques, attempting to relieve those potential critiques we brought up in Section 4.2, especially the endogeneity of "entrepreneurship capital". Before proceeding to formal panel regression analysis and its estimation results displayed in Table 4.4, this study additionally conducted stationary and co-integration tests for our panel dataset (see Table 4.2 for the

Table 4.2. Definition and sources of the data

Independent Variables	Descriptions	Data Sources
Output (Y_{it})	Provincial GDP measured in 1979 constant price	National Bureau of Statistics (NBS) of China
Physical Capital (K_{it})	Provincial capital stock measured in 1979 constant price	The author's calculation based on the data from NBS, using the Perpetual Inventory Method (Goldsmith, 1951)
Human Capital (H_{it})	Provincial population's education attainment duration in terms of year	NBS
Labor (L_{it})	Provincial number of employees as the equivalent of labor	NBS
Entrepreneurship Capital (E_{it})	The number of startups in the respective province relative to its population	*China Economic Census Yearbook 2004*

Table 4.3. Results of unit root test and co-integration test for variables in production function

Variable	Structure of the Test	Specification of the Test			
	(C, T, L)	LL	IPS	MW	HD
Y	(0, 0, 2)	14.871	−0.921	31.457	21.036***
ΔY	(0, 0, 1)	−2.571***	−1.013	34.890	11.140***
$\Delta^2 Y$	(C, T, 0)	−7.735***	−0.823	90.247***	0.342
K	(0, 0, 2)	7.970	−1.232	22.041	21.961***
ΔK	(0, 0, 1)	−5.476***	−1.360	66.825	4.520
$\Delta^2 K$	(C, T, 0)	−13.863***	−1.881**	151.562***	−2.043
E	(0, 0, 2)	−1.590*	−0.896	41.066	11.203***
ΔE	(0, 0, 1)	−6.584***	−0.915	39.089	10.555***
$\Delta^2 E$	(C, T, 0)	−21.423***	−2.974***	118.124***	−3.001
H	(0, 0, 2)	10.858	−1.233	33.874	20.908***
ΔH	(0, 0, 1)	−7.791***	−2.260	60.689	1.665**
$\Delta^2 H$	(C, T, 0)	−26.069***	−3.655***	269.083***	−3.225
ε	(0, 0, 0)	N/A	−3.276***	N/A	N/A

Note: C, T and L denote the intercept term, trend term, and the number of lag terms, respectively. *, **, and *** denote the significance level at 10%, 5%, and 1%, respectively. ε denotes the co-integration test result. The rationale of alternative specifications could refer to appendix and the author's dissertation (Yu, 2007).

content and structure of the dataset) to tease random walk risk between output and inputs (see Table 4.3 for test results). Moreover, a multi-collinearity diagnoses and a panel data model specification test have been taken subsequently, which separately suggested the replacement of traditional labor variable by a human capital embodied labor variable and the adoption of a homogeneous panel data model with varied intercepts (Hsiao, 2003). It is noticeable that such standard tests in order to ensure the validity of subsequent panel data analysis have been broadly neglected by current empirical entrepreneurship studies. Finally, we compared the estimation outcomes between static panel data model specification and dynamic panel data model specification (Blundell and Bond, 2000), choosing to accept the latter specification due to its superior compatibility with production theory and the reality of China. As is know by far, dynamic panel data model and the Generalized Method of Moments (GMM) estimation associated have exhibited higher efficiency and robustness than traditional instrumental variable (IV) method in terms of overcoming endogeneity, given a large sampled dataset (Arellano and Bond, 1991; Blundell and Bond, 2000).

Empirical results in Table 4.4 confirmed *Hypothesis I* with a significant yet comparatively small output elasticity of entrepreneurship capital. As we have expected, Kirzner-style entrepreneurship does affect the growth process, particularly in those countries experiencing institutional transition. However, once put into empirical models assuming the existence of perfect competition, there will be less opportunity to identify a significant power of arbitrage, since the mathematical derivation of these models has already represented Kirzner-style entrepreneurship. In addition, our empirical results reveal that factor accumulation approach is further limited here compared to their application in OECD countries, even with the same indicator of ME: in OECD countries, start-up rate tends to capture more implications for the Schumpeterian entrepreneurship, which is comparatively easier to be identified apart from those implicit hypothesis of the model (Ács, 2005); in China, it captures the magnitude of arbitraging entrepreneurship and thus unable to identify itself from popular growth models' free market precondition as a default.

The failure of the factor accumulation approach leads us to a second test from the TFP approach, hence yield the second part of this empirical study, i.e., the test of *Hypothesis II*. The reasoning process of this part can be outlined as follows: taking traditional physical capital and labor as input, when TFP is calculated by specific techniques in which less institutional hypothesis has been imposed, the contribution of Kirzner-style entrepreneurship will be expected to be found in TFP along with other compositions. If such is the case, proper TFP decomposition skills may screen a separate part to correspond MEC more precisely.

Table 4.4. Results of DGMM and SGMM estimation to dynamic multi-input production model

Variable	Specification I		Specification II	
	DGMM	SGMM	DGMM	SGMM
β_p	0.713***	0.989***	0.552***	1.007***
	(0.130)	(0.032)	(0.078)	(0.032)
β_1	0.867***	0.636***	0.851***	0.747***
	(0.129)	(0.053)	(0.077)	(0.060)
β'_1	−0.911***	−0.616***	−0.847***	−0.750***
	(0.123)	(0.052)	(0.010)	(0.080)
β_2	0.400***	0.019	0.202*	−0.044
	(0.118)	(0.068)	(0.111)	(0.073)
β'_2	0.447***	−0.024	0.300	0.044
	(0.125)	(0.068)	(0.081)	(0.073)
β_3			0.136***	0.100***
			(0.024)	(0.012)
β'_3			(0.051***	0.094***
			(0.017)	(0.012)
Sargan test	26.67	26.84	24.43	26.73
Dif-Sar		0.000		0.032
CRS	3.82*		4.24**	

Note: DGMM is the abbreviated term for Differenced GMM and SGMM denotes System GMM (Blundell and Bond, 2000). The model estimated is specified as

$$\ln Y_{it} = \ln A + \beta_p \ln Y_{i,t-1} + \beta_1 \ln K_{it} + \beta'_1 \ln K_{i,t-1} + \beta_2 \ln H_{it} + \beta'_2 \ln H_{i,t-1} + \beta_3 \ln E_{it} + \beta'_3 \ln E_{i,t-1} + \varepsilon_{it}$$

While other variables remain their conventional definitions in Table 4.2, $E_{i,t}$ proxies the entrepreneurship capital flow of region i in year t. As customary, Sargan test is deployed to examine the validity of instrumental variables; Dif-Sar denotes the difference Sargan test devised for testing the validity of those additional instrumental variables in SGMM; CRS tests the hypothesis of constant return to scale. Further information of these tests can be found in the reference paper and Yu (2007). *, **, and *** denote the significance level at 10%, 5%, and 1%, respectively.

In this study, we employ the Malmquist Index approach (Fare *et al.*, 1994), which belongs to the category of frontier production function estimations, to calculate and break down China's TFP from 1979 to 2004 (see Figure 4.2). Major advantages of this method entail its exemption from the institutional assumptions embedded in the Divisia index approach of growth accounting. Furthermore, it allows decomposing the change in TFP into technical progress and technical efficiency change. This distinction is crucial,

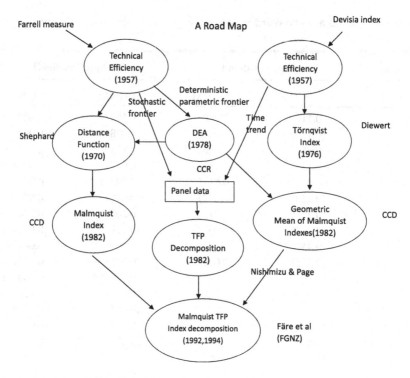

Figure 4.2.   Roadmap of Malmquist TFP index decomposition.

Source: The author's compilation.

especially for developing countries, where approaching the best practice by imitation and arbitrage in terms of technical efficiency improvement underlies TFP growth, while technical progress is still confined in pioneer regions and plutocratic SOEs (Felipe, 1997). A third advantage of our study involves the panel data nature of the provincial sample. It provides extra degrees of freedom (more than 670 observations for the reform period) in analyzing the determinants of productivity growth, technical progress, and efficiency improvement.

As we noted in *Hypothesis II*, our suspicion is that entrepreneurship in China currently contributes more to the improvement of technical efficiency. Since we have constructed the measurement of entrepreneurship using the start-up rate data from 1996 to 2004, a correlation analysis

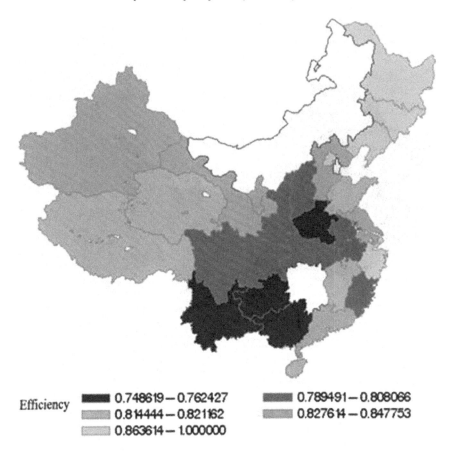

Efficiency

▆ 0.748619 – 0.762427		▆ 0.789491 – 0.808066	
▆ 0.814444 – 0.821162		▆ 0.827614 – 0.847753	
▆ 0.863614 – 1.000000			

Figure 4.3. Regional efficiency distribution of China in 1979.

Source: The author's calculations in Yu (2007).

appears to be feasible when we associate this data with the technical efficiency figures.[3]

Empirical results of this part are selectively reported considering concision. Figures 4.3 and 4.4 demonstrate the distribution of regional

---

[3]We did not regress technical efficiency on the measurement of entrepreneurship, because the selection of other control variables which may affect efficiency change is controversial in China.

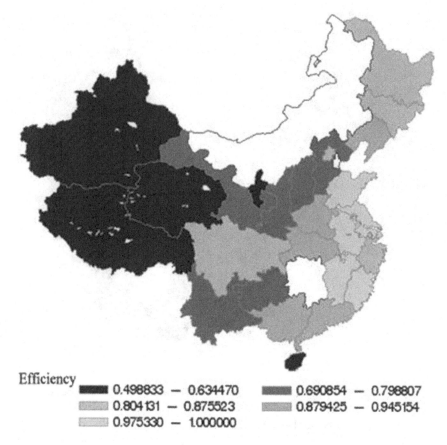

Efficiency

	0.498833 — 0.634470		0.690854 — 0.798807
0.804131 — 0.875523		0.879425 — 0.945154
0.975330 — 1.000000	

Figure 4.4.   Regional efficiency distribution of China in 2001.

Source: The author's calculations in Yu (2007).

efficiency scores across China at representative years in the reform. Table 4.5 summarizes the average mean of technical efficiency and entrepreneurship capital for 27 provinces in China through observed time span. Given the special data structure, i.e., both variables are in panel data form, this study conducts canonical correlation analysis for targeted

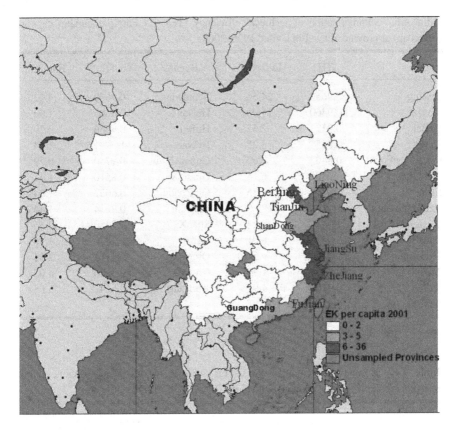

Figure 4.5. Regional entrepreneurship capital distribution of China in 2001.
Source: The author's calculations in Yu (2007).

variables so as to tease out outliers' influences to calculated coefficients. As shown in Table 4.6, entrepreneurship is positively correlated with technical efficiency change at a high significant level throughout those sampled regions while each of the variables' internal variance have been high proportionally explained, hence provides solid evidence to confirm *Hypothesis II*.

Table 4.5. Summarization of technical efficiency (TE) and Entrepreneurship capital (Entrecap) at provincial level in China, 1996–2004

Region	TE	EntreCap	Region	TE	EntreCap
BeiJing	0.9650	24.56	ShanDong	0.9600	4.22
TianJin	0.9460	15.00	HeNan	0.8605	1.93
HeBei	0.9523	2.52	HuBei	0.9566	2.29
ShanXi	0.8554	3.25	HuNan	1	1.74
Inner Mongolia	0.8403	2.60	GuangDong	0.9750	6.79
LiaoNing	0.9806	6.14	GuangXi	0.8510	1.41
JiLin	0.8704	3.35	GuiZhaou	0.6622	1.04
HeiLongjiang	1	2.69	YunNan	0.9634	1.44
ShangHai	1	38.44	ShănXi	0.7450	2.56
JiangSu	0.9581	8.01	Gansu	0.7076	1.96
ZheJiang	0.9176	9.50	QingHai	0.4151	2.52
AnHui	0.8737	1.95	Ningxia	0.5250	4.02
FuJian	0.9167	4.91	XinJiang	0.6141	3.68
JiangXi	0.9207	2.27	—	—	—

Source: The author's calculations in Yu (2007).

Table 4.6. Results of canonical correlation analysis for technical efficiency and entrepreneurship capital at provincial level in China, 1996–2004

				Redundancy Analysis	
Group	Provinces	First Canonical Correlation Coefficient	P Value (Pr>F)	Variance of EntreCap (%)	Variance of TE (%)
Northern China	BJ, TJ HB, SX	0.9939***	0.0000	96.33	75.94
Northeast China	LN, JL JS, ZJ	0.9495***	0.0010	87.68	75.98
Eastern China	AH, FJ JX, SD	0.9905***	0.0011	95.33	64.63
Southern China	HN, HB GD, GX	0.9986***	0.0000	87.06	55.13
Southwest China	GZ, YN	0.9577***	0.0006	95.06	54.03
Northwest China	ShănX, GS QH, NX	0.9989***	0.0000	59.02	35.60

Source: The author's calculations in Yu (2007).
Note: Terminologies for canonical correlation analysis can be further referred in Carroll (1968). *** indicates significance at the 0.01 level.

4.9. Concluding Remarks

The major empirical regularities of economic growth emphasize the role of TFP besides factor accumulation. Investigations on the empirics of entrepreneurship's contribution to economic growth are aware of such regularities and follow the same rationale in associated analysis. This study scrutinizes their research logics and conclusions, leading to a discovery of their individual drawbacks. Moreover, we surfaced the case of China to demonstrate those drawbacks and justify the revisions we propose accordingly.

The empirics about China, which have been developed in this study, again prove that feasible models investigating the connection between entrepreneurship and economic growth tend to be country-specific rather than follow general theories, since both terms can be intertemporal and cross-country phenomena. Therefore, the internationally empirical entrepreneurship study still has a long way to go in terms of configuring flexible and exploitable analytical models.

Additional implications from this study refer to the application of TFP decomposition skill. Separated items like technical progress, technical efficiency, and scale efficiency are promising in their employment as more accurate counterparts for heterogenous entrepreneurship measurements across different economies. TFP decomposition may be justified as suggesting directions for others to follow by growing empirical entrepreneurship literatures.

In summary, more research is needed to substantialize and then decompose the amorphous terms: entrepreneurship and TFP. Distinguishing among their country-specific meanings from different dimensions is not optional but necessary, before we can conduct reliable empirical studies to testify theories.

Appendix

Panel Data Stationary Test and Co-integration Test

Stationary test

There are several alternatives to test panel data's stationary (Yu, 2007). In this study, in order to check our results' robustness, we use four different but commonly quoted tests, i.e., one designed by Levin, Lin, and Chu (2002) (hereafter LL), another one by Im, Pesaran, and Shin (2003) (hereafter IPS), the third one by Maddala and Wu (1999) (hereafter MW) and the last one by Hadri (2000).

Considering the following model

$$y_{it} = \rho_i y_{i,t} + X_{i,t} \delta_I + \varepsilon_{i,t} \quad i = 1, \dots, N \quad t = 1, \dots, T \quad (4.3)$$

where y is our variable of interest; X is a vector of exogenous variables, including fixed effects and/or a time trend, or simply a constant, based on associated assumptions; and $\varepsilon_{i,t}$ is the error term. Following the convention, t represents time, while i proxies region.

The principle difference between LL and IPS is the assumption made on ρ_i. LL presumes that $\rho_i = \rho$, implying the coefficient of lagged dependent variable in Equation (4.3) is the same across regions, while under IPS, ρ_i is allowed to vary across regions. Given the prominent inequality in terms of production capability across China, we put more emphasis on the latter test, i.e., IPS (2003), assuming heterogeneity throughout regions.

Both LL and IPS tests belong to developed version of Augmented Dickey–Fuller test (ADF) in a panel data scenario. The formulation is as follows:

$$\Delta y_{i,t} = \beta y_{i,t} + \sum_{j=1}^{p_i} \rho_{i,j} \Delta y_{i,t-j} + X_{i,t} \delta_i + \varepsilon_{it} \quad i = 1, \dots, N \quad t = 1, \dots, T \quad (4.4)$$

LL tests the null hypothesis of $\beta = 0$, while IPS is testing that of $\beta_i = 0$ for all i. Additional t-bar statistics is used in IPS test, which are formed as a simple average of the individual t-statistics for testing in Equation (4.4), namely

$$t\text{-}bar_{NT} = N^{-1} \sum_{i=1}^{N} t_{iT} \qquad (4.5)$$

In contrast, MW constructed the so-called "combined *p*-value test", which is an exact test, to replace the asymptotic test used in LL and IPS. This further allows MW to accommodate unequal t and j among different i.

HD is a well-known test for the null of no unit root proposed by Hadri (2000). It is a residual-based Lagrange multiplier (LM) test. Consider the model,

$$y_{i,t} = r_{i,t} + \beta_i t + \varepsilon \qquad (4.6)$$

where $r_{i,t} = r_{i,t-1} + \mu_{I,t}$, a random walk. The LM statistic is formulated as follows:

$$\overline{LM} = \frac{\frac{1}{N} \sum_i^N \frac{1}{T^2} \sum_{i=1}^{T} S_{i,t}^2}{\hat{\sigma}_\varepsilon^2} \qquad (4.7)$$

where $S_{i,t} = \sum_{j=1}^{t} \varepsilon_{i,j}$ and $\hat{\sigma}_\varepsilon^2 = \frac{1}{NT} \sum_{i=1}^{N} \sum_{t=1}^{T} \hat{\varepsilon}_{i,t}^2$

$\hat{\varepsilon}_{i,j}$ is the estimated residual from Equation (4.6), $S_{i,t}$ is the partial sum of residual, while $\hat{\sigma}_\varepsilon^2$ is the estimate of the error variance. Hadri's residual-based LM test for the null of stationary is promising in that it increases the power of testing for the null of a unit root.

Co-integration test

A co-integrating relationship captures the long-run or equilibrium relationship between non-stationary variables. If variables are non-stationary, particularly in the case of time series data, but the common residual terms are stationary, then we say these variables are co-integrated and economic theory as set out in Sections 4.1 and 4.2 suggest forces which tend to keep such series together, and do not let them drift too far apart. In addition, if variables are co-integrated, our estimates are super-consistent. In other words, our estimates are not only consistent but also converge to their true values more quickly than normal (Davidson and MacKinnon, 1993).

In this chapter, we employ the extended Engle–Granger co-integration test proposed by Pedroni (2004) to complete the co-integration test. Since the mechanism of Engle–Granger co-integration test has been widely broadcasted, the author omitted detailed description on the specification of Pedroni's model for brevity.

References

Ács, Z. J., D. B. Audretsch, P. Braunerhjelm and B. Carlsson (2004). The missing link: The knowledge filter and entrepreneurship in endogenous growth. CEPR Disscussion Paper, 2–30.

Ács, Z. J., D. B. Audretsch, P. Braunerhjelm and B. Carlsson (2005). Growth and entrepreneurship: An empirical assessment. *CEPR Discussion Papers* (5409), 1–27.

Arellano, M., and S. Bond (1991). Some tests of specification for panel data: Monte Carlo evidence and an application to employment equations. *The Review of Economic Studies* **58**(2): 277–297.

Audretsch, D. B. (2002). *Entrepreneurship : Determinants and Policy in a European-US Comparison.* Boston: Kluwer Academic Publishers.

Audretsch, D. B., and M. Keilbach, (2005). Entrepreneurship capital and regional growth. *The Annals of Regional Science* **39**: 457–469.

Bai, C.-E., C.-T. Hsigh and Y. Qian (2006). The return to capital in China. *Brookings Papers on Economic Activity* (2): 61–88.

Barro, R., and X. Sala-i-Martin (1990). Economic growth and convergence across the United States. NBER.

Baumol, W. J. (1990). Entrepreneurship: Productive, unproductive, and destructive. *The Journal of Political Economy* **98**(5): 893–921.

Baumol, W. J. (1993). *Entrepreneurship, Management, and the Structure of Payoffs.* Cambridge, MA: MIT Press.

Blundell, R., and S. Bond (2000). GMM estimation with persistent panel data: An application to production functions. *Econometric Reviews* **19**(3): 321–340.

Carree, M. A., A. J, van Stel, R. Thurik and A. R. M. Wennekers, (2002). Economic development and business ownership: An analysis using data of 23 OECD countries in the period 1976–1996. *Small Business Economics* 19(3): 271–290.

Carroll, J. (1968). A generalization of canonical correlation analysis to three or more sets of variables. *Proceedings of the 76th Annual Convention of the American Psychological Association,* (3): 227–228.

Chang, P. E.-K. (1969). *Agriculture and Industrialization: The Adjustments That Take Place as an Agricultural Country is Industrialized.* New York: Greenwood Press.

Chen, E. (1997). The total factor productivity debate: Determinants of economic growth in East Asia. *Asian-Pacific Economic Literature*, 11(1), 18–38.

Chow, G. (1993). Capital formation and economic growth in China. *Quarterly Journal of Economics* 108(3): 809–842.

Chow, G., and K. W. Li (2002). China's Economic Growth: 1952–2010. *Economic Development and Cultural Change* 51(1): 247–256.

Davidson, R., and J. MacKinnon (1993). *Estimation and Inference in Econometrics*. Oxford University Press, New York.

DeLong, J., and L. Summers (1990). *Equipment Investment and Economic Growth*. Cambridge, MA: NBER.

Dollar, D., and E. N. Wolff (1993). *Competitiveness, Convergence, and International Specialization*. Cambridge, MA: MIT Press.

Easterly, W., and R. Levine, (2001). What have we learned from a decade of empirical research on growth? It's not factor accumulation: Stylized facts and growth models. *The World Bank Economic Review* 15(2): 177–219.

Fare, R., S. Grosskopf, M., Norris and Z. Zhang, (1994). Productivity growth, technical progress, and efficiency change in industrialized countries. *American Economic Review*, 81(4): 66–83.

Felipe, J. (1997). *Total Factor Productivity Growth in East Asia: A Critical Survey*. Asian Development Bank, Manila, Philippines.

Gilboy, G. J. (2004). The Myth Behind China's Miracle. *Foreign Affairs* 83: 34–41.

Hadri, K. (2000). Testing for stationarity in heterogeneous panel data. *The Econometrics Journal* 3(2): 148–161.

High, J. (2004). The roles of entrepreneurship in economic growth: Toward a theory of total factor productivity, in H. L. F. d. Groot, P. Nijkamp and R. R. Stough (Eds.) *Entrepreneurship and Regional Economic Development: A Spatial Perspective*. Cheltenham, UK and Northampton, MA, USA: Edward Elgar, pp. 46–77.

Hsiao, C. (2003). *Analysis of Panel Data*. 2nd edn. Cambridge, New York: Cambridge University Press.

Im, S., H., Pesaran and Shin, Y. (2003). Testing for unit roots in heterogeneous panel. *Journal of Econometrics* 115: 53–74.

Jorgenson, D. W. (1995). *Productivity*. Cambridge, MA: MIT Press.

Levin, A., C. Lin and J. Chu (2002). Unit root tests in panel data: Asymptotic and finite-sample properties. *Journal of Econometrics* 108: 1–24.

Li, S., and W. Zhang (2000). The road to capitalism: Competition and institutional change in China. *Journal of Comparative Economics* 28(2): 269–292.

Lu, C. (2000). *Research on the Mechanism of the Contribution of Entrepreneurship to Economic Growth*. Beijing: Tsinghua University.

Lucas, R. E., Jr. (1988). On the mechanics of economic development. *Journal of Monetary Economics* 22(1): 3–42.

Maddala, G., and S. Wu (1999). A comparative study of unit root tests with panel data and a new simple test: Evidence from simulations and the bootstrap. *Oxford Bulletin of Economics and Statistics* 61: 631–652.

Marshall, A. (1890). *Principles of Economics*. London and New York: Macmillan.

North, D. C. (1981). *Structure and Change in Economic History*. 1st edn. New York: Norton.

Pack, H. (1994). Endogenous growth theory: Intellectual appeal and empirical shortcomings. *Journal of Economic Perspectives* **8**(1): 55–72.

Pedroni, P. (2004). Panel cointegration asymptotic and finite sample properties of pooled time series tests with an application to the PPP hypothesis. *Econometric Theory* **20**(3): 597–625.

Reynolds, P., N., E., Bosma, Autio, Hunt, S., Bono, D. N. and I. Servais (2005). Global entrepreneurship monitor: Data collection design and implementation 1998–2003. *Small Business Economics* **24**: 205–231.

Romer, P. M. (1986). Increasing returns and long-run growth. *Journal of Political Economy* **94**(5): 1002–1037.

Rosenberg, N., and L. E. Birdzell (1986). *How the West Grew Rich: The Economic Transformation of the Industrial World*. New York: Basic Books.

Schumpeter, J. A., and R. Opie (1934). *The Theory of Economic Development; An Inquiry Into Profits, Capital, Credit, Interest, and the Business Cycle*. Cambridge, MA: Harvard University Press.

Sombart, W. (1929). Economic theory and economic history. *Economic History Review* January: 1–19.

Yu, J. (2007). *An Empirical Research on the Mechanism of Entrepreneurship's Contribution to China's Economic Growth*. Beijing: Tsinghua University.

Zheng, J., and A. Hu (2006). An empirical analysis of provincial productivity in China (1979–2001). *Journal of Chinese Economic and Business Studies* **4**(3): 221–239.

Chapter 5

Regional Economic Growth
and Telecommunications Infrastructure in China

Yanchun Liu
Georgetown Economic Services

5.1. Regional Economic Development in China

Dramatic economic changes have been occurring in China — the most populous country in the world — since its establishment in 1949. The substantial economic growth in China has been widely recognized by all other countries as a recent miracle (Wu, 2000). A general estimate of the average annual economic growth rate for China was around 7%–8% in the first 50 years after 1949, double that of the world on average in the same period (Wu, 2000). However, this simple rate cannot reveal the true path of China's economic development. To better elaborate on the historical perspective, this chapter references the current literature to explain China's economic development.

Zhao (1990) enunciates three phases by dividing China's economic history with its own speed of economic growth. It is noteworthy that there were no statistical releases on gross domestic product ("GDP") by statistics bureaus in China before 1978. Instead, the System of Material Product Balances ("MPS") was adopted to report economic output for both regions and the whole country. Zhao (1990) estimates the ratio between GDP and national income as 1:0.81, which is subsequently used to approximate the annual GDP levels for the period from 1949 to 1978. Although such simple conversion between GDP and national income may incur estimation bias for satisfactory data comparability, the economic development history of China can still be systematically presented. Specifically, the three phases of China's economic development are: 1949–1956, 1957–1978, and 1979–present.

- According to the estimation by Zhao (1990), the average annual economic growth rate for China was 16.8% (with GDP as the indicator) in the first phase (1949–1956). The first five-year plan was completed within this phase.
- In the second phase (1957–1978), economic growth slowed down. The average annual growth rate was 6.36% with GDP in 1957 as the base, and it was 10.44% lower than the same rate from 1949 to 1956.
- The third phase witnessed dramatic economic changes. China opened its door to the outside world and initiated a series of significant economic stimulation policies in 1978. From 1979 to 2006, the annual GDP growth rate was around 7%. In 2002, the rank of China in terms of annual GDP in the world was 6th, with the top five countries as the U.S., Japan, Germany, Great Britain, and France. It took China four years to improve its rank from sixth to fourth in terms of total GDP in 2006, after the U.S., Japan, and Germany (see International Monetary Fund database: http://www.imf.org).

The discussion in the rest of this chapter centers around the time period from 1979 to 2006, considering availability of data. As addressed later in this chapter, national economic achievements are not necessarily distributed evenly across the various provinces, municipalities, and autonomous cities from 1979 to 2006. Economic growth in China exhibits continuous upward trend from 1979 to 2006 (see Table 5.1). The data in Table 5.1 list both the nominal and real GDPs of China as well as their respective growth rates. Differences exist between nominal and real GDPs as well as their growth rates due to high inflation rates. The GDP index doubles in less than 10 years from 1978 to 1986. It is noteworthy that the GDP index is not the same as other inflation indicators such as Consumer Price Index ("CPI"). The annual GDP in 2006 (21,087.1 billion RMB) was 52 times more than that in 1979 (406.3 billion RMB). The growth rates (based on

Table 5.1. Nominal and real GDP in China

Unit: Billion RMB

Year	Nominal GDP	Nominal GDP Growth Rate (%)	GDP Index	Real GDP (in 1978 RMB)	Real GDP Growth Rate (in 1978 RMB) (%)	Consumer Price Index	Real GDP Adj. with CPI	Real GDP Growth Rate (CPI Adj.) (%)
1978	3645.2	—	100.0	3645.2	—	100	—	—
1979	4062.6	11.45	107.6	3775.6	3.58	—	—	—
1980	4545.6	11.89	116.0	3918.4	3.78	109.5	4151.3	—
1981	4891.6	7.61	122.1	4006.5	2.25	—	—	—
1982	5323.4	8.83	133.1	3998.1	−0.21	—	—	—
1983	5962.7	12.01	147.6	4039.8	1.04	—	—	—
1984	7208.1	20.89	170.0	4240.1	4.96	—	—	—
1985	9016.0	25.08	192.9	4674.2	10.24	131.1	6877.2	—
1986	10275.2	13.97	210.0	4894.0	4.70	—	—	—
1987	12058.6	17.36	234.3	5147.2	5.17	—	—	—
1988	15042.8	24.75	260.7	5770.1	12.10	—	—	—
1989	16992.3	12.96	271.3	6263.4	8.55	—	—	—
1990	18667.8	9.86	281.7	6626.6	5.80	216.4	8626.5	—
1991	21781.5	16.68	307.6	7081.9	6.87	223.8	9732.6	12.82
1992	26923.5	23.61	351.4	7662.5	8.20	238.1	11307.6	16.18
1993	35333.9	31.24	400.4	8823.9	15.16	273.1	12938.1	14.42
1994	48197.9	36.41	452.8	10644.1	20.63	339.0	14217.7	9.89
1995	60793.7	26.13	502.3	12103.5	13.71	396.9	15317.1	7.73

(Continued)

Table 5.1.   (Continued)

Unit: Billion RMB

Year	Nominal GDP	Nominal GDP Growth Rate (%)	GDP Index	Real GDP (in 1978 RMB)	Real GDP Growth Rate (in 1978 RMB) (%)	Consumer Price Index	Real GDP Adj. with CPI	Real GDP Growth Rate (CPI Adj.) (%)
1996	71176.6	17.08	552.6	12881.4	6.43	429.9	16556.5	8.09
1997	78973.0	10.95	603.9	13076.6	1.52	441.9	17871.2	7.94
1998	84402.3	6.87	651.2	12960.4	-0.89	438.4	19252.3	7.73
1999	89677.1	6.25	700.9	12795.4	-1.27	432.2	20749.0	7.77
2000	99214.6	10.64	759.9	13055.5	2.03	434.0	22860.5	10.18
2001	109655.2	10.52	823.0	13323.5	2.05	437.0	25092.7	9.76
2002	120332.7	9.74	897.8	13403.5	0.60	433.5	27758.41	10.62
2003	135822.8	12.87	987.8	13750.4	2.59	438.7	30960.28	11.53
2004	159878.3	17.71	1087.4	14702.9	6.93	455.8	35076.42	13.29
2005	183867.9	15.00	1200.8	15311.6	4.14	464.0	39626.7	12.97
2006	210871.0	14.69	1334.0	15807.7	3.24	471.0	44770.91	12.98

Source: China Statistics Yearbook series, 1979–2007.

nominal GDP) in the last four years within the examined time period (i.e., 2003–2006) are 12.87%, 17.71%, 15.00%, and 14.69%, respectively. Taking account of inflation, the real GDP growth rates (based on 1978 RMB) from 2003 to 2006 are 2.59%, 6.93%, 4.14%, and 3.24%, respectively.

Figure 5.1 shows the overall upward trend of China's real GDP from 1978 to 2006. Although the real GDP of China falls slightly in 1982, 1999, and 2000, a consistent trend of rising real GDP can best describe the recent economic development history of China since late 1970s.

As shown in Figure 5.2, the annual real GDP growth rates from 1978 to 2006 fluctuated widely, with a low of −1.27% in 1999 and a high of 20.63% in 1994. The average real GDP growth rate during the examined 29 years is 5.5%. Only three years exhibit negative growth rates — 1982, 1998, and 1999. The decade of the 1990s witnessed the fastest 10 years in terms of economic output growth, whereas economic growth began to stabilize around 3%–4% in the first several years of the 21st century.

Figure 5.2 seems to provide an "underestimated" real GDP growth rate trend for China due to the deflation of real GDPs into 1978 values, and another type of adjustment with CPI may present a better view of the economic growth in China as a whole (see Figure 5.3). Due to the lack of availability of data for 1978–1990, the CPI index only covers the 1991–2006 GDP deflation. A comparison between Figures 5.2 and 5.3 indicates that the CPI-adjusted real GDP growth rates show a comparatively flatter trend than those using the real GDPs in 1978 RMB values. In Figure 5.3, growth rates center around 10%, and there is no dramatic fluctuation within the one and half decades from 1991 to 2006.

Another way to examine China's economic development is to see the rank of China's total annual GDP in the world. The data provided by the International Monetary Fund (IMF) allow the comparison of national GDPs (see Table 5.2). From 2002 to 2006, the total GDP of China increased from U.S. $1,454 billion to U.S. $2,645 billion, witnessing an 81.95% increase within as short a period as four years. The IMF ranking of

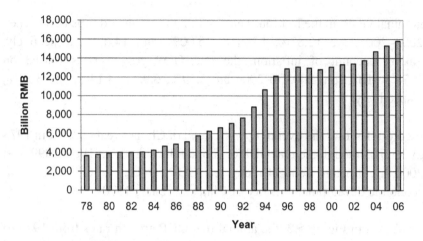

Figure 5.1. Real GDP of China: 1978–2006.

Source: *China Statistics Yearbook* series, 1979–2007.

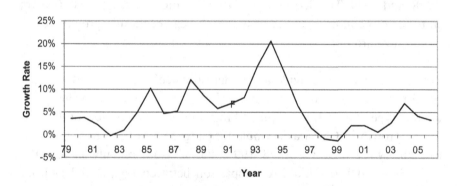

Figure 5.2. Real GDP growth rate: 1978–2006.

Note: The real GDP growth rates are calculated using 1978 RMB values.

Source: *China Statistics Yearbook* series, 1979–2007.

China also jumped from sixth in 2002 to fourth in 2006. China's importance in the world can be illustrated by the percentage contribution of
China's GDP to the world GDP: China's GDP accounted for 4.43% of the
world GDP in 2002, while this proportion increased to 5.49% in 2006. In
contrast, the proportion of the top three countries — the U.S., Japan, and
Germany — in the world GDP saw decreases from 2002 to 2006.

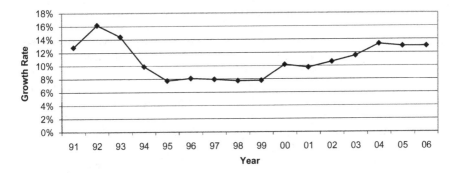

Figure 5.3. Real GDP growth rate: 1991–2006.

Note: The real GDP growth rates are calculated using GDP values adjusted by CPI.

Source: *China Statistics Yearbook* series, 1979–2007.

Given the focus of regional economic output in this study, it is necessary to examine China's regional economic growth during the period of 1978 to 2006. Maps are self-explanatory in exhibiting spatial patterns of the regional economic output. Figures 5.4, 5.5, and 5.6 present, respectively, China's regional output in 1985, 1995, and 2006. As clearly shown in the three maps, regional differences in terms of economic output are significant in all the three selected years. It is noteworthy that such differences do not decline from 1985 to 2006, which demonstrates that the rapid economic growth in China during the past three decades did not mitigate the regional economic growth disparity problem. Generally, coastal regions outperform interior regions in total output, a result of both higher population densities as well as productivity and preferential economic institutions in these coastal regions.

Another way to examine regional economic output disparity is to compare the regional economic output of the top three provinces against those of the bottom three provinces. Figure 5.7 indicates that the gap increased dramatically in the time period of 1985 to 2006. The top three provinces — Guangdong, Jiangsu, and Shandong — are located in the coastal regions of China, which account for almost all rapid economic growth. As is shown in Figure 5.7, the bottom three provinces — Tibet, Qinghai, and Ningxia — are all located in the northwest regions in China and they did not increase significantly in the past two decades. Their gaps with other developed regions grew.

Table 5.2. Top 10 countries with highest GDP in 2002

Unit: Billion U.S. Dollars

Ranking	2002 GDP Countries		% of World GDP	2006 GDP Countries		% of World GDP
	World GDP	32,813	100	World GDP	48,145	100
1	U.S.	10,470	31.91	U.S.	13,245	27.51
2	Japan	3,925	11.96	Japan	4,368	9.07
3	Germany	2,024	6.17	Germany	2,897	6.02
4	Great Britain	1,575	4.80	China	2,645	5.49
5	France	1,464	4.46	Great Britain	2,374	4.93
6	China	1,454	4.43	France	2,232	4.64
7	Italy	1,223	3.73	Italy	1,853	3.85
8	Canada	735	2.24	Canada	1,269	2.64
9	Spain	689	2.10	Spain	1,226	2.55
10	Mexico	649	1.98	Brazil	1,068	2.22

Source: International Monetary Fund database.

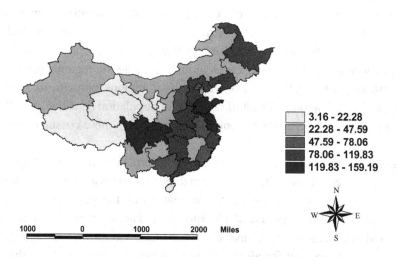

Figure 5.4. Regional outputs in China (1985).

Note: Output is measured in billions of RMB (1995 value).
Source: *China Statistics Yearbook*, 1986.

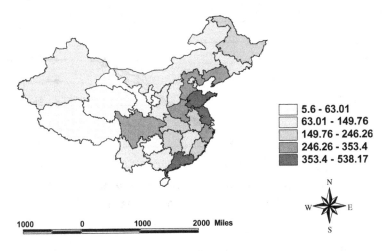

| | 5.6 - 63.01 |
| 63.01 - 149.76 |
| 149.76 - 246.26 |
| 246.26 - 353.4 |
| 353.4 - 538.17 |

Figure 5.5.   Regional outputs in China (1995).

Note: Output is measured in billions of RMB (1995 value).
Source: *China Statistics Yearbook*, 1996.

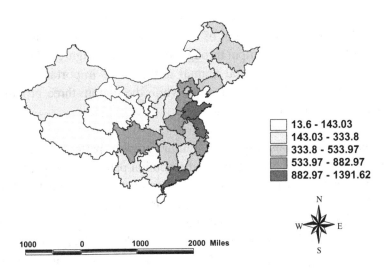

| | 13.6 - 143.03 |
| 143.03 - 333.8 |
| 333.8 - 533.97 |
| 533.97 - 882.97 |
| 882.97 - 1391.62 |

Figure 5.6.   Regional output in China (2006).

Note: Output is measured in billions of RMB (1995 value).
Source: *China Statistics Yearbook*, 2007.

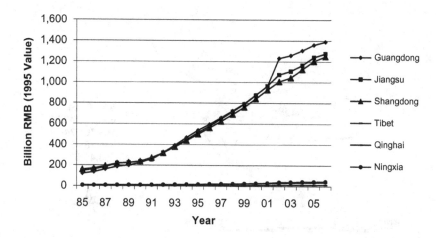

Figure 5.7. Regional output of top and bottom three provinces.

Note: Output is measured in billions of RMB (1995 value).
Source: *China Statistics Yearbook* series, 1986–2007.

The total output of the top three provinces accounted for 20%–30% of national GDP while total output of the bottom three provinces remained at around 1% of national output throughout the period. Figure 5.8 displays these trends in terms of total annual output. The importance of the top-three provinces increases steadily while the bottom-three provinces stagger at nearly negligible levels.

Different aggregations produce similar growth patterns and gaps. Figures 5.9, 5.10, and 5.11 show the distribution patterns of top 5, bottom 10, and other 15 provinces, municipalities, and autonomous cities in 1985, 1995, and 2006, respectively. The structural changes across the three selected years indicate that regional output disparities are aggravated during the time period of 1985 to 2006. Specifically, the top five provinces — Guangdong, Jiangsu, Shandong, Zhejiang, and Sichuan — increase their proportion of national output from 33% in 1985 to 39% in 1995, and 41% in 2006, whereas the bottom 10 provinces, municipalities, and autonomous cities — Yunnan, Tianjin, Inner Mongolia, Xinjiang, Guizhou, Gansu, Hainan, Ningxia, Qinghai, and Tibet — decrease their proportion of national output from 12% in 1985 to 10% in 1995 and 10% in 2006.

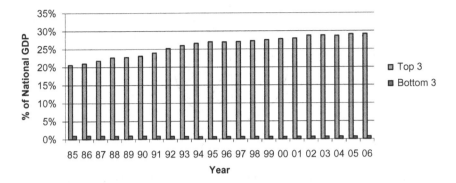

Figure 5.8. Percentages of regional output of top three and bottom three provinces to national output.

Source: China Statistics Yearbook series, 1986–2007.

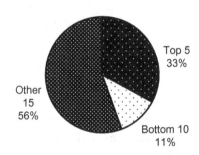

Figure 5.9. Distribution of regional output in 1985.

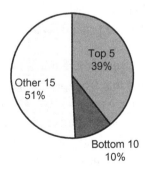

Figure 5.10. Distribution of regional output in 1995.

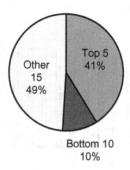

Figure 5.11.   Distribution of regional output in 2006.

Throughout the economic development history of China after 1978, rapid development of private sector in this huge country seems to be a strong impetus on the overall national economic growth. Correspondingly, the importance of state-owned enterprises (SOEs) has been decreasing during the same period, which witnessing the vibrant growth potential of the private has been simultaneously sector in China. Following the 5 special economic zones and 14 coastal harbor cities, the entire coastal region of China (e.g., Jiangsu, Zhejiang, and Guangdong) has been exhibiting tremendous economic growth potential that is characterized by entrepreneurship. From sole proprietorships and privately held corporations to large publicly held corporations, an increasing number of entrepreneurs in the private sector have been contributing to the economic development of their regions. This chapter selects some regions in the coastal and western areas in China and examines their respective industrial output structure in terms of output from SOEs and private sector in various years.

This chapter adopts the structure of a region's industrial output in terms of contribution from SOEs and that from private sector as an indicator of that region's entrepreneurship. Specifically, Guangdong, Jiangsu, and Zhejiang are selected as representative regions in the coastal area, whereas Xinjiang, Ningxia, and Qinghai denote regions in the west of China. Considering data consistency and availability, the author uses three years in the comparison analysis: 1986, 1995, and 2002.

Figures 5.12, 5.13, and 5.14 present the industrial output structures of the three selected coastal provinces.

It is clearly shown in the preceding three figures that the industrial output percentages of SOEs in all three provinces exhibit significant decreases from 1986 to 2002, with private sector dominating industrial outputs by 2002. On average, SOEs in the three provinces Guangdong, Jiangsu, and Zhejiang contributed about 40% to their overall industrial output, while such percentages dropped to 7.24%, 4.24%, and 2.93% in 2002, respectively. Therefore, these three economically vibrant provinces seem to have been benefiting from their fast-growing private sector, boosting these three provinces to be the most entrepreneurial regions in China.

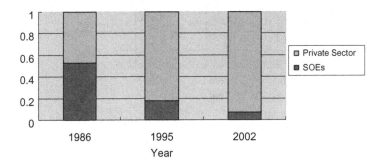

Figure 5.12.   Industrial output structure: Guangdong province.

Source: Author's calculation based on data from *China Statistics Yearbook*, various years.

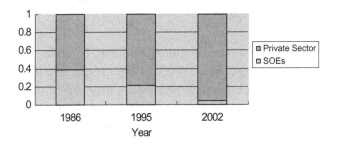

Figure 5.13.   Industrial output structure: Jiangsu province.

Source: Author's calculation based on data from *China Statistics Yearbook*, various years.

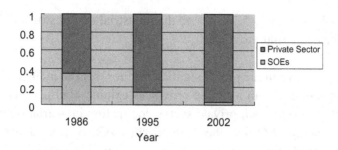

Figure 5.14. Industrial output structure: Zhejiang province.

Source: Author's calculation based on data from *China Statistics Yearbook*, various years.

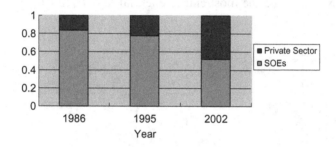

Figure 5.15. Industrial output structure: Xinjiang province.

Source: Author's calculation based on data from *China Statistics Yearbook*, various years.

On the other hand, Figures 5.15, 5.16, and 5.17 display the composition of industrial outputs of three provinces in the interior land of China — Xinjiang, Ningxia, and Qinghai.

The SOEs of the three western regions, Xinjiang, Ningxia, and Qinghai, contributed to, on average, nearly 80% of their respective industrial outputs in 1986, while such average percentage dropped to nearly 50% in 2002. Thus, a downward trend exists for SOEs of these western regions in terms of their importance to regional industrial output. SOEs still accounted for more than half of these western regions' industrial output in 2002, indicating the slow development of their regional entrepreneurship and private sector.

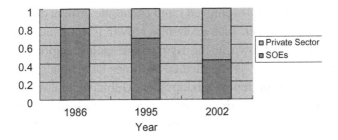

Figure 5.16. Industrial output structure: Ningxia province.

Source: Author's calculation based on data from *China Statistics Yearbook*, various years.

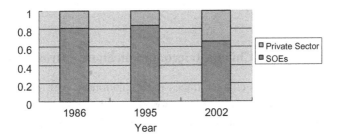

Figure 5.17. Industrial output structure: Qinghai province.

Source: Author's calculation based on data from *China Statistics Yearbook*, various years.

Comparison of the coastal and western regions reveals that the private sector in western regions developed comparatively slower than that in the coastal regions as discussed earlier. For each selected year, the coastal regions rely much less on SOEs for their regional industrial output than the western regions. The average contribution rate of SOEs is around 5% for the three selected coastal regions, contrasting with the above 50% rate for the three western regions. Furthermore, the prior discussion also purports that the coastal regions develop much faster than those in the interior land of China. Therefore, it seems reasonable to conclude that private sector, or say, regional entrepreneurship plays an important role in regional economic growth dynamics in China.

In conclusion, China has achieved rapid economic growth during the past three decades. However, such economic growth is not evenly distributed across regions. As shown in the figures and tables, regional economic development disparity is aggravated at times of China's fast growth. Similarly, regional entrepreneurship also exhibits spatial disparity, with entrepreneurs in West China contributing much less than those in the coastal area. Such similarity reveals the inherent relationship between regional economic growth and prosperity of private sector and regional entrepreneurship. After analyzing the contribution of SOEs and private sector to regional economic development, the next section of this chapter examines the history and status of telecommunications infrastructure availability across regions.

5.2. Development of China's Telecommunications Infrastructure

The second part of this chapter traces the evolutionary path of the China's telecommunications infrastructure. It is noteworthy that the development of the telecommunications sector in China was so slow before 1990s that the discussion of telecommunications infrastructure construction and availability focuses only on the time period from 1985 to 2006. The inclusion of the years from 1985 to 1990 is for consistency purpose with the dataset used in this study. Therefore, factors contributing to the earlier development or buildup of telecommunications infrastructure in China's regions prior to 1985 are not addressed. Instead, emphasis is on depicting the recent evolution of telecommunications infrastructure in China as well as the dramatic regional differences.

Some studies provide descriptive statistics on the extremely low level of telecommunications infrastructure in China in the early years after 1949. For example, Singh (1999) illustrates the status quo of telecommunications infrastructure back in 1949 with a hard number — 193,000 telephones for the over 500 million people in 1949. All of the 193,000 telephones were distributed in the "urban" areas of China. Another study by Tang and Lee (2001) extends Singh's discussion (1999) by concluding that more than 90% of counties in China did not have telephones, with 10% of counties lying in the coastal regions. The next several decades (until 1990s) witnessed the very slow development of telecommunications sector (Ding, 2005). Liu (1988) identifies as little as 0.8% of total national investment going to the telecommunications sector in the first five-year period from 1953 to 1957. The ratio never went beyond 1.5% from the 1950s to the 1960s (Tang and Lee, 2003). According to the data in He (1997), the teledensity — measured as the number of telephones per 100 habitants — was as low as 0.43 on the national level and the total number of people subscribing to telephone services did not exceed 4.1 million in 1980. The rapid growth of the telecommunication sector in China starts in the mid-1980s, which is also the reason this study selects 1986 as the starting point for its panel dataset.

In 1985, the total number of telephones in China was 6.25 million, and all these phones were fixed lines. The annual growth rates of the number of telephones from 1985 to 2006 never fell below 9%, ranging from a low of 9.4% in 2004 and a high of 50.45% in 1994. The mid-1990s was the golden period for the development of telecommunications sector in China, and the best example may be the astonishing growth rate of 50.45% in 1994. Figure 5.18 presents the annual growth rates in the 21 years from 1985 to 2005.

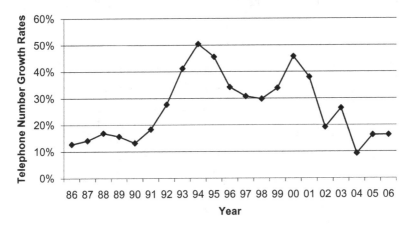

Figure 5.18. Growth rates of the number of telephones.

Note: Growth rates of 2004–2006 are estimated using telecommunications industrial capacity provided by *China Statistics Yearbook* series, 2005–2007.

Source: Comprehensive Statistical Data and Materials on 50 Years of New China, provided by National Statistics Bureau in 1999.

Teledensity is used to demonstrate the availability of telecommunications infrastructure in a region. A brief definition of this concept is the number of telephones (including both fixed and mobile lines) per 100 inhabitants. Although this study does not differentiate fixed from mobile lines in the analysis, it is noteworthy that the mobile telephones increased at an amazingly high rate from the end of 1990s. As argued by Ding (2005), the true story of China's telecommunications sector might be distorted without the inclusion of mobile line phones in the dataset (also see Giovanis & Skiadas, 2005; Ding and Haynes, 2007; Lee and Cho, 2007). The national teledensity in the examined 21 years is shown in Figure 5.19. The obviously upward trend of teledensity is self-explanatory. The increase in teledensity on the national level accelerates from 1994, and there is no single year that shows a lower teledensity than the prior year. Such rapid and continuous development in telecommunications infrastructure availability is not enjoyed by China alone. Instead, such a trend tends to be shared by other developing countries such as Brazil and Mexico (Ding, 2005). So although this study selects China as its target country for analysis of the role of telecommunications infrastructure, its results may contribute to the existing literature of other nations on the relationship between telecommunications infrastructure availability and regional economic output growth.

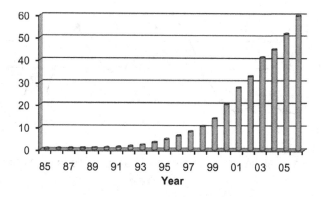

Figure 5.19.   Teledensity in China (1985–2006).

Note: Teledensities of 2004–2006 are estimated using telecommunications industrial capacity provided by *China Statistics Yearbook* series, 2005–2007.

Source: Comprehensive Statistical Data and Materials on 50 Years of New China, provided by National Statistics Bureau in 1999.

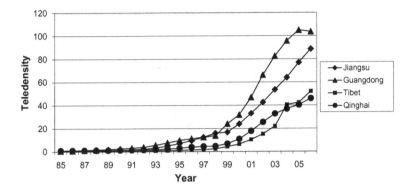

Figure 5.20. Teledensities of selected regions.

Note: Teledensities of 2004–2006 are estimated using telecommunications industrial capacity provided by *China Statistics Yearbook* series, 2005–2007.
Source: Comprehensive Statistical Data and Materials on 50 Years of New China, provided by National Statistics Bureau in 1999.

From the regions' perspective, regional disparities are as dramatic as those in regional economic output in China. Regional comparison follows the same logic as that made on regional economic output. Two relatively more developed provinces — Guangdong and Jiangsu — are picked to compare their teledensities with those of the relatively less developed provinces — Tibet and Qinghai. Figure 5.20 demonstrates the regional disparities in terms of teledensity among the four selected provinces. The comparison result is similar to that of the regional output comparison: the economically more developed provinces show generally higher teledensities than those less developed ones, and the gap increases over time. For example, the teledensity of Guangdong (103.7) is more than twice that of Qinghai (45.95). However, it is reasonable to conclude that all the four provinces — irrespective of the level of economic development— have enjoyed substantial growth in telecommunications infrastructure availability.

Maps are used again to show discrepancies in China's regional endowments in telecommunications infrastructure. Figures 5.21, 5.22, and 5.23 display the spatial distribution of telephone lines for all regions in China in 1985, 1995, and 2006. The three figures indicate the unequal regional distribution of telephones in all the three selected years. Another commonality exists in

Figure 5.21.   Distribution pattern of telephones in China (1985).

Note: The numbers of telephones of 2004–2006 are estimated using telecommunications industrial capacity provided by *China Statistics Yearbook* series, 2005–2007 (1 dot = 9,000 Telephones).
Source: Comprehensive Statistical Data and Materials on 50 Years of New China, provided by National Statistics Bureau in 1999.

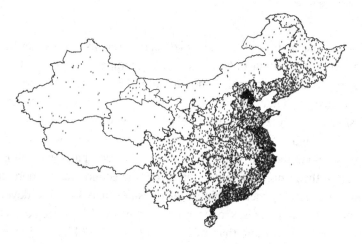

Figure 5.22.   Distribution pattern of telephone' in China (1995).

Note: The numbers of telephones of 2004–2006 are estimated using telecommunications industrial capacity provided by *China Statistics Yearbook* series, 2005–2007 (1 dot = 9,000 Telephones).
Source: Comprehensive Statistical Data and Materials on 50 Years of New China, provided by National Statistics Bureau in 1999.

that all three years exhibit a similar spatial pattern of telephone services, i.e., coastal regions tend to have the most telephone service coverage while the northwest regions have the least coverage. Comparison of the three figures reveals that all regions — regardless of their respective economic development levels — show dramatic increases in total numbers of telephones.

Figure 5.23.   Distribution pattern of telephones in China's regions (2006).

Note: The numbers of telephones of 2004–2006 are estimated using telecommunications industrial capacity provided by *China Statistics Yearbook* series, 2005–2007 (1 dot = 9,000 Telephones).
Source: Comprehensive Statistical Data and Materials on 50 Years of New China, provided by National Statistics Bureau in 1999.

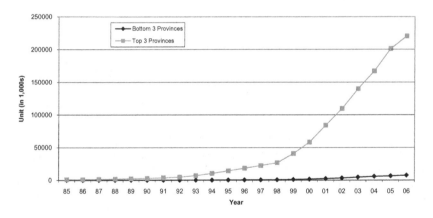

Figure 5.24.   Number of telephones: Top three versus bottom three provinces.

Note: The top three provinces are Guangdong, Shandong, and Jiangsu, while the bottom three provinces are Qinghai, Tibet, and Ningxia.
Source: Comprehensive Statistical Data and Materials on 50 Years of New China, provided by National Statistics Bureau in 1999.

Maps are also used to present spatial patterns of teledensity (see Figures 5.25, 5.26, and 5.27). The insights that can be drawn from the

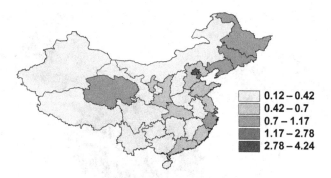

Figure 5.25.   Regional teledensity (1985).

Note: Teledensities of 2004–2006 are estimated using telecommunications industrial capacity provided by *China Statistics Yearbook* series, 2005–2007.
Source: Comprehensive Statistical Data and Materials on 50 Years of New China, provided by National Statistics Bureau in 1999.

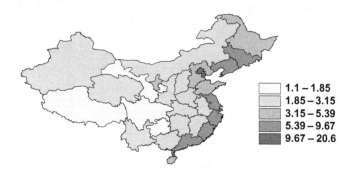

Figure 5.26.   Regional teledensity (1995).

Note: Teledensities of 2004–2006 are estimated using telecommunications industrial capacity provided by *China Statistics Yearbook* series, 2005–2007.
Source: Comprehensive Statistical Data and Materials on 50 Years of New China, provided by National Statistics Bureau in 1999.

following three figures are similar to those from Figures 5.21, 5.22, and 5.23. First, there are significant differences in terms of teledensity among regions in China in all the three selected years. Second, all regions have been increasing their teledensities during the time period from 1985 to 2006. Third, the spatial distribution pattern of teledensity follows the same track as that of telephone lines, with coastal regions outperforming

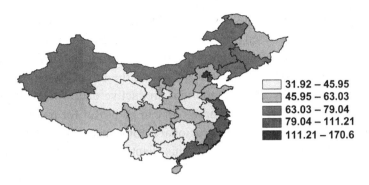

Figure 5.27.   Regional teledensity (2006).

Note: Teledensities of 2004–2006 are estimated using telecommunications industrial capacity provided by *China Statistics Yearbook* series, 2005–2007.
Source: Comprehensive Statistical Data and Materials on 50 Years of New China, provided by National Statistics Bureau in 1999.

others in telephone services access and availability. Moreover, Figure 5.24 shows that the gap in terms of telephone lines exhibits an upward trend that is similar to the gap in terms of regional output across regions.

5.3. Summary

The growth paths of regional economic output and telecommunications infrastructure during the time period from 1985 to 2006 tend to be similar. Most of the regions in China — especially those in the coastal region — achieved astounding growth in economic development in the examined period. No short-term or long-term economic recessions have occurred in this large developing country during the past three decades. The issue of regional economic income and output inequality has been a major policy target for policymakers, and the most famous example is China's Western Development program. Besides, entrepreneurship seems to contribute to regional economic growth, and the more entrepreneurial coastal regions also outperform the less entrepreneurial interior regions.

This chapter attempts to link the regional economic performance discrepancy to one of its contributory factors — telecommunications infrastructure. The rationale lies exactly in the similar evolutionary path and spatial pattern between regional output and telecommunications infrastructure availability. Rapid growth in telecommunications sector in nearly all regions in China does not mitigate the dramatic regional disparities in availability of this important productive endowment. Insights from the relationship between these two can be useful for policymaking explorations of lessening China's regional income inequality, which is one of the most important contribution of this chapter to the existing literature.

References

Ding, L. (2005). Telecommunications infrastructure and regional economic development in China. Dissertation. School of Public Policy, George Mason University, Fairfax, VA, USA.

Ding, L., and K. E. Haynes (2007). Modeling the spatial diffusion of mobile communications in China. Working paper.

Giovanis, A. N., and C. H. Skiadas (2005). A new modeling approach investigating the diffusion speed of mobile telecommunication service in EU-15. *International Symposium on Applied Stochastic Models and Data Analysis*, Brest, France.

He, Z. (1997). A history of telecommunications in China: Development and policy implications, in P. S. N. Lee (Eds.) *Telecommunications and Development in China*. Cresskill, NJ: Hampton Press, Inc.

Lee, M., and Y. Cho (2007). The diffusion of mobile telecommunications services in Korea. Available at: http://temap.snu.ac.kr/data/science/bbs/9.%20Lee-Cho%20 The%20-Diffusion%20of%20Mobile%20Telecommunications%20Services%20in%20Korea.pdf

Liu, T. (1988). *Transportation and Communication in National Economy*. Chongqin: Chongqing Press.

National Statistics Bureau (Multiple years). *China Statistics Yearbooks* (for multiple years).

Singh, J. P. (1999). *Leapfrogging Development? The Political Economy of Telecommunications Restructuring*. Albany, NY: State University of New York Press.

Tang, H. S., and P. S. N. Lee (2003). Growth in adversity: Non-economic factors in telecommunications development in China. *Telematics and Informatics* **20**: 19–33.

Wu, B. (2000). Developments of Chinese economy and economics in the recent 50 years. Academic Newspaper by Shanghai Administration Institute (1).

Zhao, D. (1990). Economic development stability and growth rate. *Journal of the Zhongnan University of Finance and Economics* **4**.

Part IV

Financial Environment
of Entrepreneurship in China

Chapter 6

Entrepreneurship Financing — Innofund

Emily Xiaoxia Wang

International Finance Corporation

Recognizing the powerful combination of entrepreneurship and techno-logical innovation, the governments of both industrialized and develop-ing the countries have devised programs to support entrepreneurship in technology-based small and medium enterprises (TSMEs). One cate-gory of these programs is public or government venture capital pro-grams that finance entrepreneurs to commercialize technological innovations, as pioneered in the U.S. and widely adopted in Europe. China ventured into this area in the 1990s in the backdrop of the initial success of reforming and restructuring its science and technology infra-structure in the 1980s. Researchers and the government were fervently drawing a blueprint of a national innovation system and introducing and testing various foreign experiences. China established its largest public venture capital program, the Innovation Fund for Small (and Medium) Technology-Based Firms (Innofund) in 1999 to provide and catalyze funding to technology-related entrepreneurial activities by TSMEs. This chapter will first briefly discuss theoretical, international, and national context for Innofund, more specifically the public-venture capital pro-grams in China, and then elaborate on how Innofund operates and how effective it has been in funding TSMEs.

6.1. Theoretical and International Context

Theoretical consensus exists that TSMEs face a significant funding gap (Moore, 1994; Murray and Lott, 1995; Sohl, 1999; Hall, 2002). The cause is multidimensional, including the institutional design of traditional financial institutions that were meant to serve large and mature companies rather than SMEs, information gap in finding sources of funding and presenting their cases (Bovaird *et al.*, 1995), technological and commercial uncertainty and different interests of entrepreneurs and financiers (Moore and Garnsey, 1993), and high costs of financing (although justifiable economically but nevertheless hinder SMEs from borrowing enough). TSMEs have additional challenges (Westhead and Storey, 1997): lack of managerial and entrepreneurial skills, the novelty of the product or service, shorter life cycle of products or services; and requirement of R&D funding.

To fill the funding gap left by the private sector, various public programs have been set up. Governments typically provide free funding for feasibility study, innovation promotion, and capacity building. As to larger funding needs for R&D, working capital, and capital expenditure, governments support soft bank loans or equity investments. Equity is a better solution for TSMEs because of their special characteristics (Moore and Garnsey, 1993; Carpenter and Petersen, 2002). Venture capital has been an important source of external equity for entrepreneurs and an effective channel to inject risk capital into TSMEs. In the 1990s, venture-capital–backed technological start-ups such as Apple Computers, Cisco Systems, Genentech, Netscape, and Sun Microsystems achieved huge commercial successes. These successes were attributed to the combination of entrepreneurs' technological expertise and venture capitalists' commercial experience and advice to enhance TSMEs' viability and value.

However, the private-sector supply of venture capital was insufficient, which prompted the governments to enhance the venture capital industry through direct measures such as incentivizing the creation of public venture capital funds and indirect measures such as improving the regulatory environment and providing tax incentives for venture capital investment.

Many countries have set up public venture capital programs, which have become an important part of venture capital industry and entrepreneurial financing.

These programs use a broad range of instruments that fall into five categories: free finance (e.g., grants and loan interest subsidies), debt finance (e.g., loans), equity finance, guarantees (e.g., loan and equity guarantees/insurance), and hybrid finance (e.g., participating preferred securities, convertibles, and equity with put or call options). More often than not, these programs use a combination of two or more instruments to cater to TSMEs' various financial needs. Specific program designs depend on the economic and institutional characteristics of individual countries.

6.2. China Context

Unlike the U.S. and other western countries, China never had an extended period when capitalism and the market mechanism could fully develop. Thus it initially lacked a strong economic base of numerous vibrant SMEs. It is in the realm of S&T policies that entrepreneurs found more systematic policy and financial support for the purpose of maintaining the nation's S&T competitiveness. The government set up the first public venture capital firm in 1985 and, in 1991, started to encourage domestic and international venture capital investors to set up venture capital funds and firms in high and new technology zones (Wang, 2004). Around the mid-1990s, venture capital was included in the national and regional innovation systems as one of the important elements and cleared the way for Sino–foreign joint-venture venture capital. In 1996, the State Council pointed out, "the S&T venture capital mechanism needs to be proactively explored in order to foster the commercialization of S&T research output".

The year 1999 marked a turning point for public venture capital programs with the promulgation of two new policies: the 1999 Resolution to Enhance Technological Innovation, Develop High Technology, and Realize Commercialization, and the 1999 Comments on Establishing China's Venture Capital System. The government began to take a systematic approach to address the hurdles for the venture capital industry and to build an growth-enabling environment. First, the central government strengthened and/or realigned the existing programs, created new public venture capital programs, and shifted its orientation to constructing an enabling environment and developing TSMEs. Second, the investor base was greatly broadened with increasing participation from local governments, universities, domestic companies, and individual investors (or angel investors). Third, local governments took initiatives to build productivity promotion centers (PPCs) and S&T business incubators that provide various intermediary services to entrepreneurs. As a result, the public venture capital programs evolved into a dynamic and comprehensive system (Figure 6.1) and central and local governments strengthened cooperation in developing venture capital industry and helping entrepreneurs.

Public venture capital programs are either wholly owned by governments/wholly state-owned enterprises (WSOEs) or joint ventures with the private sector. Those wholly owned by governments/WSOEs were usually established before 1999 and make up 20% of the total number of venture capital companies while public–private joint ventures accounted for 34%.[1] Public sources contribution to the total capital under management increased from 35% in 2002 to 39% in 2004 and amounted to RMB 19.5 billion in 2004.

Meanwhile, the government has put complementary pieces together in order to create a holistic enabling environment for entrepreneurs. These include policy bank lending; creating SME lending capacity, products, and services in commercial banks; developing a commercial credit guarantee system; and setting up the SME board in the Shenzhen Stock Exchange.

Different parts of the public venture capital system have worked together to support TSMEs and their entrepreneurial activities. For example, government budget programs supported seed- to early-stage TSMEs, which receive second- or third-round private equity financing from public and

---

[1] Based on the numbers provided in China Venture Capital Investment Report, 2004.

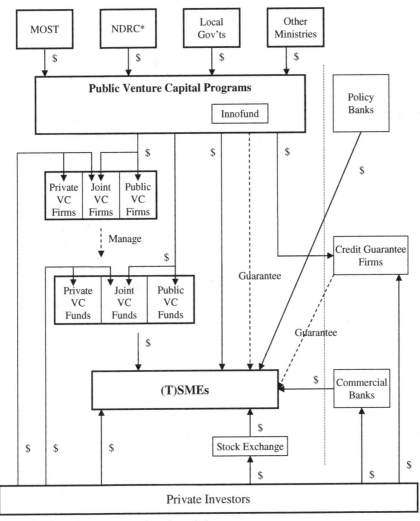

Figure 6.1. China's Public Venture Capital Program.

* National Development and Reform Commission

private venture capital companies. They may also obtain public guarantees and loans from banks. After they have grown enough to satisfy the SME board listing requirement, they may undertake an initial public offering (IPO).

6.2.1. *Establishment and Operation of Innofund*

In 1999, the Ministry of Science and Technology (MOST) and the Ministry of Finance (MOF) jointly issued "the Provisions for the Technological Innovation Fund for Science & Technology-Based Small and Medium-Sized Enterprises" (the "Provisions"). Shortly after, MOST established Innofund as the largest national-level public venture capital fund. The establishment of Innofund was good news to technology-based entrepreneurs and became a model for China's public venture capital programs.

The objectives of Innofund were set in the Provisions: (i) it shall catalyze investments in TSMEs' innovation from local governments, enterprises, venture capital companies, and other financial institutions so as to establish venture capital; and (ii) it shall not seek profits but seek to improve TSMEs' innovative capacity by supporting their innovation projects. Innofund's awards take three forms: grant, loan interest subsidy, and equity. However, only the first two forms have been actively used and equity investments are close to nil with only two cases as of 2004. The MOST directly supervises Innofund and sets annual project guidelines.

Innofund's funding comes from the central government's budget and the interest accrued to the budgeted funds. Innofund's total budget between 1999 and 2004 amounted to RMB 3.8 billion. The actual total amount of awards during the same period was RMB 4.3 billion, equivalent to 46% of all venture capital under management, or 22% of all private equity. If the local governments' matching fund of RMB 2.7 billion during the same period is included, Innofund-related government funding is equivalent to 74% of all venture capital under management (which excludes Innofund), or 14% of all private equity.[2] Thus, Innofund was a key source of funding to entrepreneurs.

---

[2]Includes 1999–2003 amount only because 2004 amount is not available. The actual total amount from local governments is greater than this number.

Table 6.1.   Innofund budget

(RMB million)

Year	1999	2000	2001	2002	2003	2004	Total
Innofund Budget[a]	1,000	800	500	500	500	500	3,800
Total S&T Programs Budget	4,399	4,576	5,258	5,582	5,900	6,525	32,240
Innofund % of Total S&T Programs	22.7%	17.5%	9.5%	9.0%	8.5%	7.7%	12.83%
Innofund Awarded Amount[a]	816	660	783	540	664	827	4,290

[a]Innofund's budget and granted amount differs because of inter-year budget transfer and the inclusion of interest earned in granted amount.
Source: (i) China Science and Technology Statistics (http://www.sts.org.cn); (ii) 1999–2003 Innofund Annual Reports (http://www.innofund.gov.cn); and (iii) 2004 Innofund project information (http://www.innofund.gov.cn).

Applicants for Innofund must satisfy the following eligibility requirements:

1. Domestically registered TSMEs;
2. Projects highly innovative and competitive in the market with potentially large economic and social benefits and the prospect to form a new industry;
3. Project implementation period between one and three years;
4. Less than 500 employees with over 30% having undergraduate and/or above degrees in S&T;
5. Core business in R&D and production and services of high and new technologies with annual R&D input of no less than 3% of sales and 10% workforce in R&D; and
6. Good financial management system.

These requirements incorporate the public venture capital experiences of other countries. They reflect the government's intention to (i) focus on innovation and commercialization and not to veer away from Innofund's objective (a lesson learned from previously failed public venture capital programs); (ii) encourage entrepreneurs to establish and grow TSMEs; (iii) prevent government awards from crowding out industry R&D

spending; and (iv) minimize the chance of awardees' operational failure by requiring a demonstrated good financial management system.

The selection of the awardees follows the principle of open competition. Every application needs to be recommended by an official sponsor, usually a local government's counterpart of the MOST or management committees of high and new technology zones. The application is then reviewed and evaluated by technological specialists and appraisers selected from Innofund's expert pool. Based on the result, the Innofund Administrator, a not-for-profit legal entity, proposes candidates to the MOST and MOF, who jointly approve final awardees.

Local governments play an important role. Each year, they launch campaigns to advocate Innofund participation and recommend high-quality applicants. Their endorsement of applicants obliges them to check the reliability of application information and share the responsibility of applicants' failure. China's centralized political structure and accordingly strong upward accountability motivate local governments to do a good job. Local governments also have an incentive to obtain as much central funding as possible in order to develop their local economy. Second, local governments are required to match 50% of Innofund's award for each project, which, in addition to drawing additional finances from localities, further aligns local and central interests. Third, the Innofund Administrator is obliged to monitor the whole implementation process of each project but, due to limited resources, has to delegate its daily monitoring responsibility to official sponsors, often local governments who in part are recipients and responsible for outcomes. The multidimensional involvement of local governments and various incentives all increase the chance of Innofund's success.

However, Innofund's virtual ride on the existing bureaucratic system differs from typical lean and flat venture capital management firms and thus may not as effective as private venture capital. The massive involvement of government also increases the chance of rent-seeking and regulatory capture. This scenario, together with lack of venture capital personnel in governments, raises the question of the governments' ability to perform well to support entrepreneurs.

In addition to the objectives stated in its founding documents, Innofund is required to give priority to:

- TSMEs founded by research personnel or overseas returnees who can transfer their scientific achievements from abroad;
- Cooperation projects among industries, universities, and research institutions; and
- Project using new technologies to revive traditional industries and create jobs.

Innofund also carries the policy goals of developing West China and providing micro-financing. While some of these missions may alleviate the geographical herding of venture capital to more economically developed regions, others may overburden Innofund and make it difficult to assess Innofund's performance and hold Innofund accountable for its performance.

6.3. Performance of Innofund

How effective has Innofund been in supporting entrepreneurs in TSMEs? To answer this question, a logic model of Innofund evaluation is constructed as shown in Figure 6.2. using the evaluation model concept in (Ruegg and Feller, 2003). The Innofund operation mechanism is set up to implement its goals of financing and catalyzing financial resources to TSMEs, building innovation capacity in TSMEs, developing market mechanism in financing entrepreneurial endeavors in innovation, and supporting development in Western China. These goals serve, at a higher order, the public policy strategy of the government and social goals. In assessment, hypotheses were developed with regard to various aspects of Innofund's goals and information and data were collected at the operational level to test these hypotheses. Specifically, we would like to know how much direct financial support Innofund has given to TSMEs and how much other financial resources Innofund has catalyzed to TSMEs; what external factors affects the TSMEs' chance of getting Innofund awards; and whether Innofund has contributed to developing the capital market for TSMEs and entrepreneurs.

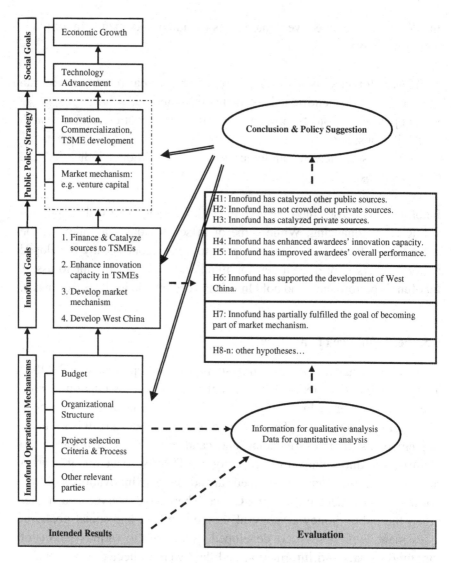

Figure 6.2. Logic model for Innofund evaluation.

6.3.1. *Innofund's Direct Financing of TSMEs*

Innofund received 25,189 applications during 1999–2004 and approved 4,946 (Table 6.2), translating in to a 25% approval rate compared to 17% for SBIR Phase I applications (Cooper, 2003) and 15% for SMART Phase

Table 6.2. Innofund statistics

	1999	2000	2001	2002	2003	2004	Total
No of Applications	3,221	4,898	3,681	4,215	4,249	4,925	25,189
No of Awards	1,089	872	1,008	780	1,197	1,464	6,410
No of Grants	759	713	767	596	963		3,798
No of Loan Interest Subsidies	330	159	241	184	234		1,148
% Approved	33.8%	17.8%	27.4%	18.5%	28.2%	29.7%	25.4%
Total Amount Applied for (RMB million)	3,874	5,420	3,589	4,040	3,776		20,699
Total Amount Approved (RMB million)	816	660	783	540	664	827	4,290
Total Amount of Grants (RMB million)	552	533	583	404	517		2,589
Total Amount of Loan Interest subsidies (RMB million)	264	127	200	136	147		874
% Approved	21.1%	12.2%	21.8%	13.4%	17.6%		16.7%
Average Size of Award (RMB)	749,633	756,491	777,083	692,615	554,570	564,891	669,267
Average Size of Grant (RMB)	727,167	747,630	760,326	677,852	536,833		681,706
Average Size of Loan Interest Subsidy (RMB)	801,303	796,226	830,415	740,435	628,419		761,716

Source: 1999–2003 Innofund Annual Reports, 2004 project information. Available at http://www.innofund.gov.cn.

I application (Moore and Garnsey, 1993). This implies that it is easier for Chinese TSMEs to receive government support in a comparable government program. A total of RMB 4.3 billion was awarded, with 75% in the form of grants and 25% in the form of loan interest subsidies. The average size of award is RMB 669,267.

6.3.2. *Catalyzing Other Funds to TSMEs*

In addition to directly funding TSMEs, Innofund is proposed to catalyze more funding from local governments, enterprises, venture capital companies, and financial institutions to TSMEs. To assess whether this purpose has been served and if so, to what extent, three hypotheses are tested: (i) Innofund has not crowded out private sources; (ii) Innofund has catalyzed other public sources; and (iii) Innofund has catalyzed private sources.

Hypothesis 1: Innofund has not crowded out private sources.

Innofund's target market is seed to early-stage TSMEs. How large is this market? Is it possible that the market is so small that Innofund basically takes many or all good deals that the private sector could have been invested in? In other words, has Innofund crowded out the private sources?

To answer these questions, we need to analyze the demand and supply of TSMEs' funding. Since there are no statistics specific to TSMEs and their funding, estimates must be made through the statistics of private technology-based companies and/or industrial SMEs in general. As shown in Table 6.3, in 2004, there are 141,353 private technology-based companies in China, with total assets of RMB 53,003 billion and total sales of RMB 4,808 billion. The average total assets and sales are RMB 37 million and RMB 34 million, respectively. On an average, each company employs 80 people. Since the average total assets and employees meet Innofund's eligibility requirements, all technology-based companies are used as an upper limit for estimating TSMEs funding. The total assets for all technology-based companies increased by 18.6% or RMB 8,178 billion in 2004. With an average debt ratio of 53%, this translates to a funding of RMB 441 billion in 2004. Innofund's awards in 2004 totaled RMB 4 billion, roughly 0.9% of all estimated funding.

Table 6.3.   Estimation of 2004 funding need of technology-based companies

	All Technology-Based Companies	Technology-Based Companies with Sales <RMB 1 million
No of firms	141,353	81,884
Total Assets (RMB bln)	5,300	208
Total Sales (RMB bln)	4,808	
Average Assets (RMB mln)	37	
Average Sales (RMB mln)	34	
% Increase in Total Assets	18.6%	
Increase in Total Asset over 2003 (RMB bln)	832	33
Average Debt Ratio	53.0%	
Funding need in 2004 (RMB bln)	441	17
Innofund's Award in 2004	4	
Innofund's Contribution	**0.9%**	**23.0%**

Source: China Science and Technology Statistics. Available at http://www.sts.org.cn/tjbg/qtzx/documents/2004/0401.htm.

Among all technology-based companies, 58%, or 81,884 firms, have sales below RMB 1 million, which can be used as a lower limit in estimating TSMEs' funding need. They had total assets of RMB 209 billion in 2004, about a RMB 33 billion increase over 2003 if using the average 18.6% asset growth ratio for all firm sizes. This translates into at least RMB 17 billion new debts for TSMEs in 2004 if using the average 53% debt ratio for all firm sizes. Innofund's 2004 award of RMB 4 billion contributed about 23% of TSMEs financing need. Hence, Innofund provides 0.9% to 23% of the funding need of TSMEs. This is insufficient to crowd out private sources in any more than a limited way if at all possible. The possibility of crowding out depends on whether the private sector can provide more than RMB 13–437 billion funding to TSMEs.

Estimation from industrial SMEs in general provides additional insight into demand and supply of TSMEs' funding. As Table 6.4 shows, there are 275,189 industrial SMEs as of 2004, with total assets of RMB 13,582 billion, an increase of RMB 3,329 billion over 2003. As the average debt

Table 6.4. Statistics of China's industrial SMEs

	2001	2002	2003[a]	2004[a]
No of Firms	162,667	172,805	194,238	275,189
Total Output (RMB bln)	3,975	4,113	4,737	5,063
Total Asset (RMB bln)	8,660	9,253	10,253	13,582
Total Sales (RMB bln)	6,325	7,286	9,062	12,769
Total Profits (RMB bln)	264	337	450	643
Total Profits and Paid Taxes (RMB bln)	592	710	880	1,178

[a]Based on new classification standards starting from 2003.
Source: Based on data from the National Bureau of Statistics of China. Available at http://www. stats.gov.cn/tjsj/ndsj/; 2001–2004 Development of China's Industrial SMEs, December 9, 2005. Available at http://sme.gov.cn.

ratio for China's SMEs is 70% and 80% of debt is from banks, this translates to a need of RMB 1,864 billion bank loans by all SMEs in 2004.[3] However, the Industrial and Commercial Bank of China (ICBC) lent only RMB 4.8 billion to SMEs in 2004. ICBC's market share of RMB loans is 22.5%, thus SME loans from all banks in 2004 cannot exceed RMB 21.3 billion, about 1.1% of all SMEs loan needs.[4] Thus, there is a significant funding gap for SMEs. TSMEs as a high-risk sub-category of SMEs have more difficulty in obtaining bank loans. From Tables 3.d.3 and 3.d.4, TSMEs account for 29.8% of SMEs in the number of firms and 1.5% of SMEs total assets. Thus only RMB 0.3–6 billion out of RMB 21.3 billion will go to TSMEs. This is not enough to meet the RMB 13 billion condition for Innofund to crowd out private sources and leaves a RMB 7–12.7 billion funding gap for TSMEs. So Innofund has not crowed out private sources but helped fill in the funding gap.

Additionally, Innofund focuses on supporting TSMEs at seed to early stages. According to Zero2ipo's 2004 China Venture Capital Annual Report, seed- to early-stage investments accounted for only 21.3%, or $0.27 billion (RMB 2.2 billion) of the total invested amount for the whole private equity

[3]Solution to SMEs' Financial Difficulty (*zhongxiao qiye rongzi nan pojie*). Financial News. March 21, 2005. http://financialnews.com.cn.
[4]CLSA Emerging Markets. September 2002. Banking in China. http://www.clsa.com.

industry in 2004, only less than a third of those funds invested in expansion and later-stage projects. Thus, seed- to early-stage projects represent a niche for the private equity industry, which Innofund helps to support.

Based on the above analysis, it is unlikely that Innofund crowds out private sources. Instead, it may well fill a huge funding gap for TSMEs.

Hypothesis 2: Innofund has catalyzed other public resources

Innofund awardees raised capital from local governments, financial institutions (predominantly banks), awardees' own capital, and other sources as well. The planned funding from these sources from 1999 to 2004 is listed in Table 6.5. On average, Innofund and local governments provide 14.1% and 5.4%, respectively, for awardees.

Table 6.5. Financial sources of Innofund's awardees

		1999	2000	2001	2002	2003	2004	Average
Funding Sources (RMB mln)								
1	Innofund	1,278	949	1,032	782	1,044	1,222	1,051
2	Local	521	226	356	316	440	548	401
3	FIs	5,448	2,111	2,578	1,715	2,289	2,055	2,699
4	Own Capital	4,004	2,483	2,920	2,405	3,212	3,932	3,159
5	Other	404	140	68	35	73	28	125
6	Total	11,655	5,909	6,952	5,253	7,058	7,784	7,435
Funding Sources (%)								
7	Innofund	11.0	16.1	14.8	14.9	14.8	15.7	14.1
8	Local	4.5	3.8	5.1	6.0	6.2	7.0	5.4
9	FIs	46.7	35.7	37.1	32.6	32.4	26.4	36.3
10	Own Capital	34.4	42.0	42.0	45.8	45.5	50.5	42.5
11	Other	3.5	2.4	1.0	0.7	1.0	0.4	1.7
12	Total	100.0	100.0	100.0	100.0	100.0	100.0	100.0
13	**(1)+(2)**	**1,799**	**1,175**	**1,388**	**1,099**	**1,485**	**1,769**	**1,452**
14	**(3)+(4)+(5)**	**9,856**	**4,734**	**5,565**	**4,155**	**5,573**	**6,015**	**5,983**
15	**Private/Public (14)/(13)**	**5.5**	**4.0**	**4.0**	**3.8**	**3.8**	**3.4**	**4.1**

Source: Innofund.

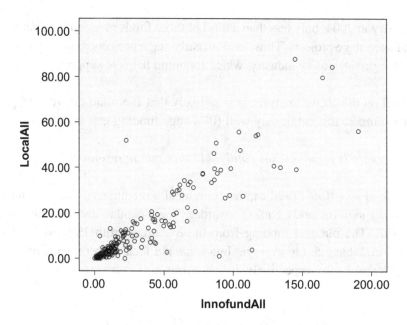

Figure 6.3. Scatter plot: Innofund versus Local government.

Because local governments are required to match at least 50% of Innofund's awards, there should be a causal link between the two sources. To test this hypothesis, data of different fund sources at provincial level during 1999–2004 are used, yielding a total of 181 valid observations of 186 possible observations. These data are planned data, not actual disbursement, because planned data are better at reflecting the underlying relationships among different sources. The scatter plot of Innofund and local government funding clearly indicates a positive linear relationship (Figure 6.3).

Accordingly, a regression analysis is conducted between the two variables with the results shown in Table 3.d.6. With an R-squared value as high as 0.783, the model is sufficient to test the causal relationship between Innofund and local government funding.

To control for regional difference, four dummies variables are introduced into the regression model in Table 6.6 to represent the Beijing–Tianjin

Table 6.6. Regression results: Innofund versus local government

Model Summary

Local All = α + β Innofund All + ε

R	R-Squared	Adjusted R-Squared	Std. Error of the Estimate
0.89	0.78	0.78	7.77

Anova

	Sum of Squares	df	Mean Square	F	Significance
Regression	39,133.01	1	39,133.00	648.66	0.00
Residual	10,859.16	180	60.33		
Total	49,992.17	181			

Coefficients

Predictors	Unstandardized Coefficients		Standardized Coefficients		
	B	Std. Error	Beta	T	Significance.
(Constant)	−0.21	0.78		−0.26	0.79
InnofundAll	0.39	0.02	0.89	25.47	0.00

area (DumBjTj), the Yangtze River Delta (DumYangtze), the Pearl River Delta (DumPearl), and the West (DumWest). The first three dummies represent the top three regions where economic development level is the highest and venture capital activities are the most active. However, the enhanced model does not yield significant coefficients of the dummies. Then the first three dummies are dropped and only DumWest is retained. The resulting enhanced model is shown in Table 6.7. The coefficient of DumWest is negative and significant at 5% level. So western provinces do match less, 30% compared to 40% for non-western provinces as shown in Table 6.8. This ratio is less than the 50% target. This implies that Innofund does not enforce the matching ratio vigorously: Only 2 of 21 non-western provinces satisfy the 50% matching requirement.

Table 6.7. Regression results: Innofund versus local government with DumWest

Model Summary

Local All = α + β Innofund All γ DumWest +ε

R	R-Squared	Adjusted R-Squared	Std. Error of the Estimate
0.89	0.79	0.79	0.62

Anova

	Sum of Squares	df	Mean Square	F	Significance
Regression	247.12	2	123.56	324.92	0.00
Residual	65.41	172	0.38		
Total	312.53	174			

Coefficients

Predictors	Unstandardized Coefficients		Standardized Coefficients		
	B	Std. Error	Beta	T	Significance
(Constant)	−0.94	0.14		−6.64	0.00
InnofundAll	−0.97	0.04	0.87	23.76	0.00
DumWest	−0.22	0.11	−0.07	−2.04	0.04

Thus there is a possibility for local governments to match less. However, between 1999 and 2004, the local matching ratios are increasing: 41%, 24%, 35%, 40%, 42%, and 45%, respectively. Thus the local governments' desire to develop local economy outweighs the possibility of moral hazard. Innofund's relaxing of local matching ratio may be based on a mutual understanding that local governments increase their matching ratios over the year until the required 50% is satisfied.

In summary, Innofund does catalyze local government funding for TSMEs: local governments match on average 38% of Innofund's awarded amount. However, the catalytic effect is less than expected because the local matching requirement is not rigorously enforced. However, the local matching ratios are increasing over the year, reflecting local governments

Table 6.8. Innofund and local government funding 1999–2004

(RMB mln)	Innofund (1)	Local Government (2)	[(2)/(1)] × 100 (%)
Beijing City	904	318	35%
Tianjin City	92	36	39%
Hebei Province	109	35	32%
Shanxi Province	52	15	29%
Inner Mongolia Autonomous region	73	17	23%
Liaoning Province	283	122	43%
Jilin Province	186	65	35%
Heilongjiang Province	121	4	35%
Shanghai City	446	135	30%
Jiangsu Province	596	240	40%
Zhejiang Province	503	260	52%
Anhui Province	99	39	39%
Fujian Province	88	76	87%
Jiangxi Province	86	34	40%
Shandong Province	412	159	39%
Henan Province	94	33	36%
Hubei Province	280	112	40%
Hunan Province	187	73	39%
Guangdong Province	449	216	48%
Guangxi Zhuang Autonomous Region	38	14	38%
Hainan Province	7	3	45%
Sichuan Province	490	159	33%
Chongqing City	118	24	20%
Guizhou Province	44	14	31%
Yunnan Province	37	11	31%
Xizang Autonomous Region	11	3	31%
Shaanxi Province	327	81	25%
Gansu Province	68	21	32%
Tsinghai Province	14	4	33%
Ningxia Hui Autonomous Region	37	21	57%
Xinjiang Uyghur Autonomous Region	57	2	38%
Subtotal — Non-West	**5,105**	**2,046**	**40%**
Subtotal — West	**1,202**	**361**	**30%**
Total	**6,307**	**2,407**	**38%**

Source: Innofund.

increased incentive to use Innofund to development local TSMEs and economy, which overcomes the possible moral hazard among local governments.

Hypothesis 3: Innofund has catalyzed private resources.

Financial institutions

Among awardees' private sources, financial institutions (FIs) provide for 32%–47% of total funding, awardees' own capital account for 34%–51%, and other sources account for 0%–4% between 1999 and 2004. First, correlations between Innofund's awards and these private sources are calculated to test if Innofund has a direct effect on them. Then, correlations between local governments' funding and private sources are calculated to find whether the local governments' funding has direct effects on private sources and whether Innofund has indirect effects through local governments. The calculated correlations are summarized in Table 6.9.

The correlation analyses show that there is statistically significant correlation of Innofund award, local government funding, and the two added up with FIs' financing, respectively. Local government funding has stronger

Table 6.9. Summary of correlations

Private Sources	Correlations	Pearson Correlation	Significance (2-tailed)
FIs	(Innofund) vs. (FI)	0.71	0.00
	(Local) vs. (FI)	0.72	0.00
	(Innofund + Local)vs. (FI)	0.73	0.00
Awardees' Own Capital	(Innofund) vs. (Own)	0.92	0.00
	(Local) vs. (Own)	0.87	0.00
	(Innofund + Local) vs. (Own)	0.92	0.00
Other Sources	(Innofund) vs. (Other)	0.50	0.00
	(Local) vs. (Other)	0..43	0.00
	(Innofund + Local) vs. (Other)	0.49	0.00

effect than Innofund awards. Innofund award and local government funding combined achieve the strongest effect. This can be explained by the closer interaction and relationship between local governments and FIs at the local level, which is quite understandable because of the fact that FIs typically finance enterprises through local branches whose representative know both local governments and enterprises better.

Awardee's Own Capital

Correlation results in Table 6.9 show that Innofund has stronger effect on Awardees' own capital than local governments. This may be because the central endorsement rather than local endorsement gives awardees more confidence about the projects under development, and awardees are therefore more willing to put in their own money. Innofund and local governments combined again show the strongest effect on awardees' own capital.

Other Sources

The effect of Innofund and local governments on other sources respectively and combined is significant but of small magnitude, i.e., less than 0.5 as shown in Table 6.9. Moreover, other sources account for only 0%–4% of awardees' funding. So other sources can be dropped from this research.

In summary, the likelihood of Innofund crowding out private sources is small. Instead, there is evidence that Innofund catalyzes local government funding. Innofund has not fully achieved its expected catalytic effect on local governments because it does not enforce the matching ratio vigorously. This may create moral hazard among local governments. However, local governments' increasing ratios in the past years indicate that this possibility has been overcome by local governments' desire to develop local economy via increasing support for TSMEs. With regard to catalyzing private sources, Innofund's effect is not as strong as local governments in inducing FIs' funding but is stronger than local governments in encouraging awardees to put in more own capital. In both cases, Innofund and local governments combined can achieve the best catalytic effect on private sources.

6.3.3. *External Factors Affecting Innofund Awards*

Table 6.10 provides the regional distribution of Innofund applications and awards in 2003. All 31 provinces have obtained Innofund's awards. However, there is a high degree of concentration, with the top six regions

Table 6.10. Regional distribution of Innofund awards 2003

	# of Applications	# of Awards	% of Awards	Ranking	Amount Applied (RMB mln)	Amount Awarded (RMB mln)
Beijing City	2,226	677	13.7%	1	2,413.5	500.6
Tianjin City	388	83	1.7%	15	403.0	54.3
Hebei Province	436	77	1.6%	17	451.4	53.8
Shanxi Province	245	40	0.8%	24	276.1	25.9
Inner Mongolia Autonomous Region	228	46	0.9%	21	250.1	30.4
Liaoning Province	983	227	4.6%	10	993.3	157.5
Of which: Dalian City	184	52	1.1%		196.6	36.2
Jilin Province	472	149	3.0%	11	477.7	106.0
Heilongjiang Province	485	91	1.8%	14	524.4	61.5
Shanghai City	1,652	353	7.1%	5	1,570.8	237.7
Jiangsu Province	2,050	523	10.6%	2	2,032.9	384.2
Zhejiang Province	1,335	406	8.2%	3	1,263.9	297.7
Of which: Ningbo City	133	49	1.0%		129.8	36.4
Anhui Province	274	72	1.5%	18	283.3	50.4
Fujian Province	364	80	1.6%	16	349.1	51.4
Of which: Xiamen City	109	32	0.6%		107.3	17.3
Jiangxi Province	187	60	1.2%	20	190.1	40.8
Shandong Province	1,410	331	6.7%	6	1,478.8	236.1
Of which: Tsingtao City	201	62	1.3%		225.1	45.1
Henan Province	447	66	1.3%	19	470.8	46.0
Hubei Province	1,001	229	4.6%	9	993.1	167.9

(*Continued*)

Table 6.10.   (*Continued*)

	# of Applications	# of Awards	% of Awards	Ranking	Amount Applied (RMB mln)	Amount Awarded (RMB mln)
Hunan Province	524	140	2.8%	12	587.4	96.9
Guangdong Province	1,396	283	5.7%	8	1,606.1	203.8
Of which: Shenzhen City	519	126	2.5%		667.8	90.7
Guangxi Zhuang Autonomous Region	160	33	0.7%	26	167.5	22.7
Hainan Province	42	5	0.1%	31	49.1	3.4
Sichuan Province	1,562	401	8.1%	4	1,537.7	257.9
Chongqing City	513	92	1.9%	13	525.0	60.4
Guizhou Province	101	27	0.5%	27	103.1	18.3
Yunnan Province	138	35	0.7%	25	124.1	19.5
Xizang autonomous Region	15	7	0.1%	30	17.3	4.8
Shaanxi Province	1,165	291	5.9%	7	1,060.8	193.2
Gansu Province	187	45	0.9%	22	217.2	29.5
Tsinghai Province	32	10	0.2%	29	31.4	7.2
Ningxia Hui Autonomous Region	94	24	0.5%	28	97.3	16.6
Xinjiang Uyghur Autonomous Region	152	43	0.9%	23	153.3	27.4
Total	20,264	4,946	100.0%		20,699.4	3,463.4
Top 6 Regions			54.4%			

Source: 1999–2003 Innofund Annual Reports.

receiving 54.5% of all awards. A further comparison with the regional preferences of international venture capitalists and the whole venture capital industry (Table 6.11) shows that Innofund's top investment regions are similar to those chosen by international venture capitalists and overall venture capital industry. However, there is one region, Sichuan, which is among Innofund's top six focus regions but does not normally appear on

Table 6.11. Venture capital focus regions

Rank	Innofund[a]	Total VC[b]	International VC[c]
1	Beijing	Shanghai	Beijing
2	Jiangsu	Guangdong	Shanghai
3	Zhejiang	Zhejiang	Guangdong
4	Sichuan	Beijing	Zhejiang
5	Shanghai	Jiangsu	Jiangsu
6	Shandong	Hubei	Shandong

Source: [a]1999–2003 Innofund Annual Reports ; [b]2003 China Venture Capital Investment Report; [c]Zeng (2004).

private venture capitalists' top lists (Table 6.11). In addition to special support to Sichuan province, Innofund also gives preferential treatment to other western provinces. This reflects Innofund's effort to correct the herding problem in the venture capital industry.

Besides location, the S&T development level determines a region's overall innovation capacity and activity and therefore the number of TSMEs that are eligible for Innofund's awards. A good indicator of the S&T development level is the regional S&T index published by MOST every year, which incorporates 27 factors in five categories: S&T environment, S&T input, S&T output, commercialization of high and new technologies, and S&T's effect on economic development. Gross domestic product (GDP) reflects a region's economic size, while GDP per capita reflects the economic development level. Both of them relate to ultimate resources available to local governments and can affect Innofund's awards. The size of a region as denoted by population is often a factor in central allocation of public resources as is the case with SBIR's awards (der Vlist *et al.*, 2004). The following analysis examines how these factors (variables) and regional dummies affect Innofund's awards. Yearly data from 2002–2004 are used excepted where otherwise stated. Table 6.12 lists all variables and their explanation.

To identify predictors of Innofund awards, a two-step correlation analysis is conducted. First, correlations between Innofund awards and other variables are calculated with the results presented in Table 6.13. Population, GDP, GDP per capita, and STindex have significant correlations with Innofund

Table 6.12. List of variables

	Variables	Explanation
1	Award#	Number of Innofund awards
2	STindex	S&T Indices published by the MOST
3	GDP	Gross domestic product in RMB billion
4	Population	Based on 2000 Census, in million
5	GDP per capita	Calculated by dividing GDP by population in 2000
6	DumWest	Dummy of 9 western provinces and 1 western city
7	DumYangtze	Dummy of 3 provinces in the Yangtze River Delta
8	DumPearl	Dummy of 2 provinces in the Pearl River Delta
9	DumBjTj	Dummy of Beijing and Tianjin

Table 6.13. Correlations between Innofund awards and other variables

Factors	Innofund	Pearson Correlation	Significance level
Population	Award#	0.23	0.03
GDP	Award#	0.53	0.00
GDP per capita	Award#	0.63	0.00
STindex	Award#	0.76	0.00

awards. STindex has the highest correlation, which may indicates that they have the strongest explanatory power.

To avoid multicolinearity among these potential predictors, correlations among them are calculated to find if they are significantly correlated with each other, especially between the STindex and other variables. The correlation results are shown in Table 6.14. Because only population is uncorrelated to STindex, both variables are retained as predictors. Other variables are dropped. To adjust for regional differences, the multiples of regional dummies and STindex (DumPearlST, DumYangtzeST, DumBjTjST, and DumWestST) are used instead of simple regional dummies. Because the former can reflect regional differences in slopes, which are more meaningful in reflecting the relationship between predictors and awards.

The regression results are shown in Table 6.15. The model has an R-squared of 0.73, indicating the adequacy of the model in predicting

Table 6.14.   Correlation among significant factors

Factors	Factors	Pearson Correlation	Significance level
STindex	Population	−0.01	0.96
STindex	GDP	0.45	0.00
STindex	GDP per capita	0.88	0.00
GDP	Population	0.74	0.00

Consequently, the following regression models are developed and estimated:

Award# a + bSTindex + cPop + dDumWestST + eDumYangtzeST + fDumPearlST + gDumBjTjST + ε

Table 6.15.   Regression results: Number of awards

Model Summary

R	R-Squared	Adjusted R-Squared	Std. Error of the Estimate
0.85	0.73	0.71	21.68

Anova

	Sum of Squares	Df	Mean Square	F	Significance Level
Regression	106,816.50	6	17,802.75	37.86	0.00
Residual	40,435.50	86	470.18		
Total	147,252.00	92			

Coefficients

Predictors	Unstandardized Coefficients		Standardized Coefficients	T	Significance Level
	B	Std. Error	Beta		
(Constant)	−83.57	12.53		−6.67	0.00
STindex	2.72	0.43	0.78	6.34	0.00
Pop	0.49	0.10	0.32	5.01	0.00
DumPearlST	−0.45	0.26	−0.12	−1.73	0.09
DumYangtzeST	0.47	0.24	0.17	1.92	0.06
DumBjTjST	0.08	0.29	0.03	0.28	0.78
DumWestST	0.82	0.19	0.27	4.27	0.00

Innofund awards. The coefficients of STindex, population, and DumWestST are all positive and statistically significant at 1% level. Thus, TSMEs' chance of getting Innofund awards depends on their regional technological development level, population, and whether it is a west province/city. The insignificance of other three dummies proves that Innofund does not have the herding problem that private venture capitalists have. The large numbers of awards in those regions are simply because of higher technological development level and large sizes (measured by population). The 10 western provinces and city do have preferential treatments from Innofund. This explains the appearance of Sichuan province on the list of Innofund focus regions. Thus, Innofund effectively avoids the herding problem pertaining to private venture capitalists.

From supply–demand perspective, the awards represents supply of Innofund and the applications represent demand. The correlation between the number of awards and the number of applications are statistically significant and as high as 0.94. Thus at provincial level, the supply of Innofund is also driven by demand, i.e., the number of applications. What determines various demands or applications across provinces? To answer this question, we look further into the key component factors of STindex, namely the percentage of GDP used for R&D, the percentage of local governments' budget dedicated to S&T activities, the percentage of sales that companies expend on R&D, and the S&T transaction amount. Again, GDP per capita, GDP, population, and four dummies are included as possible determinants (Table 6.16)

To decide which variables to be included in regression analysis, Pearson correlations are calculated with the results shown in Table 6.17. The variable (R&D/GDP) shows the highest correlation of 0.69 and is selected as a determinant. Its correlations with other variables are calculated and also shown in Table 6.17. The results show that the percentage GDP used for R&D is significantly correlated to GDP per capita, S&T transaction amount, and the percentage of companies' sale used for R&D, which are thus dropped from the list of determinants. The remaining variables are the percentage of local governments' budget used for S&T, GDP, and population. Further correlation analysis dropped GDP since it is statistically correlated to the percentage of local governments' budget used for S&T.

Table 6.16. List of variables for applications

	Variables	Explanation
1	R&D/GDP	Percentage of GDP used for R&D
2	STBudget/LocalBudget	Percentage of local governments' budget dedicated to S&T activities
3	CompR&D/Sales	the percentage of sales that companies expend on R&D
4	STTradeAmt	the S&T transaction amount
5	GDP per capita	Calculated by dividing GDP by population in 2000
6	GDP	Gross domestic product in RMB billion
7	Population	Based on 2000 Census, in million
8	DumWest	Dummy of nine western provinces and one western city
9	DumYangtze	Dummy of three provinces in the Yangtze River Delta
10	DumPearl	Dummy of two provinces in the Pearl River Delta
11	DumBjTj	Dummy of Beijing and Tianjin

Thus the demand for Innofund is driven by a region's R&D spending level (as denoted by percentage of GDP dedicated to R&D), local government's emphasis on S&T (as denoted by the percentage of local budget dedicated to S&T), and population. The Pearl River Delta and Yangtze River Delta show especially strong demand for Innofund over other geographical regions. The West dummy is not statistically significant for the number of applications but is statistically significant for the number of awards. Hence Innofund plays a redistribution role. It should be noted that the relationships analyzed above are the same when using the amounts of awards and applications. Thus such analysis of the amounts is not repeated here.

6.3.4. *Innofund's Contribution to the Capital Market Development for TSMEs*

Innofund's ultimate goal is to become part of venture capital industry and foster the development of capital market that serves TSMEs and entrepreneurs. The adoption of open competition, use of external advisors, and

Table 6.17. Correlations between Innofund applications and other variables

Factors	Factors	Pearson Correlation	Significance Level
Appl#	R&D/GDP	0.69	0.00
Appl#	GDP per capita	0.64	0.00
Appl#	STTradeAmt	0.60	0.00
Appl#	CompR&D/Sales	0.57	0.00
Appl#	STBudget/LocalBudget	0.45	0.00
Appl#	GDP	0.64	0.00
Appl#	Population	0.32	0.01
R&D/GDP	GDP per capita	0.51	0.00
R&D/GDP	STTradeAmt	0.88	0.00
R&D/GDP	CompR&D/Sales	0.59	0.00
R&D/GDP	STBudget/LocalBudget	0.22	0.09
R&D/GDP	GDP	0.09	0.50
R&D/GDP	Population	−0.12	0.34
STBudget/LocalBudget	GDP	0.46	0.00
STBudget/LocalBudget	Population	0.25	0.05
GDP	Population	0.74	0.00
GDP per capita	STBudget/LocalBudget	0.31	0.02
GDP per capita	Population	−0.12	0.26

Note: The regression analysis of applications will use the percentage of GDP used for R&D (R&D/GDP), the percentage of local budget used for S&T (STBudget/Local Budget), population (Pop), and the four dummies as determinant variable. The regression model and results are shown below.

$Award\# = a + b(R\&D/GDP) + c(STBubget/Localbugge\,t) + dpop + eDumWest + fDumYangtz\,e + gDumPearl + hDumBjTj + \varepsilon$

emphasis of commercialization potential give a flavor of market mechanism. But this effort pales in the face of Innofund's strong government-style organization and bureaucratic operational structure. Thus it is likely that rent-seeking behaviors exist. However, so far there is no evidence of significant rent-seeking behaviors. This may be attributed to Innofund's safeguard measures, including anonymous appraisal of applications, disbursing the second tranche of funding only when the awardees meet the preset landmarks, project completion appraisal, and a complaint system.

In addition, the absence of venture capital professionals in Innofund's formal management structure and the declaration of "not for profit" make it

Entrepreneurship and Economic Growth in China

Table 6.18. Regression results: Number of applications

Model Summary

R	R-Squared	Adjusted R-Squared	Std. Error of the Estimate
0.92	0.89	0.85	53.48

Anova

	Sum of Squares	Df	Mean Square	F	Significance Level
Regression	1,027,543.37	7	146,791.91	51.3	0.00
Residual	154,444.11	54	2,860.08		
Total	1,181,987.48	61			

Coefficients

	Unstandardized Coefficients		Standardized Coefficients		
Predictors	B	Std. Error	Beta	T	Significance Level
(Constant)	−64.59	18.24		−3.54	0.00
R&D/GDP	86.40	8.47	0.71	10.20	0.00
ST/LocalBudget	2.23	1.10	0.12	2.03	0.05
Pop	1.85	.31	0.35	6.03	0.00
DumPearl	63.14	31.36	0.11	2.01	0.05
DumYangtze	206.77	25.19	0.44	8.21	0.00
DumBjTj	−20.97	43.25	−0.04	−0.49	0.63
DumWest	27.30	17.05	0.09	1.60	0.12

difficult to see it as similar to the general practice of the venture capital industry. This helps explain why Innofund has not made many equity investments based on risk assessment and valuation expertise as well as the incentive to use equity to capture awardees' upside potential. Thus Innofund itself has not yet merged into the capital market.

On the other hand, Innofund does contribute to the development of the venture capital industry. Innofund has helped to nurture 9.1% of investee companies by the venture capital industry. Among the first batch of TSMEs listed in Shenzhen Stock Exchange's SME Board, over 50% of them had received Innofund awards. Innofund also collects awardees' funding need information upon the completion of projects and recommend awardees to venture capitalists who are more than happy to receive deal sourcing information from Innofund.

Thus Innofund has only marginally achieved its goal of developing market mechanism for TSME funding. While it is difficult if not impossible for a public venture capital program to operate like private venture capital, other countries experience show that there is enough room for Innofund to move closer to market mechanism. New policy actions need to be taken to achieve this goal.

6.4. Conclusion

As in other countries, TSMEs in China face a significant funding gap. The emerging public venture capital programs are tasked with building funding channels to support entrepreneurial activities in TSMEs. By the early 2000s, a system of public venture capital programs and complementary elements has been put in place and a comprehensive enabling environment for TSMEs has come into being. Both central and local governments have played an important role and committed huge resources. Innofund was established in 1999 as the largest public venture capital program to provide direct finance and catalyze other funding to TSMEs in order to enhance their innovation capacity and activity. By 2005, Innofund had sponsored 7,962 projects amounting to RMB 5.2 billion.

The likelihood of Innofund crowding out private sources is very small. Instead, there is strong evidence that Innofund catalyzes local government funding. Innofund has not fully achieved its expected catalytic effect on local governments because it does not enforce the matching ratio vigorously. This may create moral hazard among local governments. However, the local governments' increasing matching ratios in the past years indicate that this possibility has been overcome by local governments' desire to develop local economy via increasing support for TSMEs. With regard to catalyzing private sources, Innofund's effect is not as strong as local governments in inducing FIs' funding but is stronger than local governments in encouraging awardees to put in more own capital. In both cases, Innofund and local governments combined can achieve the best catalytic effect on private sources.

External factors affecting Innofund awards include technological development level and population of a region and whether it is a Western province/city. The 10 western provinces and city do have preferential treatments from Innofund. This explains the appearance of Sichuan province on the list of Innofund focus regions. Three other regions favored by private venture capitalists, i.e., the Pearl River Delta, the Yangtze River Delta, and Beijing–Tianjin area, are not particularly favored by Innofund. Thus, Innofund effectively avoids the herding problem pertaining to private venture capitalists and give more support to TSMEs in less developed West China. The awarding of Innofund also depends on the aggregate demand by TSMEs, which is determined by the general R&D spending, local governments' S&T budget, and population in a region.

Innofund has only marginally achieved its goal of developing market mechanism for TSME funding. The application of market practice in Innofund practice is very limited and its operation relies on the existing bureaucratic system. Innofund has not made many equity investments. Thus, Innofund itself has not yet merged into market mechanism. However, Innofund contributes to the development of venture capital industry by supporting TSMEs and bridging the information gap between TSMEs and venture capitalists.

Moving forward, to increase its effectiveness, Innofund should enhance its catalytic role by stringently enforcing the matching ratio requirement for local governments and finetuning the relative proportions of Innofund and local government funding for different TSMEs. It also needs a medium- to long-term plan to migrate from relying on bureaucratic system to relying on market infrastructure and mechanism. More market and management experts can be used in managing Innofund. In terms of the form of funding, equity, low-interest soft loans, and other forms should be explored to improve the utility of funding.

References

Bovaird, T. *et al.* (1995). Market Failures in the Provision of Finance and Business Services for Small and Medium-Sized Enterprises, in R. Buckland and E. W. Davis (Eds.) *Finance for Growing Enterprises*. London and New York: Routledge, pp. 13–39.

Carpenter, R. E., and B. C. Petersen (2002). Capital market imperfections, high-tech investment, and new equity financing. *The Economic Journal* **112**(February): F54–F72.

Cooper, R. S. (2003). Purpose and performance of the small business innovation research (SBIR) program. *Small Business Economics* **20**: 137–151.

der Vlist *et al.* (2004). What determines the success of states in attracting SBIR awards? *Economic Development Quarterly* **18**(1): 81–90.

Hall, B. H. (2002). The financing of research and development. NBER working paper series. Cambridge, MA, National Bureau of Economic Research, 34.

Moore, B. (1994). Financial Constraints to the Growth and Development of Small High-Technology Firms, in A. Hughes and D. J. Storey (Eds.) *Finance and the Small Firm*, London and New York: Routledge, pp. 112–144.

Moore, I., and E. Garnsey (1993). Funding for innovation in Small Firms: The role of government. *Research Policy* **22**: 507–519.

Murray, G. C., and J. Lott (1995). Have UK Venture Capitalists a Bias Against Investment in New Technology-Based Firms? *Research Policy* **24**(2): 283–299.

Ruegg, R., and I. Feller (2003). A Toolkit for Evaluating Public R&D Investment. Gaithersburg, MD: National Institute of Standards and Technology, pp. 303–305.

Sohl, J. E. (1999). The Early-Stage Equity Market in the USA. *Venture Capital* **1**(2): 101–120.

Wang, S., (Ed.) (2004). *Venture Capital Development in China 2004*. Beijing: Economy & Management Publishing House.

Westhead, P., and D. J. Storey (1997). Financial Constraints on the Growth of High Technology Small Firms in the United Kingdom. *Applied Financial Economics* **7**: 197–201.

Zeng, F. (2004). *Venture Capital Investments in China*. Santa Monica, CA: The Pardee Rand Graduate School: 136.

Chapter 7

Entrepreneurial Financing, Corporate Governance, and Firm Performance in China: With Evidence of Listed Companies on the Shenzhen Stock Exchange

Jiamin Wang
George Mason University

7.1. Introduction

Recent years have seen the rising importance of entrepreneurship and its role as "an engine of economic and social development" (Ács and Audretsch, 2003) throughout the world. Entrepreneurs, defined as those who "perceive and create new economic opportunities (new products, new production methods, new organizational schemes, and new product-market combinations), and introduce their ideas into market in the face of uncertainty and other obstacles" (Carree and Thurik, 2003), have become "the single most important player in a modern economy" (Lazear, 2002). However, entrepreneurship is usually discouraged due to lack of financial resources as nascent ventures are likely faced with credit rationing, hence the ease of capital formation in a financial market plays a significant role in stimulating new firm formation. Currently there is little literature discussing the relationship between entrepreneurial financing and the development of a country's stock market, because start-ups are more likely to get private equity financing from informal markets. Yet given venture capital (VC) funds' active participation in entrepreneurial businesses, and their preference of taking the VC-backed firms to IPO as an exit strategy, it is surprising that such a gap exists in current literature. Empirical evidence has supported the positive impact of IPOs on venture capital investments (see, for example, Black and Gilson, 1998; Gompers and Lerner, 1999; Jeng and Wells, 1998). As a new venture grows, the public market provides the entrepreneur with the opportunity of reaping entre-preneurial success through appreciation of its market value and continually expanding business with external financing. Given the public market's sig-nificant role in entrepreneurial growth, the issue should be particularly addressed by developing countries such as China, because the underdevel-opment of the stock market in those countries may have already stunted the full-fledging of entrepreneurship.

Corporate governance is a crucial indicator of the health and maturity of a country's stock market. Defined broadly, it refers to the public and pri-vate institutions, including laws, regulations, norms, and accepted busi-ness practices, that govern the relationship between investors and corporate insiders, and protect minority shareholders from being expro-priated by managers and large shareholders (Oman, 2001). Put it another way, corporate governance is a set of mechanisms through which investor protection is realized. Good corporate governance will increase corporate transparency and accountability, limit insiders' abuse of power on corporate resources, and maximize operational efficiency thus boost firm performance (Oman *et al.*, 2003). In countries with sound corporate gov-ernance, an entrepreneur's cost of raising external capital is lower due to reduced information asymmetry. Corporate governance is, therefore, an important vehicle through which a new venture can signal its credibility and strengthen investor confidence in the hope of attracting more exter-nal financing.

China's stock market has inevitably borne the impression of the original planned economy. When the stock market came into being in the early 1990s with the establishment of Shanghai and Shenzhen Stock Exchanges, it was initially built to provide financing opportunities to state-owned enterprises (SOEs) and facilitate the restructuring reform of the SOEs (Cao, 2003: p. 310). With this goal, emphasis was placed on the financing role of the stock market, whereas the need for investor protection through corporate governance was largely ignored. Principles of corporate governance were embodied in the country's Company Law and Securities Law, which nevertheless have been far from enough to provide satisfactory investor protection. Weak institutional environment and, distorted concept toward stock market, together with many publicly traded companies' relationship-based ownership structure (frequently represented by pyramidal ownership structures and cross-shareholding), have repeatedly led to corporate fraud and jeopardized the integrity of financial reporting. Investors, both domestic and international, have grown dubious, and many have either chosen to "vote with their feet" in the secondary market or hesitated to make investment. The exceptionally high degree of information asymmetry and the stock market's image of being less trustworthy have dampened entrepreneurs' future prospects of fundraising from the public market and, hence worsened their liquidity constraints and impaired their growth potential. In the recent decade, Chinese government and the China Securities Regulatory Commission (CSRC) have endeavored to strengthen the corporate governance of China's public companies and remedy the ownership structure by transferring non-negotiable shares to common shares. China's stock market will undergo fundamental reform in the near future, albeit incrementally and painfully.

This chapter explores the relationship between entrepreneurial financing and corporate governance, and addresses the issue particularly in China's context. Section 7.2 discusses how the information asymmetry problem could get exacerbated for an entrepreneurial business as a risk bearer, and what kind of positive role corporate governance could play in capital formation. Section 7.3 describes the history and status quo of China's public market, and in what ways that might place a roadblock for the growth of entrepreneurship. Section 7.4 uses historical data from 169 manufacturing companies listed on the Shenzhen Stock Exchange to empirically study the relationship between corporate governance and firm performance. Although because corporate governance data are not available for nascent ventures in China, and a sample composed of public companies is constructed instead, the empirical study still sheds light on whether corporate governance could contribute to firm growth and profitability in China's stock market. Section 7.5 concludes.

7.2. Entrepreneurial Financing and Corporate Governance

7.2.1. *Entrepreneurship and Information Asymmetry*

Agency problems are frequently found in Berle and Means type of modern corporations,[1] which are organized through separation of ownership and control (Jensen and Meckling, 1976; Fama and Jensen, 1983). Corporate insiders, such as entrepreneurs, managers, and directors, serve as the agents. They tend to exert their control rights to pursue their own interests, such as seeking higher personal compensation and diverting company resources for their own use. Such self-dealing behaviors are not aligned with the goals of the principal — the relatively dispersed investors, who aim at maximizing the market value of the shares they hold. As the firm acquires equity financing from the capital market, the insiders have the incentive to engage in wasteful expenditures because they do not bear the full consequences (Lerner, 2004). For instance, they may involve in activities that are too risky to be accepted by the investors, thus causing moral hazards. The agency problem is closely related with information asymmetry between insiders and other stakeholders. Managers and directors are always better informed regarding the financial and operating conditions of the company, whereas the investors largely rely on limited corporate disclosure to make their judgment. For any individual minority shareholder, his/her cost of monitoring the management exceeds the benefits derived from enhanced corporate governance, because the cost falls upon the individual while the benefits spill over to all the shareholders. As a result, minority shareholders have little incentive to spend their own resources to mitigate information asymmetry, a phenomenon known as the "rational apathy".

The agency problem and information asymmetry lead to credit rationing, when capital providers limit the supply of loans even if there is excess demand for capital, and not to raise the interest rate above the critical value above which profit begins to fall due to increased loan defaults

---

[1]Adolf Berle and Gardiner Means were the first to raise the agency problem derived from "separation of ownership and control." This was then popularized in the corporate governance literature.

(Stiglitz and Weiss, 1981). It will likewise affect the equity holders' willingness to provide capital, and a higher rate of return or discounted share price are usually demanded to counteract these problems. Furthermore, smaller, younger, and entrepreneurial firms are more vulnerable to such kind of rationing (Jaffe and Russell, 1976; Lerner and Merges, 1998; Petersen and Rajan, 1992).

Entrepreneurs are the group of individuals who discover, evaluate, and exploit opportunities to create future goods and services (Shane and Venkataraman, 2000). Entrepreneurial opportunities differ from other profit-seeking opportunities in that the former require discovery of new means–ends relationships, whereas the latter only concern optimization of efficiency within the existing means–ends frameworks (Kirzner, 1997). Kirzner (1997) argues that an entrepreneurial opportunity exists primarily because different members of society have made different valuations about the resources that have the potential to be transformed into a different state and an entrepreneur holds the belief that the resources have not been put into its best use and are thus priced too low. Schumpeter (1934) sees exogenous shocks as sources of opportunity because technology, social, and other types of changes offer a new supply of information revealing new ways of using resources in a more valuable way. However, due to variation in the knowledge corridor, difference in access to information, individual cognitive abilities, and social ties, the new information is unevenly distributed among people and first grasped by those who are to become entrepreneurs (Shane and Eckhardt, 2003).

Entrepreneurial opportunities also incur high risk and uncertainty. Knight (1921) distinguishes three types of uncertainties about the future: the first type could be avoided through diversification; the second type could be avoided through repeated trials and learning over time; but the third type of uncertainty, which consists of a future not only unknown, but also unknowable, are the true uncertainties that entrepreneurs are confronted with and for which they receive profit as a compensation. Sarasvathy *et al.* (2003) make a typology of entrepreneurial opportunities by the existence of demand and supply curves. In their perspective, if neither supply nor demand exists, and several economic inventions in marketing, financing, etc., are to be made in order to actualize the opportunity, true entrepreneurial opportunity is said to be created.

Because entrepreneurs base their investment on private but unverifiable information that they believe will lead to a successful venture, the investors are usually unable to identify either the true expected value of the venture (e.g., investment returns, management capabilities) or the associated degree of risk. The entrepreneurial ability is not directly observable to investors, since they lack sufficient information to differentiate between whether an entrepreneur starts a venture because of high probability of success or lower opportunity cost (Gifford, 2003). As investors perceive entrepreneurial businesses as less risk-averse and require a higher return as compensation for higher risk, Akerlof's (1970) "market for lemons" sets in, where the existence of information asymmetry prevents the capital providers from price discrimination between riskier and less risky borrowers and results in adverse selection. As a result, lenders and equity holders have to use the average expected value of the start-ups, which tend to be low, to make judgments on individual company. Moreover, in order to prolong the product lifecycle and postpone the lucrative opportunities being exhausted by entrepreneurial competition, entrepreneurs are usually eager to protect their innovative ideas and keep them away from potential competitors before the commercial launch of the new product. This consequently leads to their deliberate choice to disclose less information, which, in turn, makes investors more skeptical about the prospects of an entrepreneurial business thus grudge investments.

7.2.2. *Entrepreneurial Financing, Venture Capital, and the Public Market*

As many entrepreneurial businesses are not yet profitable and possess few tangible assets, their sustained growth depends on their access to capital. New ventures are more likely to obtain equity financing than debt financing, because they lack cash flows to pay interest. Entrepreneurs tend to obtain equity financing from informal, unregulated markets, such as through angel investors and venture capital funds. Angel investors are those wealthy individuals who invest their own money in early-stage, high-potential companies. Venture capital typically comes from institutional investors and high net worth individuals[2] and is pooled together by dedicated investment firms. Venture capital funds are organized as limited partnerships in which the managing partners invest on behalf of the limited partners (i.e., the investors who inject money into the VC fund) (Denis, 2004). Some large corporations also invest in external start-ups for either strategic or financial reasons, which are known as corporate venture capital. Later when an entrepreneurial business grows bigger, it may seek equity financing from the regulated securities markets either through private placement[3] or public offering of securities.

Generally, possible business growth stages and their corresponding financial requirements for an entrepreneurial business are classified as follows (GAO, 2000: p. 9): (1) The "seed stage", when capital is needed to prove a concept or develop a product; (2) The "start-up stage", when financing is needed for product development and initial marketing; (3) The "first stage", when commercial manufacturing and shipping are launched; (4) The "second stage" and the "third stage", when expansion of production, marketing, distribution, and product improvement set in; (5) The "bridge stage", when financing is expected to sustain major growth in a company planning to go public in 6 to 12 months; (6) The "exit stage", when either via IPO, merger, acquisition, or liquidation, the company pays back its private equity investors.

Compared to angel investors, venture capital funds tend to invest in high-growth, more mature entrepreneurial businesses that have a longer performance record to track. They play an important role from the first stage through the bridge stage, and generally expect to liquidate their investment within roughly five years (GAO, 2000). Venture capitalists are active monitors of the company they invest in (Gorman and

---

[2] High net worth individuals are those having investable assets (financial assets not including primary residence) in excess of U.S.$1 million. The number of high net worth individuals worldwide is estimated at 9.5 million, with total wealth of U.S.$37.2 trillion (Wiki). Available at http://en.wikipedia.org/wiki/High-net-worth_individual (accessed October 20, 2008).

[3] Private placement of securities is limited in distribution to certain types of investors.

Sahlman, 1989; Denis, 2004): Lerner (1995) provides evidence that venture capitalists' representation on board of directors increases during periods surrounding the replacement of the company's top executives so as to tighten oversight on these extraordinary events; Kaplan and Stromberg (2001a, 2001b) find that VCs substantially shape the management team; Gompers (1995) argues that staged capital infusion gives VCs the power of effective monitoring thus reducing potential agency problems. Besides the monitoring role, VCs could provide value-added management advice and support services to their portfolio companies (for example, design business plans, assist with the formation of strategic alliances, develop human resources functions, strengthen corporate governance structure, etc.) (Kaplan and Stromberg, 2000; Hellman and Puri, 2002; Denis, 2004). Hellman and Puri (2000) find that firms financed by VCs tend to bring their product to market more quickly. In addition, VCs can potentially make external financing more accessible to entrepreneurs by certifying the quality of a start-up (Denis, 2004). Megginson and Weiss (1991) find that VC-backed IPOs exhibit lower underpricing and lower underwriter spreads than a matched set of non-VC–backed IPOs. Therefore, entrepreneurs are usually willing to surrender substantial control rights to VCs in exchange for their equity and valuable advice, and make compromise on offers with lower valuation so as to affiliate with prominent VCs (Denis, 2004).

Exit strategy is an important component of venture capital funds' investment decisions. Venture capital can choose to exit by IPOs, acquisition, liquidation, or leveraged buy-out. Generally, IPO is the most preferable way for both the entrepreneur and the venture capitalists. A study by Venture Economics (1988) shows that every $1 invested in a firm that later goes to an IPO will generate $1.95 in return, compared to only $0.40 in return for every $1 invested in a firm that is later acquired (Zeng, 2004). Besides higher profitability, entrepreneurs, through IPO, are able to regain control rights of the company which they earlier gave up to the venture capitalists for their stake. In contrast, if investors exit through acquisition, entrepreneurs will then lose the control rights. As pecuniary rewards are not the only goal that entrepreneurs pursue, rather, many leave their secure jobs for utilities that could derive from the control rights (such as the freedom from bureaucracy, flexibility for innovation and novel business practices, prestige, leadership, and personal leverage), entrepreneurs have strong incentives to seek IPOs as the exit channel.

Empirical evidence shows that the prospect of exiting through IPOs is critical to the existence of a vibrant venture capital market (Zeng, 2004). Gompers and Lerner (1999) and Black and Gilson (1998) find strong correlation between the number of VC-backed IPOs and new venture capital commitment. Jeng and Wells (2000) conduct a cross-country analysis for 21 countries and find that IPOs are the strongest driver of venture capital investments when controlling for GDP, market capitalization growth, labor market rigidities, accounting standards, and private pension funds level. That being said, although many entrepreneurial businesses rely on private market for equity financing, public market also plays an important role in shaping a start-up's prospect of acquiring venture capital and finally using the public market as an exit. In this way, the health of a country's public market is closely related to the nurturing of entrepreneurship.

7.2.3. The Significance of Corporate Governance to Capital Formation

Corporate governance refers to those public and private institutions that underlie the relationship between corporate insiders (executives, directors, and controlling shareholders) and other stakeholders, mainly stockholders, known as the residual claimants, whose interests could only be adequately protected through effective corporate governance. Employees and creditors are in a relatively privileged position to claim their cash flow rights before shareholders, and their interests can somehow be protected by contractual relations. Since minority shareholders' interests are more likely to be at stake than large shareholders, protecting minority shareholders from expropriation becomes the primary goal of corporate governance. Principles of corporate governance normally include equitable treatment of shareholders, alignment of interests between investors and insiders, senior executives' and controlling shareholders' honesty and ethical behavior, especially during conflicts of interest, responsibility and accountability of the board of directors, integrity and transparency of information disclosure, balance of power and effective monitoring within the firm, and management's performance orientation.

Corporate governance carries twofold meaning: (1) Public companies with separation of ownership and control and more dispersed ownership structure are frequently found in countries like the U.S. and Britain. The agency problem — the conflicts between managers (as the agent) and shareholders (as the principal) — prevails in this kind of companies. Corporate governance, in this sense, focuses on monitoring and motivating the managers in a way that they will work for the benefit of outside shareholders. (2) However, dispersed ownership structure is an exception rather than a rule worldwide. Non-OECD countries, especially those in East and Southeast Asia, have much more concentrated and intertwined ownership structure through cross-shareholding and pyramidal ownership, which derive from those countries' relationship-based culture, as opposed to rule-based, and oligopolic market power. It is also a common practice in those countries to issue multiple classes of shares with unequal voting rights, giving large shareholders disproportionately more control than justified by the shares they own. Those practices give rise to a mismatch between control rights and cash flow rights and lead to the expropriation problem, in which minority shareholders' interests are harmed by not only corporate executives, but more seriously, by controlling shareholders and other large shareholders. This is because when a large shareholder owns the majority of the cash flow rights, any action he/she takes for his/her private benefits at the expense of other shareholders generates a cost that decreases the value of the shares the large shareholder himself/herself owns, thus making the expropriation behavior irrational; However, when a large shareholder's control rights far exceed his/her cash flow rights, i.e., then he/she has cheap voting rights, he/she has little incentive to make efforts to increase the value of the firm's equity (Doidge *et al.*, 2006) and will involve in seeking his/her own benefits at the expense of minority shareholders. In less mature public markets, the expropriation problem usually deteriorates the accountability of the public market more than the agency problem. Corporate governance, in such a scenario as in China, therefore, should stress protecting minority shareholders by limiting large shareholders from abusing their power.

Corporate governance plays a significant role in facilitating capital formation in emerging markets. It enhances firm performance by creating and maintaining a business environment that motivates managers and entrepreneurs to maximize firms' operational efficiency and returns on investment, and in this way generates more productivity growth and economic growth in the society (Oman 2001; Oman *et al.*, 2003). Good corporate governance will substantially increase corporate accountability and transparency, reduce information asymmetry and moral hazard, strengthen investor confidence, and make the company a more attractive candidate for external financing. As mentioned earlier, entrepreneurial businesses are more likely to suffer from information asymmetry, hence they are prone to be subject to credit rationing and find it difficult to convince investors of their growth potential. In this sense, a sound corporate governance structure, for example, in terms of stronger sense of accountability in the management, quality financial reporting based on more stringent accounting standards, and preventive measures against wastage of corporate resources and siphoning off assets for private use, will significantly improve the credibility of the new venture, dispel investors' concerns on possible corporate fraud and expropriation, and make it easier to attract more equity financing from either angel investors or venture capital funds.

Mougin (2007) shows how investor protection through better corporate governance can be used to solve the credit rationing problem that confronts entrepreneurs: the "good" entrepreneur can distinguish himself/herself from "bad" entrepreneurs by choosing a higher level of investor protection, for instance, by cross-listing in a foreign stock exchange that sets higher standards for corporate governance. A separating equilibrium can be reached in which the "good" entrepreneur sends this signal to investors, thanks to his/her low level of private benefits. Better investor protection reduces the entrepreneur's private benefits. By assuming that the diversion of corporate resources for private benefit has decreasing returns to scale and is a function of the level of investor protection, Mougin (2007) argues that because the "bad" entrepreneur extracts more private benefits than good ones, he/she will suffer more from a better investor protection. Consequently, "bad" entrepreneurs cannot choose a higher level of investor protection because their private benefits are reduced by such a great amount that the entrepreneurs' participation constraint is violated. In contrast, since the "good" entrepreneur diverts a small amount of corporate resources for his/her own benefits, he/she will not suffer as much from the reduction of private benefits due to higher investor protection, and as a result, can afford to send a positive signal by cross-listing. In this way, compliance with higher standards of corporate governance can be used to distinguish "good" entrepreneurs from "bad" ones, and credit rationing problem is solved. Doidge *et al.* (2006) investigate how a foreign firm's decision to cross-list on a U.S. stock exchange is related to the consumption of private benefits of control by its controlling shareholders, and offers empirical evidence that the probability a firm will cross-list on a U.S. exchange is inversely related to the control rights held by the controlling shareholder (used as a proxy for private benefits) and to the difference between his control rights and cash flow rights. Their findings support Mougin's (2007) argument that entrepreneurs who extract more private benefits are less likely to choose higher standards of corporate governance, and investors could use this information to single out good entrepreneurs.

Besides corporate governance's direct contribution to capital formation through reduced information asymmetry and credit rationing, it also plays an intermediary role in stimulating venture capital by building a healthier stock market. Literature (see Shleifer and Wolfenzon, 2002, for a literature review) has shown that countries with better protection to minority shareholders have more valuable stock markets (La Porta *et al.*, 1997), a larger number of listed companies (La Porta *et al.*, 1997), larger listed firms in terms of their sales or assets (Kumar, Rajan, and Zingalesm 1999), higher valuation of listed firms relative to their assets (Claessens *et al.*, 1999; La Porta *et al.*, 2002), greater dividend payouts (La Porta *et al.*, 2000), and higher correlation between investment opportunities and actual investments (Wurgler, 2000). As venture capitalists tend to prefer using IPOs to exit their investments and relinquish the control rights back to entrepreneurs, a more developed and transparent stock market will increase their chance of having successful IPOs, making them more willing to provide equity financing to new ventures. Black and Gilson (1998) argue that the venture financing market in a country is closely linked with the stock market in that country. They show that countries with well-developed stock markets, such as the U.S. and Britain, tend to have new capital committed to venture capital funds that are higher as a percentage of GDP than those countries with less developed stock markets, such as Japan, whose financial system is more bank centered. Their view is supported by Milhaupt (1997), who finds that U.S. venture capital funds tend to be larger, more actively involved in the management of their portfolio companies, more willing to invest in early-stage, innovative entrepreneurial businesses, and take larger equity stakes, when compared to those in Japan. He attributes U.S. venture capital's superior performance to its institutional environment — a more market-based orientation and a mature stock market that enables venture capital to exit more easily through IPOs (see Denis, 2004, for a literature review of the relationship between venture capital and a country's stock market).

If those arguments hold, then corporate governance is connected to the vitality of entrepreneurship through its role in establishing a healthy stock market and subsequently affecting venture capital activities. When a country has sound corporate governance with the primary goal of investor protection, investors are more confident that they will receive returns on their investments rather than being expropriated; this will in turn reduce the cost of external financing, and make capital more accessible to entrepreneurs, especially "good" entrepreneurs. The importance of corporate governance thus goes beyond the public market itself, but will optimize the allocation of financial resources and contribute to the real economy by creating an enabling business environment for entrepreneurship.

7.3. China's Stock Market: History, Transition, and Challenges for Entrepreneurship

As discussed in the Section 7.2, China's stock market, rooted in its relationship-based culture and institutional systems, is prone to pyramidal ownership structure and cross-shareholding. The fact that many Chinese-listed companies are the product of state ownership has led to exceptionally high concentration of stock ownership in the hands of few large shareholders. Therefore, in China's context, the main goal of corporate governance is to protect minority shareholders from being expropriated by controlling shareholders and to ensure that they receive investment returns and voting rights on pro rata terms. However, the development of China's stock market was largely guided by government will rather than market forces, and its unique characteristics have posed significant challenges for corporate governance and entrepreneurial financing.

Before China launched its economic reform in 1978, the concept of stock market was unfamiliar to most people. As the country underwent a transition to market economy, the stock market's role as a vehicle for extra-firm financing was gradually realized. The Shanghai Stock Exchange and Shenzhen Stock Exchange were opened in December 1990 and April 1991, respectively. B-shares[4] were also established in 1991 to allow foreign investors to own equity in China's stock market.

However, China's stock market inevitably bears the impression of the original planned economy. The 1990s were especially hard times for many state-owned enterprises (SOEs) as they were experiencing painful adjustment to the transitional economy. Some were on the brink of bankruptcy. At the same time, there emerged a pressing urge for the establishment of "modern enterprise system" in SOEs that would make them an economically independent entity and clarify their property rights. This called for restructuring and reform of many SOEs, which in turn required a great amount of additional financing. Therefore, when the stock market first came into being, it was designed to specifically meet the demand of the SOEs, and to provide a platform for them to raise money for restructuring. On the other hand, corporate governance and

---

[4]B-shares are issued by companies incorporated in mainland China and are quoted in foreign currencies, as opposed to the A-shares which are quoted in Renminbi. Initially, only foreigners could trade B-shares; but since 2001, Chinese mainlanders are also permitted to trade B-shares with legal foreign currency accounts. In contrast, A-shares initially were only allowed to be traded by Chinese mainlanders. Since 2003, licensed foreign investors called "Qualified Foreign Institutional Investors (QFII)" are also given the permission to trade A-shares on the Shanghai and Shenzhen Stock Exchanges.

investor protection, which are the building blocks for the sustainable development of a country's stock market, were largely ignored.

Until 2000, companies that wished to list in China's stock market were restricted by a quota system, by which a certain number of listings was set beforehand by the government, and these quotas were distributed to various government agencies (Zeng, 2004). Companies that sought approval for listing need to first gain recommendation from one such government agency, which incurred a lot of rent-seeking behaviors. Moreover, this quota system was strongly prejudiced against private firms, because the private sector was only viewed as an insignificant component of the national economy, whose existence was seen as against the principles of socialism. Yet with the deepening of the economic reform, the central government announced in 1997 that the private sector is "an important component" of China's economy and is expected to go hand in hand with the state-owned or collectively owned economy indefinitely. As the tone at the top changed, the quota system that strongly favored the SOEs was finally abolished in 2000, and private firms were allowed to list in the stock market since the late 1990s (Zeng, 2004).

One serious malady of China's stock market was the "split share" structure. Before the end of 2006, the stocks issued by China's public companies were divided into two broad categories: non-floating shares, which include state-owned shares and non–state-owned legal person shares; and floating shares, i.e., common shares, which are composed of A-shares, B-shares, and H-shares.[5] Unlike the western stock system, the state-owned shares and non-state-owned legal person shares could not be traded in the secondary market, and they constituted two-thirds of the total share volume. The state-owned shares were further subdivided into two categories: state shares, which were controlled by the government agencies on different levels, and

---

[5] H-shares are issued by companies incorporated in mainland China that are listed on the Hong Kong Stock Exchange or other foreign stock exchanges. Some Chinese public companies are listed simultaneously on the Hong Kong Stock Exchange and one of the two mainland stock exchanges in Shanghai or Shenzhen. H-shares are quoted in Hong Kong dollars. Price discrepancies between H-shares and A-shares are common. (Wiki) Available at http://en.wikipedia.org/wiki/H_share (accessed October 20, 2008).

state-owned legal person shares, which were owned by SOEs. The non–state-owned legal person shares, as suggested by their name, were held by non–state-owned corporations. The common shares were the only type that were negotiable and were owned by individuals, most of them being minority shareholders, and some institutional investors such as mutual funds. This unique ownership structure derived from the government's concern that if all shares were negotiable, foreign investors could possibly take over an SOE by purchasing a majority of its shares through the secondary market. For fear of such a situation, state-owned shares and non–state-owned legal person shares were made non-negotiable, so that foreign investors could never gain control of a portion of shares that is large enough for a takeover, hence the root of the socialist economy would not be shaken.

However, the split share structure created a chaos in China's stock market. China's relationship-based culture naturally provided a breeding ground for pyramidal ownership structures and cross-shareholding that tends to intensify the expropriation problem. Its unique split share structure nevertheless made the situation even worse. First, as state-owned shares and non–state-owned legal person shares were not negotiable, shareholders of those types of shares, who were also controlling shareholders and large shareholders in most cases, were faced with a mismatch between their control rights and cash flow rights. As a result, they did not care about the stock's market value or the returns on equity. They had little incentive to monitor the management's performance and uphold minority shareholders' interests. Second, the non-negotiable shares and common shares were different classes of shares that were issued at different prices: minority shareholders had to pay for a much higher per-share price than shareholders of the non-negotiable shares to purchase the common shares of the same company. As the costs of acquiring different classes of shares differed drastically, the shareholders of non-negotiable shares had much higher returns on investments than minority shareholders. This inevitably led to large shareholders' negligence of their duty for the company under control, because they bore much less financial risk than shareholders of the common shares. Third, the split share structure greatly decreased the liquidity of China's stock market, making mergers and acquisitions under the market power very difficult to happen, which seriously undermined a stock market's positive role in optimizing the allocation of financial resources hence boosting up economic productivity. Fourth, lack of liquidity of China's stock market resulted in a highly concentrated ownership structure. Typically, a public company originated from a former SOE that restructured itself and stripped part of its assets to form the new public company. Under such circumstance, the former SOE maintained its heavy-handed influence by becoming the controlling shareholder of the newly created public company and holding the state-owned legal person shares. As this type of shares was non-negotiable, the controlling shareholder could not exit its ownership through market transactions, and there was no means by which a highly concentrated ownership structure could be altered. Fifth, as the controlling shareholders' dominant position could not be challenged, and the fluctuation of common shares' market value had no effect on their benefits per se, it became inevitable that the controlling shareholders took no interest in improving the public company's performance but were rather actively involved in corporate misconducts that appropriated company recourses for private benefits at the expense of other shareholders. This gave rise to the rampancy of the expropriation problem between the controlling shareholders and minority shareholders in China's stock market.

One commonly used tactic for expropriation in China's context was to conduct unfair related-party transactions. In many cases, a listed company was closely connected to its controlling shareholder in that the two might share the same management personnel and even the same financial accounts. In this sense, the relationship between China's public company and its controlling shareholder (i.e., the former SOE before the restructuring) was similar to that between a subsidiary company and its parent company. This association enabled the controlling shareholder to easily extract resources from the public company for its own use through unfair related-party transactions, in which the controlling shareholder took advantage of its controlling power to set the rules for the transaction, which always tilted to the benefits of the controlling shareholder at the expense of the listed company. For instance, the controlling shareholder transferred its own overhead cost to the listed company, sold its own product to the listed company at a price higher than the normal market price, or purchased an intermediate product from the listed company at an abnormally lower

price. To facilitate this kind of "black" transaction, the controlling shareholder was eager to send more of its own people to the listed company's
board of directors or board of supervisors, so that it could exert tighter
control when decisions were made on related-party transactions.

China's underdeveloped stock market has created tremendous problem for
private entrepreneurial businesses that wish to raise extra-firm money by
getting listed and for venture capital funds that seek IPOs as a way to exit
their investments. First, poor corporate governance, as represented by low
level of investor protection and the extremely serious expropriation of controlling shareholders to their portfolio companies and minority shareholders, makes China's stock market an unappealing choice for candidate firms
that are considering where to get listed, because of the fear that their returns
may not be adequately protected. Second, in a stock market where corporate fraud is frequently found, investors tend to grudge trust especially to
those smaller and younger firms that suffer more from information asymmetry. With investors' dubious attitudes, newly listed entrepreneurial businesses will find their stocks lack of investor interest, undervalued, and
thinly traded, and to raise additional capital through follow-up offerings is
difficult. Third, as mentioned earlier, in China's stock market, state-owned
shares and non–state-owned legal person shares were non-negotiable, and
only common shares held by minority shareholders and institutional
investors could be traded in the secondary market. The equity held by the
venture capital funds is usually stipulated as the non–state-owned legal person shares, and its illiquidity made venture capital funds virtually impossible to exit their investments in China's stock market. This seriously crippled
venture capitalists' enthusiasm in investing in China's start-ups and hampered the growth of entrepreneurship in the country. Fourth, China's stock
market used to have an SOE-favored quota system, which substantially
diminished private start-ups' chances of getting listed. As a result, entrepreneurial businesses were discouraged from using the stock market as a channel for external financing, but forced them to seek alternative ways to fill
the financial gap, for instance, remain private or get acquired. Consequently,
entrepreneurial businesses in China had less growth opportunities, and their
innovative momentum was more likely to cease after being acquired by
incumbents. Fifth, China's stock market has not developed more

complicated financial instruments that have been widely used in Western countries to facilitate firm growth. For instance, venture capital firm is organized in such way that the investors serve under limited partnership and the investment managers serve under general partnership. However, China so far has not allowed raising money through limited partnership (Zeng, 2004). Also, employee stock option is a commonly used practice to motivate corporate insiders, but it is not allowed in China, which restricts venture capitalists' ability to monitor the portfolio firm's performance.

All the above-mentioned obstacles have caused many China's entrepreneurial businesses to choose overseas stock market to list. Yet not being able to list in the domestic market will reduce their valuation because investors tend to strongly prefer local companies which they find it easier to get access to information and monitor performance (Coval and Moskowitz, 1999; Zeng, 2004). Therefore, it is high time Chinese policymakers lift these obstacles and make the stock market a friendlier place for new ventures. The most pressing issue is to change people's stereotype toward stock markets and to let them realize the fundamental role corporate governance and investor protection play in building up a healthy stock market. Efforts required to achieve this goal include the engagement of all market players such as public companies, large shareholders as well as minority shareholders, institutional investors, intermediary market institutions, and policymakers. This also calls for a more market-based institutional environment that is built upon rule of law rather than relationship-based culture. In practice, the split share structure, which has directly led to the expropriation problem and all kinds of malfunctioning of China's stock market, might be the first thing that policymakers should resolve.

Fortunately, the government is already taking positive steps to address these concerns. Reform to abolish the split share structure was officially initiated in 2005, and there were preliminary attempts well before that. The primary goal of the reform is to make all types of shares negotiable. To mitigate the diluted effect on earnings per share due to expanded outstanding share volume, the reform is designed cautiously so that blockholders who own at least 5% of total shares of a company will be able to trade their shares freely three years after they are approved to be negotiable, and the buffer period for those who own less than 5% is one year. Currently, this reform is still in progress, and there is no one-size-fits-all solution; Instead, each public company needs to work out its own plan to reach an agreement between large shareholders and minority shareholders on how to settle the issue, for instance, through shareholder proxy voting.

China's stock market is also making great strides in launching a long-awaited second board on May 1, 2009.[6] The proposal of establishing a NASDAQ-like "second board" stock exchange, in addition to the "main board", was put forth more than a decade ago. The newly born second board is specifically targeted at innovative firms, and is expected to provide a platform for smaller, entrepreneurial firms to get listed and raise extra-firm capital. Illuminated by the successful role model of U.S.'s NADSAQ and many legendary success stories like Yahoo! and Amazon.com, the second board will facilitate new ventures' IPOs by lowering entry requirements.

7.4. Corporate Governance and Firm Performance: Evidence from Shenzhen Stock Exchange

7.4.1. *Data and Methodology*

To empirically test the importance of corporate governance for China's stock market, we further use historical data from 2003 to examine the relationship between corporate governance and firm performance. We would like to take a more direct approach by using data from private entrepreneurial businesses and see if higher level of corporate governance is related with more external financing. However, data on private enterprises, especially smaller ones, are extremely hard to obtain in China, hence we have to use the data of public companies as an approximation and investigate whether an individual company's corporate governance level has any positive effect on its performance in China's weak institutional environment where legal system is inadequate to protect minority investors. The year 2003 is used because this is the year before the reform to abolish split share structure started, so that it enables us to observe the negative effect brought by split share. We establish an index

---

[6]See http://www.china.org.cn/business/news/2009-03/31/content_17527764.htm (accessed May 13, 2009).

system to evaluate public companies' corporate governance level based on detailed data hand collected from companies' annual reports and proxy statements. The China Securities Regulatory Commission (CSRC) categorizes all the companies listed on the Shenzhen and Shanghai Stock Exchanges into 13 industries, with manufacturing being the largest industry. By the end of 2003, the manufacturing companies listed on the Shenzhen Stock Exchange accounted for 59.3% of the total listed companies and 58.7% of the total market value of the Shenzhen Stock Exchange. For this study, we select the manufacturing companies listed on the Shenzhen Stock Exchange as a sample, because to compare firm performance across industries sometimes could be misleading due to the unique characteristics of each industry. By confining our sample companies within one industry, the empirical results could be more consistent. The companies whose stocks were labeled Special Treatment or Particular Transfer[7] are excluded from the sample so as to minimize the influence of those outliers.

A linear regression model is adopted to estimate the impact of corporate governance on firm performance:

$$\text{Performance} = \alpha_0 + \beta_1 \text{Governance} + \beta_2 \text{Size} + \beta_3 \text{Leverage} + \varepsilon \quad (7.1)$$

In Equation (7.1), the dependent variable "performance" is measured by Return on Equity (ROE),[8] Return on Assets (ROA),[9] and Earnings per Share (EPS),[10] respectively.

The independent variable of interest, "governance", measures the level of corporate governance of each company in the sample. To quantify this

---

[7]As prescribed by Shenzhen and Shanghai Stock Exchange, the stocks issued by the companies whose financial conditions are deemed as abnormal will be labeled Special Treatment (ST) or Particular Transfer (PT). During the ST or PT period, restrictions are set on trading those stocks and their transaction terms are different from regular stocks.
[8]Return on Equity indicates the financial returns to shareholders.
[9]Return on Assets indicates the efficiency of business operations.
[10]Earnings per Share is calculated by dividing net income by the number of common shares outstanding.

variable, an appraisal index system is set up which includes 4 aspects and 10 questions. The first aspect — "the independence of the company from its controlling shareholder" — specifically addresses the expropriation problem in China's stock market, which derives from controlling shareholders' abuse of power. The other three aspects are commonly assessed for corporate governance level, and the questions have been catered to China's context. Below lists the components of the appraisal system:

I. The independence of the company from its controlling shareholder (30%)

(1) Does the Chairman of the board of directors or the General Manager of the listed company come from the controlling shareholder[11]'s party?[12]

---

[11]If the company's ownership structure is dispersed and there is no controlling shareholder, we substitute it with the largest shareholder. If a single shareholder holds more than 50% of the total shares of a company, we call that shareholder the absolute controlling shareholder and the ownership structure a highly concentrated one; If a single shareholder holds less than 50% of the total shares, but the shares he owns is more than the aggregation of the shares held by the second to fifth largest shareholders, we call that shareholder the relative controlling shareholder and the ownership structure a relatively concentrated one. If the shares held by the largest shareholder is no more than the aggregation of the shares held by the second to fifth largest shareholders, we call the ownership structure a dispersed one with no controlling shareholder.

[12]The chairman of the board and the general manager can control the strategy and the daily operations of the company. If they come from the controlling shareholder's party, they are more inclined to take the controlling shareholder's stand and ignore the interests of minority shareholders. The interests of the controlling shareholder do not accord with those of the minority shareholders when its residual control right exceeds its residual claim right such as the cash flow right, which is the situation commonly seen in China now. In this case of cheap voting right, the controlling shareholder has no incentive to supervise and promote the operation of the listed company. Rather, it has a strong inclination to exploit minority shareholders by various means such as unfair related party transaction so as to create private benefits for itself. Thus, in China's scenario, the origin of the listed company's Chairman or the general manager somehow indicates its willingness to protect minority shareholders.

(2) Do more than one half of the supervisors in the board of supervisors come from the controlling shareholder's party?[13]
(3) Does the Chairman get paid from the controlling shareholder instead of from the listed company?[14]

II. The internal motivation mechanism and balance of power (30%)

(4) Is it true that the Chairman or the General Manager does not own the shares issued by the listed company?[15]
(5) Do independent directors account for less than one-third of the board of directors?[16]
(6) Is the Chairman of the board also the General Manager of the listed company?[17]

---

[13] The board of supervisors functions as an internal supervisory body to protect both the large shareholders and minority shareholders. Yet if many of the supervisors come from the controlling shareholder's party, they will uphold the interests of the controlling shareholder at the cost of the minority shareholders. The determination of 50% as a threshold is based on the relevant standard of Credit Lyonnais Securities' index system (Klapper *et al.*, 2002: p. 28).

[14] If the Chairman's interests such as salary and bonus are paid by the controlling shareholder's party, they are more likely to set up management strategies that benefit the controlling shareholder while sacrificing the interests of the minority shareholders.

[15] The separation of ownership and control in modern corporations create the insider control problem. Managers could have their own interests different from those of the shareholders. The plan of stock ownership, which allows senior management members to own some stocks of the company, can reduce this kind of agency cost.

[16] Independent directors are supposed to speak for the minority shareholders. The China Securities Regulatory Commission stipulates that independent directors should account for no less than one-third of the board of directors by June 2003. However, some listed companies still have not complied with this rule.

[17] In companies where the Chairman of the board and the general manager is the same person, the insider control problem is usually more serious. If the Chairman, usually appointed by the controlling shareholder, sets up some policies that benefit the controlling shareholder but harm minority shareholders, the management team virtually cannot resist these policies because the Chairman is also the general manager.

III. The information disclosure quality of the company (30%)

(7) Does the external auditor present qualified audit opinion on either the 2002 or 2003 annual report of the company?[18]

(8) Are financial statements presented without further adjustment to the International Financial Reporting Standards?[19]

(9) Is the 2003 annual report released after March 1, 2004?[20]

IV. Returns to the outside investors (10%)

(10) The average pay-out level of the cash dividend for the year 2002 and 2003[21]

The grade generated by this index system ranges from 0 to 10. One point is given to each question from question 1 to 9 if the answer is "Yes",[22] and

---

[18] The annual report is the most important method of information disclosure by a company. Minority shareholders usually look into the operation of their invested companies through the annual report. Therefore, the quality of the annual report is a strong indicator of the information disclosure transparency of the company. The bottom line for the credibility of an annual report is that it should be given unqualified audit opinion. This indicator examines the situation of two years, because usually only a very small portion of the listed companies get qualified audit opinion, and an examination of two years will enlarge this portion and make the data more informative.

[19] It is generally believed that if the financial statements presented in the annual report are also in accordance with the International Financial Reporting Standards, the annual report tends to have higher credibility and transparency.

[20] The annual report should be released in a timely manner so that minority share-holders can make correct decision on investment. The China Securities Regulatory Commission requires all listed companies to release its annual report no later than April 30 of the next year. Each accounting year concludes on December 31. We select March 1 as the threshold to judge the timeliness of a listed company's information disclosure.

[21] A reasonable pay-out level of cash dividend is seen as appropriate investment return to outside shareholders. The dividend plan could be influenced by the company's business expansion plan that year. Hence to reduce extraordinary factors, we examine the situation in both 2002 and 2003.

[22] For question (1), in case of pyramidal ownership structure, if the Chairman or the general manager comes from the controlling shareholder of the listed company's direct controlling shareholder, one point is also given.

zero point is given if the answer is "No". For question 10, if the company did not pay a cash dividend consecutively for years 2002 and 2003, one point is given. If the average pay-out of cash dividend is equal to or more than 1 RMB per 10 shares, zero point is given. If the average pay-out level is less than 1 RMB per 10 shares, 0.5 point is given. *In this way, the higher a grade a company gets in this index system, the lower its corporate governance level is, in terms of investor protection.* We refer to Klapper and Love (2002), Shi and Situ (2004), and the Chinese Corporate Governance Index[23] in deciding the weighting scheme of the four aspects. Two control variables "size" and "leverage" are included in Equation (7.1), according to the literature. "Size" is calculated by the natural logarithm of the book value of the company's total assets at the end of the given year, and "leverage" denotes the debt ratio of that year. The sample includes 169 manufacturing companies, after dropping observations with missing values.

7.4.2. *Results*

The corporate governance level of the 169 companies in the sample is assessed respectively based on the index system presented in Section 7.4.1. The distribution of the grades approximates to a normal distribution (see Figure 7.1), with 1.0 point as the minimum and 8.0 points as the maximum. The mean is 4.44 points, and the median is 4.5 points, while the standard error is 1.34. The corporate governance grades of almost one third of the sample companies fall between 4.5 and 5.0 points, suggesting that the majority of the sample companies provided a mediocre level of investor protection.[24]

Table 7.1 presents the estimation of Equation (7.1) by running three regressions with ROE, ROA, and EPS as the dependent variable, respectively.

---

[23]This index system, abbreviated as CCGI, was established by the Corporate Governance Research Center of Nankai University, China.
[24]Recall that the index system is designed in such a way that the higher a grade a company gets in this index system, the poorer its corporate governance is, hence less protection it provides to outside investors.

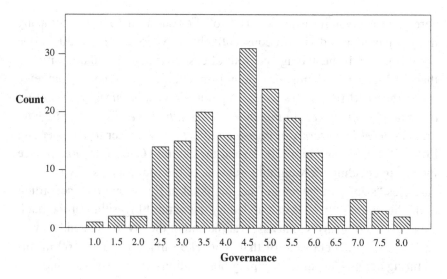

Figure 7.1. The distribution of the corporate governance grades of the sample companies.

Table 7.1. Relationship between corporate governance and firm performance

	(1) ROE	(2) ROA	(3) EPS
Constant	−0.336***	−0.191***	−2.331***
Governance	−0.012***	−0.008***	−0.041***
Size	0.021***	0.015***	0.132***
Leverage	−0.004	−0.077***	−0.165*
N	169	169	169
Adjusted R-Squared	0.19	0.23	0.35

Note: * Statistically significant at 0.10.*** Statistically significant at 0.01.

The coefficient on "governance" is statistically significant at 0.01 in all three regressions.[25] The results show that the variable "governance" is negatively related with firm performance, meaning higher corporate governance grades tend to be related with worse firm performance. Put it another way, poor firm performance is more likely to be found among

---

[25]The regression models display no serious multi-collinearity and heteroscedasticity problems.

companies whose corporate governance structure is less favorable to outside investors, which is in line with our expectation. The variable "size" shows positive sign, and the research of Chen and Jiang (2000), Chen and Xu (2001), and Bin and Shu (2003) shows similar results.

7.4.3. *The Uneven Distribution of Corporate Governance Level in China: By Region*

As the empirical study reveals a positive statistical relationship between corporate governance level and firm performance, we are further interested

Table 7.2.   Regional differences of public companies' corporate governance grades

Region	Number of Obs.	Mean Value of the Corporate Governance Grades	t-test
Companies from East and Mid China	134	4.332	−2.213**
Companies from West China	35	4.857	(0.031)

Note: **Statistically significant at 0.05; *p*-value in the parentheses. China's three mega regions — East China,[26] Mid China,[27] and West China[28] — have long been noticed for their salient regional economic disparity, with East China taking the lead and West China lagging behind. In this chapter, we also explore if there exists imbalanced development in corporate governance of the public companies coming from those three regions. Table 7.2 shows that the corporate governance grades for those from East and Mid China were significantly lower than those from West China, meaning compared to public companies from West China, those from East and Mid China had significantly better corporate governance structure in terms of investor protection. However, there is no significant difference between the corporate governance level of the public companies from East China and those from Mid China, suggesting that the country's regional difference in corporate governance is not as salient as its regional economic disparity, although the former roughly follows the pattern of the latter. This may be attributed to China's overall rather poor corporate governance level.

---

[26]East China includes eight provinces — Liaoning, Hebei, Shandong, Jiangsu, Zhejiang, Fujian, Guangdong, and Hainan, and three municipalities — Beijing, Tianjin, and Shanghai.
[27]Mid China includes eight provinces — Shanxi, Henan, Anhui, Hubei, Hunan, Jiangxi, Heilongjiang, and Jilin.
[28]West China includes 11 provinces — Sichuan, Guizhou, Yunnan, Tibet, Shaanxi, Gansu, Qinghai, Ningxia, Xinjiang, Inner Mongolia, and Guangxi, and one municipality — Chongqing.

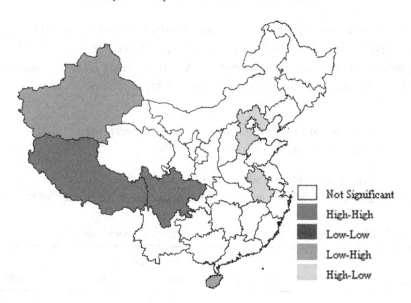

Figure 7.2. LISA cluster map of the corporate governance grades of Mainland China's public companies.[29]

in what types of listed companies are more vulnerable to corporate governance weakness in China's context and wish to seek possible means of improvement. The distribution of corporate governance level will be analyzed by region and by ownership structure in turn.

Figure 7.2 presents the LISA[30] cluster map of the corporate governance grades of the sample companies. Tibet and Sichuan Province had high grades, meaning their public companies' corporate governance levels were relatively low, and their neighboring provinces (mostly West China provinces) also had poor corporate governance. Hebei Province in East China and Anhui Province in Mid China had high grades, but their surrounding provinces (half of them coastal provinces) tend to have low grades, meaning Hebei and Anhui had low corporate governance level

---

[29]Hong Kong, Macao, and Taiwan are not shown on the map, because data are not available for those places.
[30]Local Indicators of Spatial Association.

while their neighbors did a better job. An exception is Xinjiang, which had low grade being, meaning high corporate governance level, while surrounded by other Western provinces that tend to provide poor investor protection. The empirical evidence indicates that public companies from West China generally had worse corporate governance when compared to those from the coastal area, and this regional disparity deserves attention in the policymaking process.

7.4.4. *The Uneven Distribution of Corporate Governance Level in China: By Ownership Structure*

To further analyze whether certain ownership structure could have led to poorer corporate governance, comparisons are made to see if there is a statistically significant difference between the mean value of corporate governance grades of the companies whose controlling shareholder held state shares or state-owned legal person shares and the companies whose controlling shareholder held non–state-owned shares (including non-state-owned legal person shares and common shares).

The comparisons of the mean values are made pair by pair, and all are significant at the 0.05 level. Table 7.3 shows that while the corporate governance grades of the companies whose controlling shareholder held state-owned legal person shares were higher than the companies whose controlling shareholder held non–state-owned shares, meaning the former

Table 7.3. Ownership structure and corporate governance: By the type of controlling shareholder

The Type of the Shares the Controlling Shareholder Held	Number of Obs.	Mean Value of the Corporate Governance Grades of this Group
State shares	32	3.167
State-owned legal person shares	96	4.690
Non–state-owned shares[31]	41	4.110

---

[31]Including non–state-owned legal person shares and common shares.

had a corporate governance structure that was less favorable to investor protection than the latter, the companies whose controlling shareholder held state shares actually had the best corporate governance, i.e., the lowest average grade, among the three groups. One explanation for such phenomenon is that the majority of the sample companies whose controlling shareholder held state shares appeared to be large companies that manufacture products critical and fundamental to the national economy, such as petroleum refinery and machinery building. Compared to other medium-sized and smaller manufacturing companies in consumer industries like beverage and clothing, these big companies were exposed to more public scrutiny, and many were under direct supervision from the central government. As a result, they constantly felt the pressure to provide more transparency and protection to outside investors through improving their corporate governance.

The owners of the state-owned legal person shares were mainly SOEs, which previously stripped a portion of their assets and set up a new public company of which they became the controlling shareholder. As discussed in Section 7.3, there was a prevailing misconception in China that the stock market was established to facilitate the restructuring of SOEs and a public company's role was to provide financing to their state-owned controlling shareholder, the SOEs, whose presence in public companies was represented by their ownership of the state-owned legal person shares. Under such a misconception, SOEs frequently involved in expropriation behaviors to extract public companies' resources for their own benefits, and one way of doing this was through unfair related-party transactions. Therefore, it is not surprising to find from Table 7.3 that public companies whose controlling shareholder held state-owned legal person shares had the worst corporate governance among the three.

This argument is further supported by a comparison of the mean value of the independence grades[32] between the companies whose controlling

---

[32]The independence grade comes from the first aspect of the index system, "the independence of the company from its controlling shareholder." It ranges from 0 to 3 points.

shareholder held state-owned legal person shares and the companies whose controlling shareholder held non-state-owned shares. The mean value of the former group is 1.81, whereas the mean value of the latter group is 1.07, and the difference is statistically significant at 0.01. The results indicate that public companies whose controlling shareholder held state-owned legal person shares were less independent, which facilitated their controlling shareholder's expropriation for private benefits. Therefore, efforts to improve corporate governance of China's public companies should focus on reducing the dominance of the controlling shareholders who held state-owned legal person shares by abolishing the split share structure and making public companies truly independent business entities whose retained earnings would not be taken away at discretion.

7.5. Conclusion

This chapter discusses the relationship between entrepreneurial financing, corporate governance, and firm performance. Entrepreneurial businesses, as the risk-bearer, are more likely to find it hard to acquire extra-firm financing because they tend to suffer more from the information asymmetry problem. Yet by opting into a higher level of corporate governance, a new venture could signal its credibility and strengthen investor confidence, thus attracting more capital to increase its growth potential. On the other hand, venture capital funds play a crucial role in financing and stimulating entrepreneurial businesses, and they have strong preference of using IPOs as an exit strategy. Committed venture capital investments are positively related with the degree of maturity of a country's stock market, and sound corporate governance will help build a healthier and more developed stock market and protect investors' interests by reducing the agency problem and expropriation problem. This will, in turn, make it easier for entrepreneurial businesses to successfully launch IPOs and use the stock market as a source for financing. Therefore, sound corporate governance lowers the cost of capital formation and grows a country's entrepreneurship by making financial resources more accessible to entrepreneurs.

The chapter then examines the history of China's stock market, the transitions it is going through at present, and the challenges it poses to entrepreneurship. China's stock market was established under the misconception that it was to provide financing to the restructuring reform of the SOEs. Corporate governance and investor protection hence were ignored, and repeated corporate fraud slashed investor confidence, making them less willing to invest in smaller and younger firms. The split share problem, together with cross-shareholding and pyramidal ownership structures rooted in China's relationship-based culture, gave rise to serious expropriation problem in which controlling shareholder drained away public companys' resources at the expense of other shareholders. Institutions poorly equipped to corporate governance have greatly hampered entrepreneurial businesses' growth and quenched angel investors and venture capital funds' enthusiasm in this emerging market. Fortunately, the Chinese government has taken positive measures in recent years to address the corporate governance problem.

An empirical study on the public companies listed on the Shenzhen Stock Exchange sheds light on the important role of corporate governance on firm performance in China's weak institutional environment. Major findings include: (1) Corporate governance level is positively related with firm performance, when controlled for firm size. (2) Public companies from East and Mid China had significantly better corporate governance than those from West China. (3) Public companies whose controlling shareholder held state-owned legal person shares had the poorest corporate governance. Although data on public companies are used as a substitute because private firms' data especially that of start-ups, are extremely hard to obtain in China, the empirical evidence nevertheless points a direction for policymakers who are endeavoring to make China's stock market a better one, which will, in turn, boost investor confidence and lead to an enabling environment for entrepreneurial growth. To strengthen corporate governance, focus should be particularly placed upon West China's public companies and those with a controlling shareholder that holds state-owned legal person shares. Once China's stock market becomes more trustworthy, it will facilitate the capital formation of entrepreneurial businesses and encourage venture capital funds, both international and domestic, to make more investments on China's start-ups.

The study is one of the few that links corporate governance to entrepreneurship and discusses it in China's context. Given the significance of corporate governance to entrepreneurial financing, this chapter hopes to bridge the gap in current literature and contribute to policymakers' deeper understanding of the issue. Best practices of corporate governance in China's context may include, but are not limited to:

(1) Listed companies becoming truly independent business entities that carry the goal of maximizing shareholder values. They are the fundamental market players through which the capital market realizes efficient allocation of financial resources.
(2) Large shareholders and minority shareholders being treated equally and equitably: investment returns and voting rights being distributed on pro-rata terms. No privileges should be granted based on controlling shareholder's government-backed identity, for instance, being a government agency or a state-owned enterprise.
(3) The information disclosure integrity assuming importance. As illustrated by the Enron scandal, this could never be overemphasized. Financial reporting should be accurate, transparent, timely, easily accessible, and presented in plain language without overcomplicated technical jargon.
(4) An effective intra-firm monitoring system should be established that maintains balance of power, and executives' remuneration should be based on performance rather than seniority.

While these are common corporate governance principles, they appear to be crucial in China's relationship-based culture. In the long run, sound corporate governance will build a healthy and sustainable public market, infuse confidence and a sense of trust into investors, and stimulate entrepreneurship by providing the ease of capital formation through either venture capital funds or the public market.

References

Ács, Z. J., and D. B. Audretsch (2003). Introduction to the handbook of entrepreneurship Research, in Z. J. Ács and D. B. Audretsch (Eds.) *Handbook of Entrepreneurship Research: An Interdisciplinary Survey and Introduction*. Boston, Dordrecht, London: Kluwer Academic Publishers.

Akerlof, G. A. (1970). The market for "Lemons": Quality uncertainty and the market mechanism. *Quarterly Journal of Economics* **84**: 488–500.

Bin, G., and Y. Shu (2003). Ownership split, firm performance and investor protection. *Management World* **5**: 101–108.

Black, B. S., and R. J. Gilson (1998). Venture capital and the structure of capital markets: Banks versus stock markets. *Journal of Financial Economics* **47**: 243–277.

Carree, M. A., and A. R.Thurik (2003). The impact of entrepreneurship on economic growth, in Z. J. Ács and D. B. Audretsch (Eds.) *Handbook of Entrepreneurship Research*. Boston, Dordrecht, London: Kluwer Academic Publishers.

Chen, X., and D. Jiang (2000). The ownership diversification, firm performance and industrial competitiveness. *Journal of Economic Research* **8**: 28–35.

Chen, X., and X. Xu (2001). Ownership structure, corporate performance and investor protection. *Journal of Economic Research* **11**: 3–11.

Claessens, S., S. Djankov, J. Fan and L. Lang, (1999). Expropriation of minority shareholders in East Asia. The World Bank.

Coval, J. D., and T. J. Moskowitz (1999). Home bias at home: Local equity preference in domestic portfolios. *Journal of Finance* **54**(6): 2045–2073.

Denis, D. J. (2004). Entrepreneurial finance: An overview of the issues and evidence. *Journal of Corporate Finance* **10**: 301–326.

Doidge, C., G. A. Karolyi, K. V. Lins, D. P. Miller and R. M. Stulz (2006). Private benefits of control, ownership, and the cross-listing decision. NBER Working Paper 11162.

Fama, E., and M. Jensen (1983). Separation of ownership and control. *Journal of Law and Economics* **26**: 301–325.

GAO (U.S. Government Accountability Office). (2000). Small business efforts to facilitate equity capital formation. GAO.GGD-00-190.

Gifford, S. (2003). Risk and uncertainty, in Z. J. Ács and D. B. Audretsch (Eds.) *Handbook of Entrepreneurship Research: An Interdisciplinary Survey and Introduction*, Boston, Dordrecht, London: Kluwer Academic Publishers, pp. 37–53.

Gompers, P. (1995). Optimal investment, monitoring, and the staging of venture capital. *Journal of Finance* **50**: 1461–1489.

Gompers, P., and J. Lerner (1999). *The Venture Capital Cycle*. Boston: MIT Press.

Gorman, M., and W. Sahlman (1989). What do venture capitalists do? *Journal of Business Venturing* **4**: 231–248.

Hellman, T., and M. Puri (2000). The interaction between product market and financing strategy: The role of venture capital. *Review of Financial Studies* **13**: 959–984.

Hellman, T., and M. Puri (2002). Venture capital and the professionalization of start-up firms. *Journal of Finance* **57**: 169–197.

Jaffe, D. M., and T. Russell (1976). Imperfect information, uncertainty and credit rationing. *Quarterly Journal of Economics* **90**: 651–666.

Jeng, L., and P. Wells (1998). The determinants of venture capital funding: Evidence across countries. NBER Working Paper.

Jensen, M., and W. Meckling (1976). Theory of firm: Managerial behavior, agency costs and ownership structure. *Journal of Financial Economics* **3**: 305–360.

Kaplan, S., and P. Strömberg (2000). How do venture capitalists choose investments? University of Chicago.

Kaplan, S., and P. Strömberg (2003). Financial contracting meets the real world: An empirical analysis of venture capital contracts. *Review of Economic Studies* **70**(2): 281–315.

Kaplan, S. N., and P. Strömberg (2001). Venture capitalists as principals: Contracting, screening, and monitoring. *American Economic Review* **91**(2): 426–430.

Kirzner, I. (1997). Entrepreneurial discovery and the competitive market process: An Austrian approach. *Journal of Economic Literature* **35**: 60–85.

Klapper, L., and I. Love (2002). Corporate governance, investor protection, and performance in emerging markets. World Bank Policy Research Working Paper 2818.

Knight, F. (1921). *Risk, Uncertainty and Profit*. New York: Houghton Miffin.

Kumar, K., R. Rajan and L. Zingales (1999). What determines firm size? NBER Working Paper 7208.

La Porta, R., F. Lopez-de-Silanes, A. Shleifer and R. Vishny (1997). Legal determinants of external finance. *Journal of Finance* **52**: 1131–1150.

La Porta, R., F. Lopez-de-Silanes, A. Shleifer and R. Vishny (2000). Agency problems and dividend policies around the world. *Journal of Finance* **55**: 1–33.

La Porta, R., F. Lopez-de-Silanes , A. Shleifer and R. Vishny (2002). Investor protection and corporate valuation. *Journal of Finance* **57**(3): 1147–1170.

Lazear, E. P. (2002). Entrepreneurship. NBER Working Paper.

Lerner, J. (1995). Venture capitalists and the oversight of private firms. *Journal of Finance* **50**: 301–318.

Lerner, J. (2004). When bureaucrats meet entrepreneurs: The design of effective "Public Venture Capital" programs, in D. Holtz-Eakin and H. Rosen (Eds.) *Public Policy and the Economics of Entrepreneurship*, Cambridge, MA: MIT Press, pp. 1–22.

Lerner, J., and R. P. Merges (1998). The control of technology alliances: An empirical analysis of the biotechnology industry. *Journal of Industrial Economics* **46**(2): 125–156.

Leslie, A., P. Jeng and C. Wells (2000). The determinants of venture capital funding: Evidence across countries. *Journal of Corporate Finance* **6**: 241–289.

Megginson, W., and K. Weiss (1991). Venture capitalist certification in initial public offerings. *Journal of Finance* **46**: 879–903.

Milhaupt, C. (1997). The market for innovation in the United States and Japan: Venture capital and the comparative corporate governance debate. *Northwestern University Law Review* **91**(3): 865–898.

Mougin, F. (2007). Asymmetric information and legal investor protection. *Economics Letters* **95**: 253–258.

Oman, C., S. Fries and W. Buiter (2003). Corporate governance in developing, transition and emerging-market economies. OECD Development Center, Policy Brief No. 23.

Oman, C. P. (2001). Corporate governance and national development. OECD Development Center, Technical Papers No. 180.

Petersen, M. A., and R. G. Rajan (1992). The benefits of firm-creditor relationships: Evidence from small business data. University of Chicago.

Sarasvathy, S., N. Dew, S. R. Velamuri, and S. Venkataraman (2003). Three views of entrepreneurial opportunity. In Z. J. Ács and D. B. Audretsch (Eds.) *Handbook of Entrepreneurship Research: An Interdisciplinary Survey and Introduction*. Boston, Dordrecht, London: Kluwer Academic Publishers, pp. 141–160.

Schumpeter, J. (1934). *Capitalism, Socialism, and Democracy*. New York: Harper and Row.

Shane, S., and J. Eckhardt (2003). The individual-opportunity nexus. In Z. J. Ács and D. B. Audretsch (Eds.) *Handbook of Entrepreneurship Research: An Interdisciplinary Survey and Introduction*. Boston, Dordrecht, London: Kluwer Academic Publishers, pp. 161–191.

Shane, S., and S. Venkataraman (2000). The promise of entrepreneurship as a field of research. *Academy of Management Review* **25**(1): 217–226.

Shi, D., and D. Situ (2004). Empirical study on Chinese listed companies' governance and its impact on firm performance. *World Economy* **5**: 69–79.

Shleifer, A., and D. Wolfenzon (2002). Ownership, economic entrenchment and allocation of capital. *Journal of Financial Economics* **66**(1): 3–27.

Stiglitz, J., and A.Weiss (1981). Credit rationing in markets with imperfect information. *American Economic Review* **71**: 393–410.

Wurgler, J. (2000). Financial markets and the allocation of capital. *Journal of Financial Economics* **58**: 187–214.

Zeng, F. (2004). *Venture Capital Investments in China*. Unpublished Doctoral Dissertation. The Pardee Rand Graduate School.

Part V

Other Factors Related to Entrepreneurship and Economic Growth in China

Chapter 8

Regional Disparities of New Firm Formation in China

Jian Gao and Shi Shude
Tsinghua University

8.1. Introduction

A new firm is an important driving force of local economic development
and can provide abundant job opportunities, and this has become a consensus among policy makers and academic researchers. How can a large
number of new firms be created in a region? To clarify this issue, we need
to analyze why in some places, so many new firms are generated, while
others have only few new firms. New firm formation rates (NFFRs) are
not equal in different regions. It provides rare materials to dig out what are
determinants of regional variations in NFFR. This chapter aims to analyze
the characteristics of these regions with different level of NFFR to find
out the reasons behind the variation in NFFR. Here, we are only concerned about the variation in NFFR across regions in China.

It is true that many scholars have paid attention to this phenomenon and
performed researches on regional variations in NFFR in their home country context (Dean *et al.*, 1993; Hart and Gudgin, 1994; Keeble and Walker,
1994; Armington and Ács, 2000; Sutaria and Hicks, 2004; Okamuro and
Kobayashi, 2005; Lobo and Costa, 2005). However, there is still no coher-
ent conclusion. The explanations for variations in NFFR are disparate in
different countries. The determinants that have been confirmed in the U.S.
include demand (Bartik, 1989; Sutaria and Hicks, 2004), human capital
(Armington and Ács, 2000), per capital local saving in bank (Sutaria and

Hicks, 2004), and mean establishment size (Armington and Ács, 2000; Sutaria and Hicks, 2004). In Britain, demand (Keeble and Walker, 1994; Dean *et al.*,1993), industrial restructuring (Dean *et al.*, 1993), and housing wealth (Keeble and Walker, 1994; Roboson, 1994) are significant influences on entrepreneurial activities. The results found in Germany are human capital (Audretsch and Fritsch, 1994), innovation activities (Fritsch and Mueller, 2005), mean establishment size (Fritsch and Falck, 2002), and entrepreneurial climate (Fritsch and Mueller, 2005). Related researches have also been pursued in some other countries, such as Ireland (Hart and Gudgin, 1994), Sweden (Davidsson and Wiklund, 2000), France (Guesnier, 1994), Portugal (Lobo and Costa, 2005), and Japan (Okamuro and Kobayashi, 2005). However, the determinants found in these countries are disparate. More empirical researches are needed to provide evidence and new findings to perfect the present theoretical frame.

Another characteristic of the present researches is that most of them are analyzed for developed countries. In developing countries, however, there are still few studies in this field. The reason may be a lack of available data relevant to new firms or that researchers in developing countries give less regard to regional entrepreneurship. It is interesting to conduct such a research in a developing country. Actually, China has pronounced variations in NFFRs across different regions. There are two basic characteristics: one is that the developed regions in the east of China have active entrepreneurial activities and their NFFRs are far larger than the undeveloped regions in the west of China; the other is that the disparity of NFFR between the two categories of regions was expanding overtime.[1] The reasons leading to these two characteristics are just the focus questions to be analyzed in this chapter.

In the following section, the state of new firm formation in China will be analyzed, which is to show the current situation of entrepreneurial activities in China. In Section 8.3, we review previous studies for the purpose of analyzing the theoretical relationships between a set of explanatory variables and NFFR. Then, in Section 8.4, we account for data, indicators'

---

[1]In Section 8.3, the disparity between the developed regions and the undeveloped regions is explained.

measurement and empirical method. In Section 8.5, we examine the determinants of regional variations by panel data modeling regression across 29 provinces between 1996 and 2006. And in Section 8.6, we separately test the determinants for two categories of regions and for two stages to understand for further the characteristics of determinants over time and in China.

8.2. The State of New Firm Formation in China

The labor market approach is used to measure NFFRs across regions,[2] which standardizes the number of new firms with respect to the size of the labor force. NFFR is calculated for each of 29 provinces in the mainland of China, based on the number of increasing private firms in each region during a year. Private firms are the results of start-ups owned by private individuals. In this study, we view the number of increasing private firms as new firms. The number of increasing private firms is standardized by the number of population aged 15 to 64 years old. The data are used from *China Statistics Yearbook*, published by China National Bureau of Statistics. Finally, NFFR is calculated as the number of new firms per 10,000 members of the labor force.

According to *China Statistics Yearbook*'s data, till 2006 there have been 4.98 million private firms, with over 0.68 million new private firms being established in the whole year. NFFR in 2006 was about 5.17 new firms per 10,000 people (Figure 8.1). However, in 1996, the total number of private enterprises was just 0.82 million and NFFR was 1.33 new firms per 10,000 people. During the 1996–2006 period, there were about 0.378 million start-ups on average per year. Over the years, the number of new

---

[2]Two approaches have been generally adopted to measure NFFR across regions. One is to standardize the number of new firms relative to the number of establishments already in existence, termed as the ecological approach. The other is the labor market approach, i.e., standardizing the number of new firms with respect to the size of labor force. Compared to the labor market approach, the ecological approach would result in higher NFFR in regions where the establishment size is relatively high and lower in regions where the average establishment size is relatively low (Armington and Ács, 2002).

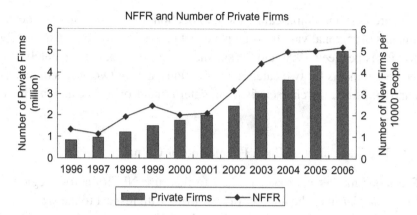

Figure 8.1. NFFR and total private firms number in China 1996–2006.
Note: NFFR is the new firm formation rate.

firms increased, with a relatively distinct rise between 1996 and 2001 and between 2002 and 2006. The average growth rate of new firms between 2002 and 2006 was 21.4%, larger than 13.3% between 1996 and 2001. On the whole, NFFR in China shows an uptrend of fast increase over the 11 years, except 2000 with a decrease.

There are large variations in NFFR across different regions in China. Based on the level of economic development,[3] this study defines six provinces as the developed regions (DRs), including Beijing, Tianjin, Shanghai, Jiangsu, Zhejiang, and Guangdong. These provinces are located in the coast of East China, and they represent the highest level of economic development in mainland China. The other 23 provinces are defined as the undeveloped regions (UDRs). We calculate NFFRs for the two categories of regions (DRs and UDRs) between 1996 and 2006, which are shown in Figure 8.2. The difference between the two regions is large. In 1996, NFFR in DRs was 3.3 new firms per 10,000 people, whereas in UDRs, it was just 0.66, and the difference was 2.64 new firms per 10,000 people. However, in 2006, the difference reached 13.17 new firms per 10,000 people. Over the years, the difference in NFFR has been expanding rapidly. It can be

---

[3]It is measured by per capital GDP. In 2006, per capital GDP in these six provinces are far larger than in other provinces.

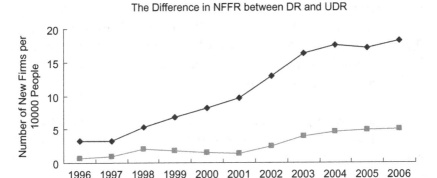

Figure 8.2.   The expanding trend of disparity between DR and UDR from 1996 to 2006. *Note:* NFFR is the new firm formation rate; DR is the developed regions; UDR is the undeveloped regions.

concluded from the increasing trend in Figure 8.2 that the disparity between DR and UDR would go on in the following a few years. Why are the differences among regions so large? Why does the rapid expansion of the disparity in NFFR occur? In the following sections, we will theoretically analyze and empirically examine the determinants.

8.3. The Determinants of Variations in NFFR

Favorable environment conditions encourage entrepreneurs to start up new firms (Romanelli, 1989). Turbulent environment, such as technological changes, political and regulatory changes, and social and demographic changes, can disrupt the competitive equilibrium that exists in a market or industry, and thereby form opportunities (Kirzner, 1973; Shane, 2003; Alvarez and Barney, 2007). When these opportunities and entrepreneurs with abilities needed in the entrepreneurial action synthesize, new firms may come into being (Reynolds, 1995). In addition to opportunities, other resources in external environment also affect the formation and growth of a new firm. For example, entrepreneurs need to acquire labor force, financial capital, and material from the outside of organization.

When environmental resources are munificent in a region, a new firm can be formed easily and a large number of new firms might follow. Therefore, we need to analyze regional characteristics and the composition of regional environment to explore the reasons why there exist significant differences in NFFR.

On the basis of reviewing the previous literatures, nine regional factors are identified as the influences on new firm formation. They are key components of regional environment conditions affecting entrepreneurial activities.

8.3.1. *Demand Growth*

Demand growth offers entrepreneurs a favorable market condition, where they are more likely to perceive entrepreneurial opportunities and easier to acquire cheaper resources (Romanelli, 1989). Opportunities can be created in the process of demand growth (Eckhardt and Shane, 2003). Increasing market for products or service stimulates entrepreneurs to start up new firms to meet customer's demand because new niches may be generated in this condition (Christensen and Bower, 1996), or the increased capacity in the present market needs new firms to fill the gap (Drucker, 1985). Once entrepreneurs perceive these opportunities, they would try to seek essential resources and start new firms for the pursuit of profit.

Population growth is an important proxy of demand growth, which has been widely used in the present literature (Reynolds *et al.*, 1994). Population growth increases the number of potential customers for purchasing product or services. Using a database of U.S. Bureau of the Census, Armington and Ács (2002) discovered that population growth was an significant variable influencing regional differences in NFFR. Keeble and Walker's (1994), in their analysis of new firms in the U. K.'s 11 regions in the 1980s, found a positive relationship between population growth and NFFR. Lee *et al.* (2004) also found that population growth rate was an important variable explaining regional variations in NFFR. *Income growth* is another important proxy of demand growth (Reynolds *et al.*, 1994). As people's income grows, customers will have more and more disposable money, leading to increasing demand for products and services. And the consuming habits of people may change in the process of income growth, such as pursuit of comfort and feeling new wants. Armington and Ács (2002) have verified the positive relationship between income growth and entrepreneurial activities.

Pertaining to demand growth, the following hypotheses are stated:

H1a: a region's population growth is positively related to its NFFR
H1b: a region's income growth is positively related to its NFFR

8.3.2. *Human Capital*

An entrepreneur's human capital determines his/her abilities in discovery or creation, evaluation, and exploitation of entrepreneurial opportunities. Entrepreneurial decisions involve the creation or identification of new ends and means (Eckhardt and Shane, 2003). Baumol (1990), Holmes and Schmitz (1990), and Gifford (1993) discussed differential entrepreneurial abilities and argued that people with greater such abilities would tend to self-select as entrepreneurs. Individuals with high human capital are more likely to create or identify new ends and means, and start up new firms to exploit profit opportunities. Formal education, such as attending a university, is an important and effective means to improve an individual's human capital. Knowledge improves an individual's cognitive abilities, leading to more productive and efficient potential activities (Schultz, 1959). Cooper *et al.* (1994) hold a view that education is related to knowledge, skills, problem-solving ability, discipline, motivation, and self-confidence. Training in education can enhance an individual's abilities in searching information and receiving new thinking (Davidsson and Honig, 2003). Moog (2002) verified that a founder with better education has stronger abilities of acquiring, evaluating, and utilizing information, and he/she is more effective to obtain entrepreneurial capital from banks, private investors, or venture capitalists. Guesnier (1994) found that the propensity of entrepreneurship was positively related with entrepreneurs' education degree. Fothergill and Gudgin (1982) found that enterprises whose founders had undergraduate university degrees grew faster than those whose founders had lesser education.

These insights focus on the effect of entrepreneurs' human capital on new firms. At the regional level, human capital also influences the quality level of labor force. The regions with higher average education level usually contain plenty of skillful people and management talents, where entrepreneurs can easily find qualified employees. The cost of searching for an employee in these regions, including time and capital, may be cheaper than in other regions with low level of education. New firms can be more easily formed and can succeed in these regions. Some empirical researches, such as Okamuro and Kobayashi (2005), Lobo and Costa (2003), and Ács and Armington (2006) have confirmed that regions with more university graduates have more new firm formation.

Pertaining to human capital, the following hypotheses are stated:

H2: a region's rate of labors with higher education is positively related to its NFFR

8.3.3. *Unemployment*

Many researchers have analyzed the effect of unemployment. The present idea argues that there are two opposite effects on new firm formation: one was that unemployment might promote the unemployed to start their own business; the other was that it could hinder new firm formation (Reynolds *et al.*, 1994; Sutaria and Hicks, 2004).

When a person loses his/her job and fails to find another one in time, he/she may well decide to create a new employment opportunity by starting a business. Therefore, unemployment incites self-employment, and regions with higher unemployment rate may have larger rate of entrepreneurial activity (Storey, 1991; Roboson, 1994; Fritsch and Mueller, 2005). On the other hand, a high local level of unemployment has a negative effect on new firm formation. Unemployment reduces people's aggregate disposable income and effectively reduces local demand for goods and services, leading to decreased new firm formation (Ritsilä and Tervo, 2002; Armington and Ács, 2002; Sutaria and Hicks, 2004). Under the influences of these two categories, the final presented result of their impact on new firm formation may be positive, negative, or ambiguous, depending on which of the two effects is dominant.

Pertaining to unemployment, the following hypotheses are stated:

H3: a region's unemployment rate is related to its NFFR, but the direction of this relationship is indeterminate.

8.3.4. *Technological Development*

Technological development is an important source for entrepreneurial opportunities. Schumpeter (1934) viewed technological change as the basis for a new good, a new method of production, the opening of a new market, the use of a new source of supply, or the development of a new organizational form. Shane (1996) suggested that invention and technological change created opportunities for new combinations of factors of production. When entrepreneurs perceive these opportunities of new combinations, they will be inspired to start new firms to seek profit. In other words, entrepreneurial opportunities created by technological change attract new entrants to exploit new products and processes (Highfield and Smiley, 1987). Technological development relative to an industry can promote the emergence of new firms within that industry (Dean *et al.*, 1996).

The empirical evidences also support the argument that the technological development level is positively related to entrepreneurial activities in a region. Blau (1987) analyzed self-employment rates in the U.S. over a two-decade period and found that an increase in the rate of technological change led to an increase in the self-employment rate. Dean *et al.* (1996) found that rapid technological change was significantly related to high rates of venture formations in U.S. manufacturing industries. Shane (1996) examined rates of entrepreneurship over time from 1899 to 1988 in the U.S. and found technological change, measured as the number of invention patents issued, had a positive effect on rates of entrepreneurship.

Pertaining to technological development, the following hypotheses are stated:

H4: a region's technological development level is positively related to its NFFR

8.3.5. *Industry Restructuring*

Changes in industrial structure favor the increase of self-employment rate (Blau, 1987). Service companies usually need less capital to start and face lower technological difficulties than manufacturing companies, leading to a lower entry barrier. The shift from manufacturing employment to services could increase NFFR (Armington and Ács, 2002). Compared with manufacturing, service industries tend to have relatively higher entry rates (Fritsch and Mueller, 2006; Fritsch and Falck, 2002). Reynolds *et al.* (1995) and Evans and Leighton (1989) verified that consumer services, construction, and retail have higher birth rates than manufacturing or distributive services. Johnson (2004) examined regional differences in recent business formation activity in the U.K. over the period 1994–2001 and found the highest formation rates were in "Hotels and restaurants" and in "Real estate, renting, and business activities", and the lowest rates were in "Agriculture, forestry, and fishing" and in "Manufacturing".

Empirical researches also have examined the positive relationship between industrial structure and entrepreneurial activity. Egelin *et al.* (1997) tested the determinants of business start-ups in former West Germany 1989–1994, and obtained the result that the existing industry structure, measured by employment share of services and employment share of retailing/wholesaling, was an important explaining factor for regional differences of start-ups. Okamuro and Kobayashi (2005) analyzed regional factors of the start-up ratio in Japan and found the share of manufacturing establishments was negatively related to regional start-up ratio.

Pertaining to services development, the following hypotheses are stated:
H5: a region's service growth is positively related to its NFFR

8.3.6. *Private Wealth*

Private capital, including entrepreneurs' self-wealth and borrowing from family members and friends, is an important financing resource for an entrepreneur to start a new venture (Basu and Goswami, 1999; Bates, 1995). Due to a low level of credit evaluation and lack of fixed assets as mortgage, new firms find it difficult to obtain a loan from bank. And venture capital is more difficult for them to finance, because investors favor new firms with high growth potential. The fact is that just a few from a thousand of business plan can fortunately obtain venture capital investment. Private capital is always the easiest way for entrepreneurs to get access to. The private wealth level of entrepreneurs and people around them exert important influence on whether entrepreneurs can get enough entrepreneurial capital. Generally, entrepreneurs are easier to finance in regions with higher level private wealth (Reynolds *et al.*, 1994; Garofoli, 1994). Per capita bank saving is a proxy for regional private wealth. Sutaria and Hicks (2004) found that the level of per capita bank saving had a positive relationship with NFFR in a region.

Pertaining to private wealth, the following hypotheses are stated:

H6: a region's per capital bank saving is positively related to its NFFR

8.3.7. *Entrepreneurial Culture*

Entrepreneurial culture is defined as a social context where entrepreneurial behavior is encouraged. It motivates individuals in a society to engage in entrepreneurial behaviors. Under different environmental context, people's value to entrepreneurship may distinct due to their varied attitudes to innovation and achievements. Start-up firms in regions with better entrepreneurial culture may be encouraged, while in the conservative regions, it may be disliked (Lipset, 2000). Entrepreneurial culture is closely related to regional entrepreneurial activities. Regions with a high population of venturing firms could stimulate new firm formation, due to a large number of entrepreneurs as role models. Employees in small firms or private enterprises can be affected by those successful models. Then they can influence their friends, neighbors, and colleagues. And entrepreneurial climate in the region gradually improves. This chapter uses shift of employment to private firms to represent regional venturing firms' collectivism.

Pertaining to entrepreneurial culture, the following hypotheses are stated:

H7: a region's shift of employment to private firms is positively related to its NFFR

8.4. Methodology

8.4.1. *Dependent Variable*

NFFR is used as the dependent variable in the study. It is measured by the number of new firms per 10,000 labor force in a region, representing the active level of entrepreneurial activities. When NFFR is larger, the level of entrepreneurial activities is higher and more new firms are owned by people in a region. The measurement of NFFR is an adaptation of labor market approach widely used in the present literature to measure the level of entrepreneurial activities. The labor market approach is to standardize the number of new firms with respect to the size of the labor force (Robson, 1994; Davidsson and Wiklund, 2000; Armington and Ács, 2002; Lee *et al.*, 2004; Fritsch and Mueller, 2005). In this study, due to the lack of exact new firm registering data and labor force data, we have to use the number of increasing private firms as the number of new firm and the population aged from 15 to 64 years as the labor force.

8.4.2. *Independent Variables*

Demand growth is measured by two indicators: population growth and consumption growth. This is consistent with the present literature, and a combination of these two indicators to measure demand growth (Reynolds *et al.*, 1994; Armington and Ács, 2002). Population growth in a region is calculated by standardizing the population change during one year with respect to the total population in the last year (Keeble and Walker, 1994; Lee *et al.*, 2004). Consumption growth is measured as the annual rate of per capital income change during one year. *Unemployment rate* is the proxy for the level of unemployment in the region, defined as the average number of the unemployed divided by the number of labor force. It is a usual measurement of unemployment, used in many papers, such as Kangasharju (2000), Gayglslz and Koksal (2003), and Armington and Ács (2002). *Human capital* is measured by the college degree share in the region. It is calculated as the percentage of the employed with college degree in the total employed population. This is analogous to Fritsch (2004), Armington and Ács (2002), and Hart and Gudgin (1994). *Private wealth* is measured by per capita private saving in the banking system (Lobo and Costa, 2003), calculated as the private saving in the banking system divided by the population in the region. *Entrepreneurial culture* is difficult to measure. Till now, there has been no one widely accepted region-level proxy. In this study, we measured it by the shift of employment to private firms, calculated as the share of employment increase in private firm in the total employed population. *R&D intensity* is the proxy for technological development in the region (Dean and Meyer, 1996). It is calculated as the ratio of R&D input to the regional GDP. *Industrial restructuring* is measured by service growth, defined as service industrial output growth divided by the total industrial output growth.

8.4.3. *Data Collected*

In order to examine the factors influencing regional new firm formation, we use panel data to test the hypotheses analyzed above, data combined by 29 provinces[4] of the mainland in China and 11 years from 1996 to 2006. The data of independent variables, however, need to lag behind the dependent variable data for one year, as indicators selected would take one year to influence localized process of new firm formation (Sutaria and Hicks, 2004). Hence, the period of independent variables data is actually from 1995 to 2005.

The data in the paper are all from the public statistics yearbook published by National Bureau of Statistics. Basic data of population growth, income growth, unemployment rate, the shift of employment to private firms, and the share of service growth are from *Chinese Statistics Yearbook* (1995–2006). College degree share data come from *China Labor Statistical Yearbook* (1995–2006). And basic data for per capita private saving are based on *Chinese Finance Yearbook* (1997–2004). As for R&D intensity, R&D output data are from *China Statistical Yearbook on Science and Technology* (1995–2006) and GDP data are from *Chinese Statistics Yearbook* (1995–2006).

---

[4]Xizang and Chongqing are not included, due to their data is incomplete between 1996 and 2006.

8.4.4. *Research Technique*

Three steps will be taken to test the hypotheses. The first is to examine the determinants of regional variations in NFFR for the whole sample, including 29 provinces. The second is to take panel data model regressions separately for each of the two categories of regions (DRs and UDRs). As we have analyzed earlier, these two regions have disparate levels of economic development and own different NFFRs (Table 8.2). With separate test, we can make the judgement that whether the determinants between them are different. The third is to examine the models separately for two stages, 1996–2001 and 2002–2006. This division is the result of observing Table 8.1. We can find that 2001 is a turning point. NFFR in the first stage fluctuates and increases slowly, but it has a quick growth in the second stage. Using separate test for the two stages is to explore whether the determinants are different between the two stage.

A correlation description of selected variables is presented in the Table 8.2. Three correlation coefficients of the variables, human capital, private wealth, and technological development in the matrix, exceed an absolute level of 0.6. To reduce the influence of potential muticollinearity, these three variables are separated into different models. That is the reason that there are three models to in the same examination, each of which individually includes human capital, or private wealth, or technological development.

In panel data regression, it is difficult to make the choice between fixed and random effect models. There has been intensive discussion in the literature (e.g., Wooldridge, 2002). Generally, the most common choice is made on the basis of the Hausman specification test. We also use this test to make the choice between fixed and random effect models for each model. For example, in model 1' Hausman test of Table 8.3, we get the results of $Chi^2 = 142.78$ and Prob> $Chi^2 = 0.000$. It shows that the null hypothesis of random effect is rejected and fixed effect model is better.

Likelihood-ratio test is used to test heteroskedasticity in the models. For example, in model 1 of Table 8.3, we get the result of LR $Chi^2 = 568.29$, and Prob > $Chi^2 = 0.0000$. We obtain a highly significant test result supporting

Table 8.1. Variables influencing new firm formation

Start-up Mechanisms	Variable Name	Expected Effect	Definition	Data Source
Demand growth	Population growth	+	Annual rate of population change	*Chinese Statistics Yearbook*
	Consumption growth	+	Annual rate of per capital income change	*Chinese Statistics Yearbook*
Unemployment	Unemployment rate	+/−	Share of the unemployed in labor force	*Chinese Statistics Yearbook*
Human capital	College degree share	+	Share of college degree in labor force	*China Labor Statistical Yearbook*
Private wealth	Per capita private saving	+	Per capita local private deposits in the banking system	*Chinese Finance Yearbook*
Entrepreneurial culture	Shift of employment to private firms	+	Share of private firm employment increase in the total employed population	*Chinese Statistics Yearbook*
Technological development	R&D intensity	+	Ratio of R&D input to regional GDP	*China Statistical Yearbook on Science and Technology*
Industrial restructuring	Service growth	+	Share of service sector output growth in the total industrial output growth	*Chinese Statistics Yearbook*

Table 8.2.   Correlation Coefficients

	Rate	(1)	(2)	(3)	(4)	(5)	(6)	(7)
Population growth	0.185**							
Income growth (ln)	0.354**	−0.004						
Unemployment rate	−0.052	−0.128*	−0.040					
R&D intensity	0.498**	0.059	0.267**	−0.312**				
Per capital local saving	0.711**	0.176**	0.357**	−0.135*	0.621**			
College degree share	0.714**	0.192**	0.343**	−0.164**	0.717**	0.781**		
Shift of employment to private firms	0.635**	0.143*	0.259**	−0.003	0.364**	0.589**	0.522**	
Service growth	0.101	−0.025	−0.048	−0.126*	0.170**	0.090	0.118*	0.046

Note: $^{\dagger}p < 0.10$, $^{*}p < 0.05$, $^{**}p < 0.01$

the existence of heteroskedasticity in the model. Hence, it is better to estimate the model by feasible generalized least squares (FGLS). In other models, we also observe the presence of heteroskedasticity by Likelihood-ratio test and find that it is a common problem in our models needed to be corrected. Therefore, we use FGLS to estimate the models in the paper. In addition, we test serial correlation by Wooldridge test. For example, in model 1, the result of Wooldridge test is $F(1,28) = 4.4$ (Prob $>F = 0.05$) and the null hypothesis of no serial correlation is rejected at a confidence level of 95%. It is better to add AR (1) in the model to decrease the influence of serial correlation. We use the same way to test serial correlation the other models and decide whether to add AR (1) as an extra explained variable.

8.5. Model Estimation: Results and Interpretation

Table 8.3 shows the estimated results of three models for the whole sample including 29 provinces. T-statistics is given in the bracket to justify whether the estimated coefficient is statistically significant. The coefficients are relatively stable in three models.

The coefficient for income growth is positive and statistically significant, indicating that regions with larger income growth have a higher new firm formation rate. The result is consistent with Lee *et al.* (2004) and Armington and Ács (2002), and supports the hypothesis that a region's income growth is positively related to its new firm formation rate. However, the coefficient for population growth is positive but not statistically significant, indicating that population growth has not yet become an important factor of influencing regional variations in new firm formation rate.

The coefficient for R&D intensity, a proxy for technological development, is positive and statistically significant, suggesting that regions that have higher R&D intensity will have higher new firm formation rates. This is consistent with Dean and Meyer (1996) and Shane (1996). It shows that technological development has become a significant influencing factor to new firm formation in regional level of China.

The coefficient for service growth, calculated by the share of service output growth in the total industrial output growth, is statistically insignificant.

Table 8.3.   Model results: The determinants of new firm formation

Independent Variables	Model 1	Model 2	Model 3
C	−0.10	−3.31	−5.14
Population growth	0.064	0.052	0.155
	(1.41)	(1.37)	(1.16)
Income growth	0.233**	0.238**	0.439†
	(2.96)	(3.42)	(1.73)
R&D intensity	1.775*		
	(2.20)		
Service growth	−0.108	0.610	0.406
	(−0.27)	(1.55)	(0.25)
College degree share		0.589**	
		(9.81)	
Unemployment rate	0.874**	0.840**	1.434**
	(4.41)	(6.60)	(3.21)
Per capital local saving			3.218**
			(4.47)
Shift of employment to private firms	0.824**	0.846**	0.889**
	(2.96)	(4.16)	(3.82)
AR(1)	0.220*		
	(3.17)		
Adjusted R^2	0.661	0.725	0.674
F-statistic	17.07	23.37	18.57
	(0.0000)	(0.0000)	(0.0000)
Hausman test	142.78	75.90	93.57
	(0.000)	(0.000)	(0.000)
Wooldridge test	4.04	1.25	1.345
	(0.05)	(0.27)	(0.26)
Observations	290	290	290

Note: t-values are reported in parentheses below the coefficient estimate. †$p < 0.10$, *$p < 0.05$, **$p < 0.01$.

It does not support the hypothesis that service growth is positively related to new firm formation rate. Perhaps, the reason is that the service development in China is in low level at the recent stage and manufacturing is in the predominant position. Therefore, the role of service growth still presents insignificant influence to new firm formation.

The coefficient for human capital, as measured by share of college degree, is positive and statistically significant, indicating that regions with higher education level will have higher new firm formation rate. The result is consistent with Okamuro and Kobayashi (2005), Lobo and Costa (2003), and Armington and Ács (2002). It suggests that a region needs to develop its education to enhance human capital level, which exert important role in its new firm formation development.

The coefficient for unemployment rate is positive and statistically significant. Although unemployment has two opposite effects on new firm formation, the result here indicates that in China the impetus effect of unemployment is dominant and presents a positive relationship with new firm formation rate. This is consistent with Storey (1991), Robson (1994), and Fritsch and Mueller (2005).

The coefficient for private wealth, as measured by per capita local saving, is positive and statistically significant, indicating that regions with higher level of private wealth have a higher new firm formation rate. At the early stage of a new firm, financing private capital is very important to entrepreneurs. Generally, when residents in a region are richer, entrepreneurs can easily obtain the needed capital from private wealth.

The coefficient for entrepreneurial culture, measured by shift of employment to private firms, is positive and statistically significant, consistent with the hypothesis. Entrepreneurial culture can be improved by encouraging collective venturing firms and generating more employment in them. This study uses shift of employment to private firms to represent regional venturing firms' collectivism. The result indicates that regions with more employment in private firms will have higher new firm formation rate.

Based on the above analysis, we can come to the conclusion that income growth, technological development, human capital, unemployment, private wealth, and entrepreneurial culture evidence the hypothesized relationships with new firm formation rate. These influencing factors are determining the regional variations in new firm formation rate in China.

8.6. Accessing Determinants by Regions and Stages

In this section, two steps will be taken to analyze the determinants for further. The first is, if we separately see the determinants in DR and in UDR, to examine whether the results of the two categories of regions are different. If significant differences exist, it shows that factors determining the development of entrepreneurial activities between DR and UDR are varied. DR and VDR tests need to be performed using the same model as in the previous section. Then comparing the regression results can facilitate in making the judgment. The second is to see whether the determinants change in different periods. We divide the time of 1996–2006 into two stages, 1996–2001 and 2002–2006, and separately test the models for them.

8.6.1. *Two Categories of Regions*

The results are shown in Table 8.4. Models 1, 2, and 3 are estimated for UDR, and models 4, 5, and 6 are estimated for DR. We can find that most of coefficients in the models are similar, with the exception of R&D intensity. Five variables have positive and statistically significant coefficient results in both the models of the two categories of regions. They are income growth, unemployment rate, per capital local saving, and shift of employment to private firms, and college degree share, which indicate that these five factors are all important determinants promoting the development of entrepreneurial activities in both the developed regions and the undeveloped regions.

The other two variables, population growth and service growth, have statistically insignificant coefficient results in both the models of the two categories of regions. It suggests that population growth and industrial change measured by service growth are not important factors for the development of entrepreneurial activities in the two categories of regions. Even in the developed regions, service growth has not exerted statistically

Table 8.4. Model results: The determinants in DR and UDR

Independent Variables	UDR			DR		
	Model 1	Model 2	Model 3	Model 4	Model 5	Model 6
C	−2.78	−2.95	−2.55	−4.44	−10.18	−8.75
Population growth	0.035	0.016	0.033	0.412	0.333	0.042
	(0.80)	(0.42)	(0.81)	(1.10)	(1.19)	(0.30)
Income growth	0.154*	0.117*	0.210**	1.582†	0.945†	0.891**
	(2.25)	(2.01)	(2.83)	(1.81)	(1.70)	(3.24)
R&D intensity	3.993**			−2.893		
	(6.83)			(−0.89)		
Service growth	0.006	0.150	0.213	−0.341	4.214	6.381
	(0.02)	(0.45)	(0.56)	(−0.04)	(0.77)	(1.35)
College degree share		0.525**			0.688†	
		(9.12)			(1.81)	
Unemployment rate	0.581**	0.633**	0.909***	4.546**	2.566**	2.312**
	(4.16)	(5.38)	(6.07)	(3.09)	(2.73)	(4.23)
Per capital local saving			1.180**			4.593*
			(3.24)			(4.68)
Shift of employment to private firms	0.559**	0.446*	0.813**	1.280**	1.193**	0.804†
	(2.86)	(2.46)	(3.94)	(2.69)	(2.45)	(1.86)
Adjusted R^2	0.533	0.599	0.41	0.61	0.679	0.679
F-statistic	10.32	13.20	6.62	9.43	12.36	11.43
	(0.0000)	(0.0000)	(0.0000)	(0.0000)	(0.0000)	(0.0000)
Hausman test	27.59	17.34	11.00	—[5]	—	—
	(0.000)	(0.008)	(0.088)			
Wooldridge test	0.45	0.423	0.470	0.44	2.37	2.25
	(0.51)	(0.52)	(0.50)	(0.51)	(0.18)	(0.19)
Observations	230	230	230	60	60	60

Note: t-values are reported in parentheses below the coefficient estimate. *DR is the developed region; UDR is the undeveloped region.* †$p < 0.10$, *$p < 0.05$, **$p < 0.01$.

[5]Model fitted on these data fails to meet the assumptions of the Hausman test.

significant influence to entrepreneurial activities. This result is not the expected, that it should have been a determinant in the developed regions.

The most surprise result, however, is that R&D intensity has a positive and statistically significant coefficient in the undeveloped regions, while it has a negative but statistically insignificant coefficient in the developed regions. The result may be partly influenced by the limited sample because just six provinces in the cross section have been considered. The other reason may be that these six provinces have a close R&D intensity, which does not explain the differences of NFFR at the statistical level.

8.6.2. *Two Stages*

In order to make sure whether the dominants changes over time, we examined the models for the two stages, including the first stage from 1996 to 2001 and the second stage from 2002 to 2006. The results given in the Table 8.5 suggest that the determinants of the two stages are variable. The coefficients of four variables change from the insignificant in the first stage to the significant in the second stage. These changes may be closely related to the transformation of social and economic structure within the past 10 years of economic transition in China.

The coefficient of population growth becomes statistically significant in the second stage. The reason may be that, driven by the expansion of economic disparity among different regions and increasingly convenient transportation with modern vehicles, population shifting is increasing, especially from rural area to cities, which produces change in market demand and in turn affects entrepreneurial activities. Population shifting is likely to not only cause the number of potential customer in specific market to change but also influence people's income changing. For example, rural workers migrating to urban areas can earn higher income than that in their hometown. And this improves people's purchasing power, which is in favor of entrepreneurial activities.

The coefficient of service growth also becomes statistically significant in the second stage. Service development may be a cause and effect of

Table 8.5. Model results: The determinants in different stages

Independent variables	1996–2001			2002–2006		
	Model 1	Model 2	Model 3	Model 4	Model 5	Model 6
C	5.16	−4.07	−1.83	−8.30	−5.06	−6.28
Population growth	0.049	−0.033	0.091	0.453**	0.326**	0.370**
	(1.26)	(−0.27)	(0.90)	(5.28)	(4.13)	(7.32)
Income growth	0.188*	0.117†	0.361†	0.617**	0.672**	0.469**
	(2.13)	(1.65)	(1.86)	(4.67)	(5.29)	(4.19)
R&D intensity	1.32†			1.968†		
	(1.83)			(1.72)		
Service growth	0.307	1.641†	3.43	1.875**	2.08**	1.932**
	(0.98)	(1.64)	(1.59)	(2.95)	(3.07)	(3.36)
College degree share		0.853*			0.253**	
		(2.43)			(2.85)	
Unemployment rate	0.150	0.160	−0.357	2.445**	1.531**	1.686**
	(0.65)	(0.59)	(−0.65)	(4.24)	(3.59)	(3.40)
Per capital local saving			2.931			3.976*
			(1.23)			(7.73)
Shift of employment to private firms	0.336	1.93	2.292†	0.181	0.210†	0.145*
	(0.38)	(1.46)	(1.69)	(1.48)	(1.72)	(2.22)
AR(1)	−0.046					
	(−0.40)					
Adjusted R^2	0.446	0.342	0.20	0.849	0.863	0.902
F-statistic	4.31	15.95	7.28	24.79	27.82	39.96
	(0.0000)	(0.0000)	(0.0000)	(0.0000)	(0.0000)	(0.0000)
Hausman test	193.01	3.67	10.03	—	25.84	43.41
	(0.000)	(0.721)	(0.123)		(0.000)	(0.000)
Wooldridge test	3.782	4.023	3.49	0.559	0.45	0.509
	(0.06)	(0.05)	(0.07)	(0.46)	(0.51)	(0.48)
Observations	145	174	174	145	145	145

Note: t-values are reported in parentheses below the coefficient estimate. *DR is the developed region; UDR is the undeveloped region.* †$p < 0.10$, *$p < 0.05$, **$p < 0.01$.

entrepreneurial activities. In China, the service sector has rapidly developed in recent years. The development speed of service, however, varied among different regions. In developed regions, service has improved relatively poor, while it is still in the undeveloped regions. This growing disparity, which expands over time leads to the result that service gradually exerts significant influence on entrepreneurial activities.

Unemployment exerts statistically significant effects on NFFR in the second stage. This may be influenced by the unemployment growth and self-employment policies in the past 10 years. The number of unemployed people has surged since the Chinese government carried out institutional reforms in 1998. Many workers in state-owned enterprises who remained unemployed, were laid off but they needed to make a living. The central and local governments implemented preferential policies to encourage unemployed workers to be self-employed, and many chose to do small business or start new ventures. Of course, the effect of policies has a certain lag.

The effect of private wealth on NFFR is influenced by the people's income level. When the overall level of private wealth is relatively low, its impact on business would be small. But in recent years, the income and living standards of people have increased, and private wealth has grown rapidly. Entrepreneurs could borrow money easier than before from people around to start new firms. Hence, private wealth gradually becomes an important factor that drives entrepreneurial activities.

8.7. Conclusions and Implication

There are large variations in NFFRs across different regions in China. We divide mainland China into two categories of regions, the developed regions and the undeveloped regions, and find that the disparity in NFFR between them was large and expanding rapidly during the period of 1996–2006. Using panel data model, this study examined what determines the variations in NFFR across 29 provinces in mainland China between 1996 and 2006. Consistent with our hypothesized relationships, the results show that income growth, technological development, human capital, unemployment, private wealth, establishment size, and entrepreneurial culture have significant impacts on NFFR. Regional variations in NFFR in China are mainly determined by these factors.

This study also assessed the determinants for further growth. One is to separately examine the determinants for the developed regions and the undeveloped regions. We found that most of the factors had similar effect on NFFR in the two categories of regions. The other is to examine the determinants for two stages, 1996–2001 and 2002–2006. We found that four factors, population growth, service growth, unemployment, and private wealth, exerted significant effect on NFFR in the second stage but not in the first stage. This suggests that the determinants of NFFR variations change over time.

Regional differences in NFFR provide big challenges for policies makers in China. Most current policies in encouraging entrepreneurial activities are still far more limited and largely concentrated within science parks. In our view, the Chinese government should make efforts in the following areas: The first is to further improve the environment for the development of the service sector and implement policies to encourage start-ups in service, especially in modern service business. This will not only benefit the development of entrepreneurship but also be in line with the trend that the government advocates to lower energy consumption in business. The second is to explore an effective way of transforming private capital into venture capital. This will guide and encourage private wealth to be invested new venture. In China, there is a vast reservoir of private capital among people. If this resource can be efficiently used to develop entrepreneurial activities, it will reduce much difficulty for entrepreneurial attempts. The third is to strengthen entrepreneurship education and encourage people with a high level of human capital to become entrepreneurs. These people are more likely to start up high-growth new firms and create great value. Meanwhile, there are a large number of people who have completed their higher education. If entrepreneurship is encouraged in this demographic, they would create huge wealth and offer an abundant amount of jobs for our society.

References

Ács, Z., and A. Varga (2005). Entrepreneurship, agglomeration and technological change, *Small Business Economics* **24**: 323–334.

Alvarez, B. (2007). Discovery and creation: Alternative theories of entrepreneurial action. *Strategic Entrepreneurship Journal* **1**:11–26.

Armington, Z., and J. Ács (2002). The determinants of regional variation in new firm formation. *Regional Studies* **36**: 33–45.

Basu, A., and A. Goswami (1999). Determinants of South Asian entrepreneurial growth in Britain: A multivariate analysis. *Small Business Economics* **13**: 57–70.

Bates, T. (1985). Entrepreneur human capital endowments and minority business viability. *The Journal of Human Resources* **24**(4): 540–554.

Bates, T. (1995). Self-employment entry across industry groups. *Journal of Business Venturing* **10**: 143–156.

Blau, D. (1987). A time-series analysis of self-employment in the United States. *Journal of Political Economy*, **95**(3): 445–465.

Bartik, T.J., Small business start-ups in the United States: Estimates of the effects of characteristics of states, *Southern Economic Journal* **55**(4): 1004–1018.

Baumol, W. J. (1990). Entrepreneurship: Productive, unproductive, and destructive. *Journal of Political Economy* **98**(5): 893–921.

Christensen C. and J. Bower (1996). Customer power,strategic investment, and the failure of leading firms. *Strategic Management Journal* **17**(3): 197–218.

Cooper A. C., F. Javier and C. Y. Woo (1994). Initial human and financial capital as predictors of new venture performance. *Journal of Business Venturing* **9**(5): 371–395.

Davidsson, P. (1995). Culture, structure and regional levels of entrepreneurship. *Entrepreneurship and Regional Development* **7**: 41–62.

Davidsson, P. and J. Wiklund (2000). Conceptual and empirical challenges in the study of firm growth. In D. Sexton and H. Landström (Eds.) *The Blackwell Handbook of Entrepreneur-ship.* Oxford, MA: Blackwell.

Davidsson, P., and B. Honig (2003). The role of social and human capital among nascent entrepreneurs. *Journal of Business Venturing* **18**: 301–331.

Dean, T. J., G. D. Meyer and J. DeCastro (1996). Industry environments and new venture formations in U.S. manufacturing: A conceptual and empirical analysis of demand determinants. *Journal of Business Venturing* **11**: 107–132.

Dean, T. J., G. D. Meyer and J. DeCastro (1993). Determinants of new-firm formations in manufacturing industries: Industry dynamics, entry barriers, and organizational inertia. *Entrepreneurship Theory and Practice* 49–60.

Drucker, R. (1985). *Innovation and Entrepreneurship.* New York: Harper & Row.

Eckhardt, J. T., and S. Shane (2003). Opportunities and entrepreneurship. *Journal of Management* **29**(3): 333–349.

Egelin, J. *et al.* (1997). Firm foundations and the role of financial constraints. *Small Business Economics* **9**: 137–150.

Evans, D., and L. S. Leighton (1988). The determinants of changes in U.S. self-employment, 1968–1987. *Small Business Economics* **1**: 111–119.

Fothergill, S. and G. Gudgin (1982). *Unequal Growth: Urban and Regional Employment Change in the UK.* Heinemann Educational Books (London).

Fritsch, M., and O. Falck (2002). New firm formation by industry over space and time: A multi-level analysis. Technische Universität Freibeg Working Paper, 11.

Fritsch, M. (2004). Entrepreneurship, entry and performance of new business compared in two growth regimes: East and West Germany. *Journal of Evolutionary Economics* **14**(5): 525–542.

Fritsch, M., and P. Mueller (2005). The persistence of regional new business formation-activity over time-assessing the potential of policy promotion programs. Technical University Bergakademie. Freiberg Working Paper, 2005.

Garofoli, G. (1994). New firm formation and regional development: The Italian case. *Regional Studies* **28**: 381–393.

Gifford, S. (1993). Heterogeneous ability, career choice, and firm size. *Small Business Economics* **5**: 249–259.

Guesnier, B. (1994). Regional variations in new firm formation in France. *Regional Studies*, **28**(4): 347–358.

Hart, M., and G. Gudgin (1994). Spatial variations in new firm formation in the Republic of Ireland, 1980–1990. *Regional Studies* **28**(4): 367–380.

Highfield, R., and R. Smiley (1987). New business starts and economic activity: An empirical investigation. *International Journal of Industrial Organization* **5**: 51–66.

Holmes, T. J., and J. A. Schmitz Jr. (1990). A theory of entrepreneurship and its application to the study of business transfers. *Journal of Political Economy* **98**(2): 265–294.

Johnson, P. (2004). Differences in regional firm formation rates: A decomposition analysis. *Entrepreneurship: Theory and Practice* **28**(5): 431–445.

Kangasharju, A. (2000). Regional variations in firm formation: Panel and cross-section data evidence from Finland. *Regional Science* **79**(4): 355–373.

Keeble, D., and S. Walker (1994). New firms, small firms and dead firms: Spatial patterns and determinants in the United Kingdom. *Regional Studies* **28**(4):411–427

Keeble, D., (1997). Small firms, Innovation and regional development in Britain in the 1990s. *Regional Studies* **31**(3): 281–293.

Kirzner, I. (1973). *Competition and Entrepreneurship*. Chicago, IL, and London: University of Chicago Press.

Lee S. Y., R., Florida and Z. J. Ács (2004). Creativity and entrepreneurship: A regional analysis of new firm formation. *Regional Studies* **38**(8): 879–891.

Lipset, S. M. (2000). Value and entrepreneurship in Americas, in *Entrepreneurship: The Social Science View*, in R. Swedbeg (Ed.) Oxford, UK, Oxford University Press, pp. 21–33.

Lobo, C. A., and J. S. Costa (2003). New firm formation: An empirical study for Portugal. Regional Science Association International Conference, Pisa.

Mueller S., and A. S. Tomas (2001). Culture and entrepreneurial potential: A nine country study of locus of control and innovativeness. *Journal of Business Venturing* **16**(1)

Moog, P. (2002). Human capital and its influence on entrepreneurial success. *Historical Social Research* **27**(4): 157–180.

Okamuro, H., and N. Kobayashi (2006). The impact of regional factors on the start-up ratio in Japan. *Journal of Small Business Management* **44**(2): 310–313.

Okamuro, H., and N. Kobayashi (2005). Determinants of regional variations in the start-up ratio: Evidence from Japan, COE-RES Discussion Paper.

Reynolds, P. D., B. Miller and W. R. Maki (1995). Explaining regional variation in business births and deaths — U.S. 1976–88, *Small Business Economics* **7**: 389–407.

Reynolds, P., D. J., Storey, and P. Westhead (1994). Cross-national comparisons of the variation in new firm formation rates, *Regional Studies* **28**(4): 443–456.

Ritsilä, J., and H. Tervo (2002). Effects of unemployment on new firm formation: Micro-level panel data evidence from Finland. *Small Business Economics* **19**(1): 31–40.

Roboson, M. T. (1994). The determinants of new firm formation in UK construction: Evidence from quarterly VAT registrations. *International Journal of the Economics of Business* **1**(2): 233–246.

Romanelli, E. (1989). Environments and strategies of organization star-up: Effects on early survival. *Administrative Science Quarterly* **34**: 369–387.

Schultz, T. W. (1959). Investment in man: An economist's view. *The Social Service Review* **33**(2): 109–117.

Schumpeter, J. A. (1934). *The Theory of Economic Development*. Cambridge, MA: Harvard University Press.

Shane, S. (1996). Explaining variation in rates of entrepreneurship in the United States: 1899–1988. *Journal of Management* **22**(5): 747–781.

Shane, S. (2003). *A General Theory of Entrepreneurship. The Individual-Opportunity Nexus*. Edward Elgar: Northampton, MA.

Storey, D. J.(1991). The birth of new firms — Does unemployment matter? A review of the evidence. *Small Business Economics* **3**(3): 167–178.

Sutaria, V., and D. A. Hicks (2004). New firm formation: Dynamics and determinants. *The Annals of Regional Science* **38**(2): 241–262.

Chapter 9

Diversity, Innovation, and Entrepreneurship in China

Haifeng Qian*, Roger R. Stough[†], and Junyang Yuan[†]
*Cleveland State University
[†]George Mason University

9.1. Introduction

Innovation and entrepreneurship play increasingly important roles in regional economic development today. In the U.S., regions experiencing extraordinary economic performance since the 1980s (e.g., Silicon Valley, Austin, TX, and Northern Virginia) are mostly technology- or innovation-based, and generally present high new firm formation rates. This is also the case in the European Union and other parts of the developed world. Economists and regional scientists following this trend have been investigating the geographic sources of innovation and entrepreneurship (e.g., Jaffe, 1986; Ács and Armington, 2006).

Knowledge production functions developed by Griliches (1979), Jaffe (1989), and Romer (1990) suggest R&D efforts and human capital as primary determinants of innovative output. This approach further highlights the role of knowledge spillover in promoting innovation, particularly at the regional level. In relation to that, the divergent conclusions from the Marshall–Arrow–Romer (MAR) theory (defined by Glaeser *et al.*, 1992) and the Jacobs theory (1969) revolve around the question whether industrial specialization or diversity encourages the occurrence of knowledge spillovers. While there is no consensus over the role of industrial diversity, scholars have begun to examine whether social or cultural diversity may also have effects on innovative activity. Florida (Florida and Gates, 2001; Florida, 2002a, 2002b; Florida *et al.*, 2007; Mellander and Florida, 2007), in the regional context, defines the potentially important role of diversity, openness, or tolerance in attracting talented people and high-tech industries. Diversity, however, may also increase communication costs, while interpersonal interactions occur more easily within a socially cohesive group than across different social groups.

This chapter contributes to the empirical literature by investigating the determinants of regional innovation and entrepreneurship in China. In particular, the effect of social diversity on innovation and entrepreneurship is examined. Similar to innovation, entrepreneurship has been connected with commercialization of new technologies and knowledge spillovers (Ács and Armington, 2006; Audretsch *et al.*, 2006). Following Qian (2010), we employ the *Hukou* index to measure the degree of diversity or openness in Chinese regions. It is an index exclusively applicable to countries like China with an inhabitant registration system. Based on a panel dataset of provincial-level regions, we test whether social diversity is significantly associated with innovation and entrepreneurship in China after controlling for a set of potential determinants of innovative and entrepreneurial activity.

This chapter is organized as follows. Section 9.2 reviews the literature of geographically mediated determinants and measurement issues of innovation and entrepreneurship. It is followed by the introduction of data, variables and methods. Section 9.3 presents the empirical findings. Section 9.4 concludes.

9.2. Literature Review

The role of innovation in economic development has been studied by economists for a long time. Schumpeter (1934) identifies five types of innovation that he considers as the core of economic development.[1] The dynamics in which innovation drives economic development has been further investigated by the proponents of the post-Schumpeterian approach (e.g., Nelson and Winter, 1982). The neoclassical economists also recognize the importance of technology or innovation for economic growth (Solow, 1956, 1957). Recently, innovation has become one of the key topics in mainstream economics, thanks to the emergence of the new growth theory (Romer, 1990). With the growing concern over the role of innovation in economic development, factors driving innovative activity have also been extensively explored from a variety of angles, such as from a geographic perspective. Innovations occur unevenly across regions. According to the U.S. Small Business Administration (SBA) 1982 Survey, 81% of the total 4,200 U.S. innovations are concentrated in 11 states (Feldman and Florida, 1994). This section reviews the literature addressing the geographic sources of innovation. In addition, measurements of innovation and entrepreneurship are also discussed, paving the way for subsequent empirical analysis.

9.2.1. *Geographic Sources of Innovation*

Understanding why innovative activity tends to concentrate in some specific regions contributes to the making of innovation policies that promote regional competiveness. Knowledge production functions, initiated by Griliches (1979) and Jaffe (1986, 1989), shed light on geographically mediated determinants of innovation. Early models (Griliches, 1979; Jaffe, 1986, 1989) address R&D investments in facilities such as universities and firms as the key input in the knowledge production function. They highlight not only the direct role of R&D in knowledge generation

---

[1]The Schumpeterian notion of innovation addresses "the carrying out of new combinations." Such a dynamic process, according to Schumpeter (1934), includes the introduction of a new good or a new quality of a good, the introduction of a new method of production, the opening of a new market, the conquest of a new source of supply and the carrying out of the new organization of any industry. Students of innovation have been primarily focusing on the first two types, also identified as *(technological) product innovation* and *(technological) process innovation* (Schmookler, 1966).

but also the indirect role of universities, research institutes, technological parks, and knowledge-intensive industries as the locus of R&D activity. One important implication of those models from a geographic perspective is that regions attracting more R&D investments or hosting more R&D facilities tend to produce more innovations. This relationship has been supported by many analyses (Malecki, 1981; Jaffe, 1989; Ács *et al.*, 1992; Goldstein and Luger, 1990; Feldman, 1994; Feldman and Florida, 1994; Anselin *et al.*, 1997; Feldman and Audretsch, 1999).

Another type of knowledge production function, derived from Romer's model (1990), takes new knowledge output as a function of labor for research and the existing public knowledge stock. The regional stock of researchers, according to this theory, is critical to the generation of innovations. Bartel and Lichtenberg (1987), using national level data, have exhibited the important role that well-educated workers play in the creation of new technologies. In another empirical study, Zucker and Darby (1996) show that "star" bioscientists not only produce important knowledge products when they coauthor papers with research scientists from firms but also drive the commercialization of biotechnologies. In a series of empirical studies based on the region-level data, Florida (2002b; Florida *et al.*, 2007; Mellander and Florida, 2007) finds positive effects of human capital and the creative class on technology. While those talented people play an indispensable role in accelerating regional innovation, the geographic determinants of talent distribution may affect innovative activity indirectly. Those determinants may include market factors, such as wage (Florida, 2002a), and non-market factors such as local amenities (Glaeser, Kolko, and Saiz, 2001) and social diversity (Florida and Gates, 2001; Florida, 2002a, 2002b).

The importance of R&D and researchers to innovation, suggested by the two types of knowledge production functions, highlights the role of universities in innovative activity in the sense that they not only attract R&D and generate new knowledge but also provide the economy with well-educated researchers. The social benefits of universities, however, also rely on the extent to which knowledge spillover may occur. The phenomenon of knowledge spillover has recently drawn major attention from economists. A number of empirical studies based on knowledge production functions show that knowledge spillovers exist and appear to be geographically bounded (Jaffe, 1989; Ács *et al.*, 1992; Jaffe *et al.*, 1993; Anselin *et al.*, 1997; Ács, Anselin and Varga, 2002; Peri, 2005).

Glaeser *et al.* (1992) find that two technological externalities theories prevail in explaining the effect of the industrial structure on knowledge spillover. One is known as MAR externalities, following the idea of Marshall that the local concentration of production benefits producers as a result of knowledge spillovers among firms within the same industry. In contrast, Jacobs (1969) suggests that knowledge spillovers from outside the core industry are more important for innovation and the growth of cities. The diversity of geographically proximate industries in cities accordingly contributes more to innovation than specialization. Glaeser *et al.* (1992) and Feldman and Audretsch (1999) support Jacobs's emphasis on diversity. The MAR theory, which addresses specialization also receives supporting evidence, e.g., from Porter (1998) and Ács, FitzRoy, and Smith (2002).

While there is no consensus over the effect of industrial diversity on innovative activity, some scholars have shifted research focus to social or cultural diversity. Florida (Florida and Gates, 2001; Florida, 2002a, 2002b; Florida *et al.*, 2007; Mellander and Florida, 2007), in the regional context, finds the important roles that diversity, openness, or tolerance play in attracting talented people and high-tech industries. According to his theory, social diversity may encourage innovation in two ways. First, a diversified society consists of people with diverse knowledge backgrounds and diverse thinking perspectives that foster the production of new knowledge; and second, diversity signals low barriers to entry of talent from outside, thereby attracting creative people from other regions. Diversity, however, may also increase communication costs while individual interactions are easier to occur within a socially cohesive group than across different social groups. Cummings and Kiesler (2005) reveal that scientific research involving more universities or disciplines could be more problematic. To sum up, the overall effect of social diversity on innovation remains unclear, which calls for additional empirical analysis.

9.2.2. Measures of Innovation

Innovation is difficult, if not impossible, to be measured. New products might be used to measure product innovations. Scholars however face difficulties in deciding what can be considered as "new", especially in the context of incremental innovation. Nevertheless, some quantification attempts have been made from either the input or the output side of innovative activity.

The most widely used proxy for innovation is associated with patents. A patent is "a public contract between an inventor and a government that grants time-limited monopoly rights to the applicant for the use of a technical invention" (Smith, 2005). Though not all patents are eventually commercialized, the patent system provides individuals, firms, or universities with the monopolistic right to use their inventions for a specified period, e.g., 20 years. As one of the key advantages of this measure, time-series patent information has been well documented by government agencies such as the U.S. Patent Office and the European Patent Office. Using the patent data, Breschi (2000) investigates the geographic patterns of innovation in some European countries. Jaffe *et al.* (1993) exploit another advantage of the patent data when employing the patent citation as a measure for knowledge or innovation spillovers. Despite these advantages, the patent data conceptually correspond to inventions but not necessarily innovations. In other words, they cannot measure the economic value of inventions (Hall, Jaffe, and Trajtenberg, 2001). Even accepting inventions as the substitute for innovations, patent data cannot cover all inventions since not all new ideas are patented (Pakes and Griliches, 1980).

The scale of high-tech industries has also been employed as a proxy for innovation. Because innovative activity is more likely to occur in those knowledge-based high-tech industries, for instance, ICT and pharmaceutical, the relative scale of those innovative industries may represent the innovation capacity of regions or nations. This approach has been adopted in several empirical studies by Florida (2002b; Mellander and Florida, 2007). The advantage of the high-tech indicator over the patent indicator is that the former better reflects the commercialization component of innovation. This approach, however, measures innovation from the input side and thus in an indirect way. Another disadvantage of high-tech measures results from the fact that innovative activity can definitely occur outside those so-called high-tech industries (Porter, 1998).

While it is difficult to get good measures for innovation based on official statistical data, attempts to design indicators and obtain data through surveys have been made. Such surveys may only acquire innovation data for a short period and a limited number of firms, but more accurate measurement for innovation can be used. For instance, the U.S. Small Business Administration (SBA) in 1982 surveyed over 100 technology, engineering, and trade journals, through which the number of innovations for each four-digit SIC industry was documented. This survey only recorded those inventions followed with commercialization, and therefore it can better capture the definition of innovation. This dataset leads to several important empirical studies on the relationships between innovation and factors such as firm size (Ács and Audretsch, 1987, 1988), technological infrastructure (Feldman and Florida, 1994), knowledge spillover (Ács, Audretsch, and Feldman, 1994; Audretsch and Feldman, 1996; Anselin *et al.*, 1997), and industry diversity (Feldman and Audretsch, 1999). A similar survey toward the British industries had been developed even earlier by the Science Policy Research Unit at the University of Sussex. From a different approach, another survey conducted directly toward R&D laboratories of 200 U.S. firms by Adams in 1997 includes information on the number of new products as a result of the research work in those laboratories. This dataset allows for quantification of innovation through new products and empirical investigation of the sources of innovation at the micro level. Adams (2001) examines the location of knowledge spillovers using this dataset. In Europe, the OECD in the early 1990s launched the *Community Innovation Survey* (CIS) that collected various data of incremental and radical innovations from a large number of European firms. The 2002 CIS survey covers 140,000 firms, providing ample information for innovation research.

9.2.3. *Innovation and Entrepreneurship*

Innovation in the Schumpeterian notion is closely associated with entrepreneurship. Innovation consists of two indispensable components: (1) creation of new technologies and (2) commercialization of new technologies. Entrepreneurship focuses exclusively on the second component of innovation. Audretsch *et al.* (2006) and Ács and Armington (2006) developed a knowledge spillover theory of entrepreneurship, arguing that entrepreneurs endeavor to commercialize new technologies from either incumbent firms or research institutions through creating new firms. By accepting this theory, the number of new firms can be used as a measure for knowledge based entrepreneurship.

9.2.3.1. *Data, variables, and methods*

We seek to test geographic sources of innovation and entrepreneurship in China using a panel dataset highlighting economic and social indicators of 30 provincial-level regions in Mainland China for the period of 1998–2006. In particular, the effects of social diversity on innovation and entrepreneurship are investigated. The initial year of 1998 is chosen because China's latest jurisdictional adjustments occurred in 1997, when Chongqing was separated from Sichuan Province and became a municipality directly under the central government. One region in Mainland China not covered by this dataset is Tibet, which is generally excluded from similar empirical analysis (because it is always an outlier). Data for some variables are missing for some specific years (in most cases 1998 or 2006). While cities or metropolitan regions have been suggested as the best geographic unit for similar empirical analysis (Jacobs, 1969; Glaeser, 1999; Florida, 2002b), in the case of China, we are unable to base our study on cities due to data unavailability and unreliability at the municipal level. As a compromise, we control for the urbanization rate in the econometric specifications. Dependent variables are proxies for innovation and entrepreneurship. Independent variables suggested by the literature include R&D, human capital, the university, diversity or openness, amenities, and the urbanization rate. In addition, we add a dummy variable indicating whether or not a region is a municipal region directly controlled by the central government.

9.2.4. *Dependent Variables: Proxies for Innovation and Entrepreneurship*

The literature suggests four ways to measure innovation and entrepreneurship: the scale of high-tech industries, patents per capita, innovation information from surveys, and new firm formation. As far as we have been able to learn, there are no comprehensive innovation survey data available in China. We therefore use the other three measures.

High Technology. We use the proportion of value added in high-tech industries to GDP as a measure for innovation in terms of high technology. High-tech industries in China include electronic and telecommunications, computers, and office equipment, pharmaceuticals, medical equipment and meters, and aircraft and spacecraft. The high-tech value-added data for 2000–2005 are available from *China Statistics Yearbook on High Technology Industry* (2004–2007), and GDP data are available from *China Statistics Yearbook* (2001–2006).

Patents. We use the number of granted patents per 100,000 as a proxy for regional innovation in terms of patenting capability. The Chinese Patent Office grants three types of patents: inventions, utility models, and designs. The latter two account for more than 80% of total patent approvals. *China Statistics Yearbook* (1999–2007) provides both the patent data and population data from 1998 to 2006.

New Firm Formation. We use the number of new firms per 100,000 employees as a measure for entrepreneurship, or in other words, the commercialization side of innovation. Three provincial municipal regions, Shanghai, Beijing, and Tianjin take the lead in establishing new firms. New firm formation data and employment data for 1998–2004 are available from *China Economic Census* (*2004*) and *China Statistics Yearbook* (1999–2005), respectively.

Figure 9.1 presents spatial distributions of innovation and entrepreneurship in China for the year 2000.

9.2.5. *Independent Variables*

Diversity. Diversity, openness, or tolerance has been measured by the scale of the gay population in most of Florida's studies (Florida and Gates, 2001; Florida, 2002a, 2002b; Florida *et al.*, 2007; Mellander and Florida, 2007).

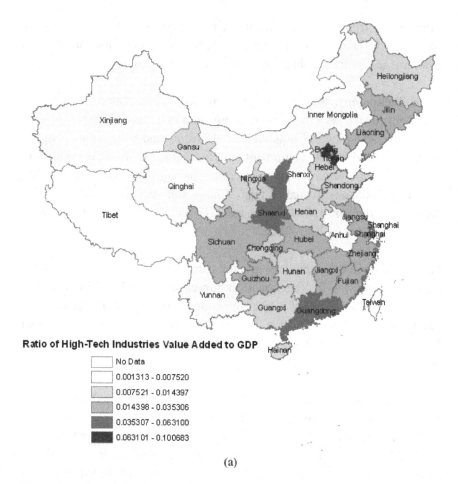

Ratio of High-Tech Industries Value Added to GDP

- No Data
- 0.001313 - 0.007520
- 0.007521 - 0.0144397
- 0.014398 - 0.035306
- 0.035307 - 0.063100
- 0.063101 - 0.100683

(a)

Figure 9.1.   Spatial distributions of innovative and entrepreneurial activities in China for the year 2000.

Ottaviano and Peri (2006) from an ecological approach adopt an index which measures the relative composition of population in terms of countries of birth. Neither of these two indexes, however, can be borrowed and used to measure diversity in China due to data unavailability. As an alternative, we use the *Hukou* index as a proxy for diversity or openness, following the work of Qian (2010). In China, each citizen has a *Hukou* status, signifying the person's place of residence. Those with a locally registered *Hukou* are generally local permanent residents and those without are generally temporary residents from the outside. The *Hukou* index measures

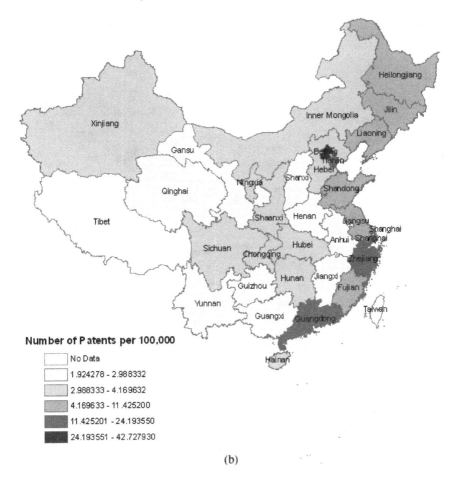

Number of Patents per 100,000

- No Data
- 1.924278 - 2.988332
- 2.988333 - 4.169632
- 4.169633 - 11.425200
- 11.425201 - 24.193550
- 24.193551 - 42.727930

(b)

Figure 9.1. *(Continued)*

the share of regional population without a locally registered *Hukou*. Data for 1998–2006 are available from *China Statistics Yearbook* (1999–2007).

R&D. R&D in firms or universities, according to the knowledge production function, is one of the key determinants of innovation. The ratio of total R&D capital stock to GDP is employed to measure R&D efforts in a region. While *China Statistics Yearbook on Science and Technology* (1993–2007) only provides new R&D investments data for each year, we assume a capital depreciation rate of 15% and use the 2000 constant value to compute the total R&D stock.

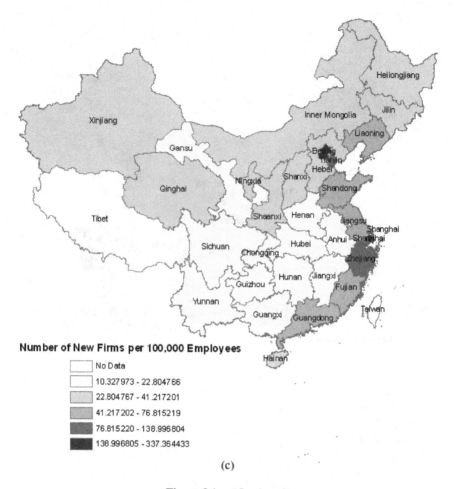

Number of New Firms per 100,000 Employees

☐ No Data
☐ 10.327973 - 22.804766
☐ 22.804767 - 41.217201
☐ 41.217202 - 76.815219
☐ 76.815220 - 138.996804
☐ 138.996805 - 337.364433

(c)

Figure 9.1. (*Continued*)

Human Capital. The stock of researchers, talent, or human capital is another key factor that may exert a major impact on innovative output. We measure the regional human capital level by the proportion of those with a college degree among the population aged 15 years and older. Data for 1998–2006 are available from *China Statistics Yearbook* (1999–2007).

University. The university plays an important role in both knowledge production and knowledge spillover and therefore is recognized as one of the key determinants of regional innovation. The scale of the university in our case is measured by the ratio of new graduates from local colleges in a particular year to local population. *China Statistics Yearbook* (1999–2007) provides such data for the period of 1998–2006.

Amenities. Local amenities, according to Kotkin (2000), can attract both high-tech industries and talented people who undertake innovative work. Amenities may refer to many types such as natural, cultural, constructional, and service. We measure service amenities using the location quotient of employment in the tertiary sector (researchers and employment in other unknown service industries excluded). Data for 1998–2006 are available from *China Labor Statistics Yearbook* (1999–2007).

Urbanization. As previously mentioned, data unavailability and unreliability do not allow us to use cities or metropolitan regions as the primary geographic unit. While innovative activity is more likely to occur in cities, the urbanization rate is expected to affect innovation. Rather than defining urbanization in terms of population, we use an urbanization rate measured by the ratio of urban employment to total employment. This way can better reflect urbanization of business activity. *China Labor Statistics Yearbook* (1999–2006) lends us the data to calculate the urbanization rate of employees for the period 1998–2005.

Dummy for provincial municipalities. China has four provincial-level municipalities directly under the central government: Beijing, Tianjin, Shanghai, and Chongqing. They present a much higher urbanization rate than other provinces. More importantly, they receive more resources and preferential policies from the central government, which put them at advantageous positions for economic and social development. We therefore employ a dummy variable to control for the economic and political effects of being such a provincial-level municipality.

With a panel dataset, we run four regressions for each of the three measures of innovation and entrepreneurship: the pooled-OLS model, the first difference model (FD), the fixed effects model (FE), and the random effects model (RE). To reduce the effect of multicollinearity on parameter estimations, a stepwise approach is employed for both the pooled-OLS model and the first difference model. Using different methods toward the same data allows for more reliable conclusions.

We further investigate whether some of the factors mentioned earlier (diversity, the university, amenities, urbanization, and dummy for provincial municipalities) have indirect effects on innovation and entrepreneurship through human capital, given the hypothesis that human capital is closely associated with innovation and entrepreneurship. In this case, human capital is considered as a function of these factors. The literature on the geography of talent suggests that market factors may also determine the extent to which a region may attract or retain human capital (Florida, 2002a). As a response, we add another explanatory variable — the natural logarithm of average wage — to reflect the market demand. Wage data are available from *China Labor Statistics Yearbook* (1999–2007). The average wage from 1998 to 2006 is converted into the 2000 constant value.

9.3. Findings

This section presents the regression results showing whether social diversity is significantly associated with innovative and entrepreneurial activity in China and what other factors may matter. The three measures of innovation and entrepreneurship as the dependent variable are discussed separately, followed by the exploration of geographic sources of human capital to see whether those variables of our interest have indirect impacts on innovation and entrepreneurship.

9.3.1. *High Technology*

Table 9.1 shows the regression results when the relative scale of high-tech value added is used as the dependent variable and a proxy for innovation. Diversity or openness across different models exhibits a positive relationship with high technology, yet significant only in the least reliable pooled-OLS model. R&D is positively and significantly associated with high

Table 9.1. Regression results (High-tech as the dependent variable)

Independent Variable	Pooled OLS (Stepwise)	First Difference (Stepwise)	Fixed Effects (FE)	Random Effects (RE)
Human capital	−0.235***		0.025	0.007
R&D	0.173**	0.854***	1.026***	0.487***
Service amenities	−0.024**		−0.006	−0.021***
Diversity	0.140***		0.004	0.004
University	7.945***		−2.465**	0.518
Urbanization			0.151***	0.058**
Provincial city (dummy)	0.021***			0.001
Number of observations	180	150	180	180
R²	0.506	0.078	0.449	0.394

*Significant at 0.1.
**Significant at 0.05.
***Significant at 0.01.

technology across all models. The urbanization rate presents a positive and significant association with high technology in both the FE and RE models. Human capital and service amenities exhibit no significant and positive effect on high technology when R&D and other factors are held constant. The role of the university in regional high technology agglomeration is unclear when the sign of its coefficient varies across different models.

9.3.2. Patents

Table 9.2 shows the regression results when the number of patents per 100,000 is used as the dependent variable and a proxy for innovation. The coefficient of diversity presents different signs and significance levels across models. The relationship between diversity and patenting therefore remains unclear based on our results. Coefficients of human capital and

Table 9.2.   Regression results (Patents as the dependent variable)

	Dependent Variable: Patents			
Independent Variable	Pooled OLS (Stepwise)	First Difference (Stepwise)	Fixed Effects (FE)	Random Effects (RE)
Human capital	68.974***		145.854***	97.844***
R&D			−43.135	−0.784
Service amenities		−10.721 **	−8.587**	−7.985**
Diversity	68.222***	−25.424***	0.393	15.057*
University	3074.304 ***		2109.553 ***	2985.945***
Urbanization			123.699***	15.516*
Provincial city (dummy)	5.568***	4.080***		4.419
Number of observations	240	210	240	240
R^2	0.717	0.123	0.496	0.399

*Significant at 0.1.
**Significant at 0.05.
***Significant at 0.01.

the university are consistently positive and significant in most models. Among other explanatory variables, the urbanization rate is positively associated with the patent count as well, although this relationship is significant only at the 0.10 level in the RE model. The coefficient of service amenities is consistently negative and significant in the FD, FE, and RE models, contrary to the findings in empirical analysis for developed countries (e.g., Shapiro, 2006).

9.3.3. New Firm Formation

Table 9.3 shows the regression results when the number of new firms per 100,000 employees is used as the dependent variable and a proxy for entrepreneurship or the commercialization side of innovation. To test the knowledge spillover theory of entrepreneurship, we add patents as an

Table 9.3. Regression results (New firm formation as the dependent variable)

	Dependent Variable: New Firm Formation			
Independent Variable	Pooled OLS (Stepwise)	First Difference (Stepwise)	Fixed Effects (FE)	Random Effects (RE)
Patents	5.566***	2.877***	6.053***	5.835***
Human capital	544.731***		334.319	412.571**
R&D	−910.115***		−556.205	−748.710***
Service amenities			23.616	17.471
Diversity		102.222***	100.216*	77.791
University	13442.46**		6197.618	6728.791
Urbanization			−70.213	6.688
Provincial city (dummy)	46.716***	19.641***		47.44**
Number of observations	210	180	210	210
R^2	0.853	0.448	0.744	0.742

*Significant at 0.1.
**Significant at 0.05.
***Significant at 0.01.

additional explanatory variable. Parameter estimations show that its coefficient is consistently positive and highly significant in all models, supporting the idea that entrepreneurs exploit the commercial value of patents by creating new firms. Diversity demonstrates a positive relationship with new firm formation in the FD, FE, and RE models, but insignificant in the RE model. Human capital and the university are positively associated with entrepreneurial activity but not significant in all models. In addition, firms are more likely to be created in those provincial municipalities as the coefficient of the dummy variable is positive and significant across all models.

9.3.4. Human Capital

According to previous results, human capital exhibits a positive and significant effect on innovation measured by the patent output and subsequently

Table 9.4.   Regression results (Human capital as the dependent variable)

	Dependent Variable: Human Capital			
Independent Variable	Pooled OLS (Stepwise)	First Difference (Stepwise)	Fixed Effects (FE)	Random Effects (RE) Effects (RE)
ln_wage	0.026***		0.035***	0 .034***
Service amenities	0.054***		0.010	0.022***
Diversity		−0.030*	0.010	0.012
University	7.866***		5.010***	5.208***
Urbanization	0.165***		0.055	0.144***
Provincial city (dummy)		0.007***		0.010
Number of observations	240	210	240	240
R^2	0.899	0.050	0.698	0.687

*Significant at 0.1.
**Significant at 0.05.
***Significant at 0.01.

contributes indirectly to entrepreneurial activity. Therefore, diversity and other geographically mediated factors, if associated with human capital, will have indirect impacts on innovation. According to Table 9.4, the sign of the estimated coefficient of diversity changes between the FD model and the FE/RE models. The wage level and the university are both positively associated with human capital and significantly in all but the FD models, suggesting their positive indirect effects on innovative and entrepreneurial activity. Service amenities, urbanization, and the dummy variable of being a municipality directly under the central government similarly exhibit positive associations with human capital, though not significant in some models.

9.4. Conclusion

There has been a growing concern over the effects of social or cultural diversity on innovation and economic growth in the developed world, especially in the U.S., a highly diversified country (Florida, 2002a; 2002b; Ottaviano and Peri, 2006; Mellander and Florida, 2007). This chapter investigates whether diversity contributes to innovation and entrepreneurship in China as it does in the U.S. China is not an ethnically diversified society to a certain extent. The *Han* ethnic group accounts for more than 90% of the total Chinese population. Neither is China a knowledge-based economy. Its R&D investments in the high-tech industries are far less than developed countries. It is however still interesting to see the relationship between diversity and innovation or entrepreneurship in China considering the diverse cultures across Chinese regions and tremendous efforts made by the Chinese government to build a "creative economy."

We use three measures of innovation and entrepreneurship — the high-tech value added relative to GDP, the patent count divided by population, and the number of new firms divided by employment — and the *Hukou* index as a proxy for diversity or openness. Our panel data analysis shows no consistent relationship between diversity and innovation or entrepreneurship. Regional innovation in China relies primarily on R&D (for high technology), human capital (for patents), and the university (for patents). Entrepreneurship is highly dependent on patents per capita in a region and is more likely to occur in the municipalities directly under the central government. The university together with the wage level is also indirectly associated with innovation and entrepreneurship through its effects on human capital.

The unclear relationship between diversity and innovation or entrepreneurship presented in our analysis might result from the way we measure diversity. The *Hukou* index, as the gay index, might be a reasonable proxy for openness but not necessarily for diversity. The latter requires a measure to reflect both the "richness" and "evenness" of diversity, such as the country of birth index used in Ottaviano and Peri (2006). Qian and Stough (2011) compare openness (the gay index) and diversity (the country of birth index) based on data of the U.S. regions, and find that it is diversity, not openness, that presents positive and significant effects on innovation. Moreover, a large proportion of those non-permanent residents without a local *Hukou* in China move to big cities actually for non-creative and low-paid jobs, therefore making limited contributions to innovation. Despite these disadvantages, the *Hukou* index reflects our best efforts to seek a measure for diversity given data availability in the context of China studies.

References

Ács, Z. J., L. Anselin and A. Varga (2002). Patents and innovation counts as measures of regional production of new knowledge. *Research Policy* **31**(7): 1069–1085.

Ács, Z. J., and C. Armington (2006). *Entrepreneurship, Geography, and American Economic Growth*. New York: Cambridge University Press.

Ács, Z. J., and D. B. Audretsch (1987). Innovation, market structure, and firm size. *Review of Economics and Statistics* **69**(4): 567–574.

Ács, Z. J., and D. B. Audretsch (1988). Innovation in large and small firms: An empirical analysis. *American Economic Review* **78**(4): 678–690.

Ács, Z. J., D. B. Audretsch and M. P. Feldman (1992). Real effects of academic research: Comment. *American Economic Review* **82**(1): 363–367.

Ács, Z. J., D. B. Audretsch and M. P. Feldman (1994). R&D spillovers and recipient firm size. *Review of Economics and Statistics* **76**(2): 336–340.

Ács, Z. J., F. R. FitzRoy and I. Smith (2002). High-technology employment and R&D in cities: Heterogeneity vs specialization. *Annals of Regional Science* **36**: 373–386.

Adams, J. D. (2001). Comparative localization of academic and industrial spillovers. NBER Working Paper 8292.

Anselin, L., A. Varga and Z. Ács (1997). Local geographic spillovers between university research and high technology innovations. *Journal of Urban Economics* **42**(3): 422–448.

Audretsch, D. B., and M. P. Feldman (1996). R&D spillovers and the geography of innovation and production. *American Economic Review* **86**(3): 630–640.

Audretsch, D. B., M. C. Keilbach and E. E. Lehmann (2006). *Entrepreneurship and Economic Growth*. New York: Oxford University Press.

Bartel, A. P., and F. R. Lichtenberg (1987). The comparative advantage of educated workers in implementing new technology. *Review of Economics and Statistics* **69**(1): 1–11.

Breschi, S. (2000). The geography of innovation: A cross-sector analysis. *Regional Studies* **34**(3): 213–229.

Cummings, J. N., and S. Kiesler (2005). Collaborative research across disciplinary and organizational boundaries. *Social Studies of Science* **35**(5): 703–722.

Feldman, M. P. (1994). *The Geography of Innovation*. Boston, MA: Kluwer Academic Publishers.

Feldman, M. P., and D. B. Audretsch (1999). Innovation in cities: Science-based diversity, specialization and localized competition. *European Economic Review* **43**(2): 409–429.

Feldman, M. P., and R. Florida (1994). The geographic sources of innovation: Technological infrastructure and product innovation in the United States. *Annals of the Association of American Geographers* **84**(2): 210–229.

Florida, R. (2002a). The economic geography of talent. *Annals of the Association of American Geographers* **92**(4): 743–755.

Florida, R. (2002b). *The Rise of Creative Class: And How It's Transforming Work, Leisure, and Everyday life*. New York: Basic Books.

Florida, R., and G. Gates (2001). *Technology and Tolerance: The Importance of Diversity to High-Tech Growth*. Washington, DC: Brookings Institution, Center for Urban and Regional Growth.

Florida, R., C. Mellander and K. Stolarick (2007). Inside the black box of regional development: Human capital, the creative class and tolerance. CESIS Electronic Working Paper Series Paper No. 88.

Glaeser, E. L. (1999). Learning in cities. *Journal of Urban Economics* **46**(2): 254–277.

Glaeser, E. L., H. D. Kallal, J. A. Scheinkman and A. Shleifer (1992). Growth in cities. *Journal of Political Economy* **100**(6): 1126–1152.

Glaeser, E. L., J. Kolko and A. Saiz (2001). Consumer city. *Journal of Economic Geography* **1**: 27–50.

Goldstein, H. A., and M. I. Luger (1990). Science/technology parks and regional development theory. *Economic Development Quarterly* **4**(1): 64–78.

Grilliches, Z. (1979). Issues in assessing the contribution of research and development to productivity growth. *Bell Journal of Economics* **10**(1): 92–116.

Hall, B. H., A. B. Jaffe and M. Trajtenberg (2001). The NBER patent citations data file: Lessons, insights and methodological tools. NBER Working Paper No. 8498.

Jacobs, J. (1969). *The Economy of Cities*. New York: Random House.

Jaffe, A. B. (1986). Technological opportunity and spillovers of R&D: Evidence from firms' patents, profits, and market value. *American Economic Review* **76**(5): 984–1001.

Jaffe, A. B. (1989). Real effects of academic research. *American Economic Review* **79**(5): 957–970.

Jaffe, A. B., M. Trajtenberg and R. Henderson (1993). Geographic localization of knowledge spillovers as evidenced by patent citations. *The Quarterly Journal of Economics* **108**(3): 577–598.

Kotkin, J. (2000). *The New Geography*. New York: Random House.

Malecki, E. (1981). Federal R&D spending in the United States of America: Some impacts on metropolitan economies. *Regional Studies* **16**(1): 19–35.

Mellander, C., and R. Florida (2007). The creative class or human capital? CESIS Electronic Working Paper Series No. 79.

Nelson, R. R., and S. G. Winter (1982). *An Evolutionary Theory of Economic Change*. Cambridge, MA: Harvard University Press.

Ottaviano, G. I. P., and G. Peri (2006). The economic value of cultural diversity: Evidence from US cities. *Journal of Economic Geography* **6**(1): 9–44.

Pakes, A., and Z. Griliches (1980). Patents and R&D at the firm level: A first report. *Economics Letters* **5**(4): 377–381.

Peri, G. (2005). Determinants of knowledge flows and their effect on innovation. *Review of Economics and Statistics* **87**(2): 308–322.

Porter, M. E. (1998). Clusters and new economics of competition. *Harvard Business Review* November–December: 77–90.

Qian, H. (2010). Talent, creativity and regional economic performance: The case of China. *Annals of Regional Science* **45**: 133–156.

Qian, H., and R. Stough (2011). The effects of social diversity on regional innovation: Measures and empirical evidence. *International Journal of Foresight and Innovation Policy* **7**: 142–157.

Romer, P. M. (1990). Endogenous technological change. *Journal of Political Economy* **98**(5): S71–S102.

Schmookler, J. (1966). *Invention and Economic Growth.* Cambridge, MA: Harvard University Press.

Schumpeter, J. A. (1934). *The Theory of Economic Development.* Oxford: Oxford University Press.

Shapiro, J. M. (2006). Smart cities: Quality of life, productivity, and the growth effects of human capital. *Review of Economics and Statistics* **88**(2): 324–335.

Smith, K. (2005). Measuring innovation, in J. Fagerberg, D. C. Mowery and R. R. Nelson (Eds.) *The Oxford Handbook of Innovation.* New York: Oxford University Press.

Solow, R. M. (1956). A contribution to the theory of economic growth. *The Quarterly Journal of Economics* **70**(1): 65–94.

Solow, R. M. (1957). Technical change and the aggregate production function. *Review of Economics and Statistics* **39**(3): 312–320.

Zucker, L. G., and M. R. Darby (1996). Star scientists and institutional transformation: Patterns of invention and innovation in the formation of the biotechnology - industry. *Proceedings of the National Academy of Sciences of the United States of America,* **93**(23): 12709–12716.

Chapter 10

The Evolution and Determinants of Private Sector Entrepreneurship in China

Shaoming Cheng
Florida International University

10.1. Introduction

The economic reform in the People's Republic of China (hereafter, China) since the late 1970s has attracted a huge influx of foreign investments and has resulted in a great number of foreign-affiliated companies. It is less known that during the same period, indigenous private firms have grown tremendously from literally non-existence before 1978 to over 6.2 million registered private businesses by the end of June 2008, with annual growth rate over 10% in 2000–2007 and over 19% in 2000–2005.[1] Much research has been done to examine the entrepreneurship development process in China and to identify unique characteristics that are different from other transitional economies (e.g., Anderson and Lee, 2008; Djankov *et al.*, 2006; McMillan and Woodruff, 2002; Tan, 1996; Yang, 2007; Yu and Stough, 2006). Nevertheless, existing studies typically attempted to explain the unique characteristics of Chinese entrepreneurship by focusing on a single set of variables, for example, institutions, culture or cultural values, or economic reform and policy changes. Such an approach, though

---

[1] *Xinhua News* on March 26, 2009. Available at: http://news.xinhuanet.com/english/2009-03/26/content_11075962.htm.

offering valuable insights, may not be adequate to recognize the interconnection between the external forces or their joint effects in China's entrepreneurship development. The purpose of this chapter, therefore, is to present the interdependence among policy, cultural, and institutional factors in the development of China's private sector entrepreneurship. It is also proposed in the chapter that a successful entrepreneur in China, at least theoretically, has to possess excellent business intelligence, cultural sense and political skills to navigate through and take advantage of the interdependence among unique policy, cultural, and institutional environments in China.

10.2. What is China's Private Sector Entrepreneurship?

Defining entrepreneurship is not an easy task primarily due to its elusive nature.[2] Joseph Schumpeter is one of the earliest and greatest theorists who intended to systematically examine entrepreneurs and their contribution to economic development. Schumpeter (1936) stressed that entrepreneurs are innovators who destroy existing market equilibrium and create business opportunities through a dynamic process of "creative destruction" by introducing "new combinations", i.e., new products or services, new markets, new means of production, or new forms of organizations. Schumpeterian entrepreneurship is a disruptive force in an economy and a major mechanism of wealth creation and economic development. Unlike Schumpeterian opportunity-creating entrepreneurs who disrupt existing market equilibrium, Kirzner (1973) argued that market equilibrium does not typically exist and entrepreneurs help move the economy toward equilibrium. Based on the economic thoughts of the Australian school regarding uncertainty (e.g., von Mises, 1959), Kirzner posits the idea of "entrepreneurial alertness" in which the entrepreneur discovers a profit opportunity that has been overlooked. Kirznerian entrepreneurial discovery theory, therefore, provides the micro-level cause of macro Schumpeterian entrepreneurship-driven economic development (Hebert and Link, 1988; Kirzner, 1999). Entrepreneurship in both Schumpeterian

---

[2] For economic history and various definitions of entrepreneurship, please refer to Hebert and Link (1988).

creative destruction and Kirznerian entrepreneurial discovery is treated as a mechanism and a process, and entrepreneurs hence are simply the bearers and executors of the mechanism and the process.

In this chapter, private sector entrepreneurship in China is defined as the process that occurs and causes changes in the private sector economy in which entrepreneurial individuals have played critical roles in privatized existing firms and newly created businesses in response to economic opportunities. The private sector is defined as non-state sector (*feigongyou jingji*) referring to "all production units that are not fully owned or fully controlled by the state" (Li, 2006; p. 128). This is a rather imprecise definition, but is able to reflect and capture intentionally ambiguous ownership arrangements in many private and quasi-collective enterprises, increasingly blurred distinctions between state-owned, collective, and private businesses, and growing privatization, both formal and informal, in China. Specifically, the private sector in this chapter consists of all firms that are not exclusively owned by the state: township and village enterprises, urban collective enterprises, individual household enterprises (*getihu*, with no more than seven employees), privately owned enterprises (*siying qiye*, with eight or more employees), spinoffs of state-owned enterprises, and public companies transformed from former state-owned enterprises. Walder (2006) contended that focusing on emerging non-state or private economy in China can reflect China's private sector entrepreneurship and new business creation because China's private economy, unlike that of former Soviet Union through rapid and large-scale privatization, has grown gradually from bottom up and through numerous initially small start-ups or spinoffs of state-owned enterprises.

Previous literature, nevertheless, attempted to characterize Chinese entrepreneurs based on individual traits or on their organizational forms. In a series of pilot yet extensive surveys in five developing and transition countries, namely, Brazil, China, India, Nigeria, and Russia, Djankov *et al.* (2006) intended to identify individual characteristics of Chinese entrepreneurs and non-entrepreneurs and compare entrepreneurs' characteristics across the five nations. They concluded that Chinese entrepreneurs are more risk-taking and are more likely to have family members or childhood friends who became entrepreneurs than their non-entrepreneur counterparts. Chen *et al.* (2006), through five national surveys in 1993, 1997, 2000, 2002, and 2004, concluded that Chinese private entrepreneurs have become more educated and better-connected in social, economic, and political networks. Hsu (2006) defined Chinese entrepreneurs based on three legal categories, including (1) *de facto* owners or partners of privatized collective and state-owned firms (*chengbao*); (2) petty capitalists (*getihu*) who own small businesses with less than seven non-family-member employees; and (3) owners of private businesses that have more than seven employees (*siying qiye*). Tsang (1996) focused exclusively on private businesses (*siying qiye*), justified by their expected greater roles in employment and economic growth compared to individual household businesses (*getihu*).

Both of the two previous approaches are limited because they may underestimate, if not significantly, the size and extent of China's private economy and entrepreneurship and therefore their impacts on China's economic development. One of the conceptual challenges to the individual-trait approach is that entrepreneurs often wear different "hats" from venture capitalists, to managers, and even to bookkeepers and accountants, so it would be difficult to identify and distinguish entrepreneurs from others. Furthermore, China's entrepreneurs tend to disguise themselves and/or their businesses due to China's previous political suppression of capitalism and private businesses, only recently established legitimacy of private businesses, and potential current political and economic gains. Concealment, as one of the most commonly used strategies, is adopted by entrepreneurs to cover up private businesses' ownership by registering them as collective or pseudo-collective enterprises (Lin and Zhang, 1989; Tsai, 2005). Bian and Zhang (2006) elaborated that some private firms hide their real status by "attaching" (*guakao*) themselves to state-owned businesses while others are registered as collective businesses to avoid discrimination or to gain privileges or protection from local governments. Zhang (1999) estimated that in 1995 registered private businesses accounted only for one third of private enterprises in China while the other two thirds were "forged collective enterprises" (p. 15). In addition, approaches based on individual traits and forms of businesses may not adequately reflect the roles and impacts of entrepreneurs in China's privatization of state-owned enterprises. Informal privatization since the 1990s through leasing or contracting out state-owned enterprises often to managers has created gray ownership, a mix of public and private ownership, and entrepreneurs inside the state and public sector (Lin, 2001; Young, 1995, 1998).

10.3. Policy Factors

China's private sector and entrepreneurship have undergone a difficult history from being prohibited prior to 1979 to strong growth nowadays. The history of China's private sector entrepreneurship can be divided into prohibition, accommodation, and encouragement. Private sector or entrepreneurs had been a political taboo in China since the late 1950s until the late 1970s and there was almost no individual or private business during this period (Guiheux, 2006; Peng, 2004). Liao and Sohmen (2001) however suggested that entrepreneurship was never completely suppressed but existed in forms of underground economy. Lu (1994) maintained that such black-market businesses or entrepreneurship may be unproductive to the economy due to their rent-seeking nature and behaviors, in line with Baumol's (1990) classification of productive and unproductive entrepreneurship.

In 1978, the Third Plenary Session of the Eleventh Central Committee of the Chinese Communist Party (CCP) marked the beginning of the official accommodation of private businesses. It for the first time since 1949 recognized private businesses' and private sector's positive role, despite marginal, in China's economic modernization and growth. The private sector, however, was regarded as a supplement to the mostly state-owned economy to "fill in the gaps" in the distribution of consumer goods and services (Tsang, 1996) and to provide employment opportunities to a huge number of urban unemployed resulting from the Cultural Revolution, such as urban-educated youth who were sent to the countryside (Malik, 1997). Individual household businesses (*getihu*), which by law were limited to hire no more than seven employees, were the dominant legal form of privately owned firms. The legal definition of household businesses itself, however, reflected widespread ideological prejudice and political bias against private businesses, despite their potential roles in addressing pragmatic concerns of economic stability and employment. Socialist ideology and doctrine had to be reinterpreted carefully and prudently to accommodate the development of private sector economy and entrepreneurs. Li (2006) suggested the "no more than seven employees" requirement was determined based on anecdotal evidence in Marxist doctrine that hiring fewer than eight non-family members does not constitute exploitation. Even with the reinterpretation, individual household businesses were often considered for and associated with individuals who had limited options in finding jobs, such as school drop-offs and people with criminal records (Anderson and Lee, 2008; Kshetri, 2007). Not until 1988 were private businesses and entrepreneurs constitutionally legitimate when the constitution was revised in March 1988. In June 1998, the *Tentative Stipulations on Private Enterprises* (TSPE) was issued by the State Council. TSPE lifted up many restrictions for private businesses and provided legal basis for private ownership. According to TSPE, a privately owned firm hiring more than eight employees was regarded as a private enterprise (*siying qiye*) in contrast to household businesses (*getihu*), and the private economy hence complements (*buchong*) socialist state-owned economic system.

The development of China's private sector has boomed since Deng Xiaoping's "Southern Tour" in 1992. Private enterprises have become an important and rapidly growing element of China's "socialist market economy" in contrast to being merely complementary to the state-owned economy in the 1980s (Guiheux, 2006). Entrepreneurs, most of them were business founders and managers, have stepped up in the economic and political arenas and played increasingly significant roles in economic and political policy making. During the eightieth anniversary of the CCP on July 1, 2001, former President Jiang Zemin officially called for all qualified private entrepreneurs and other individuals, independent of their social class or status, to join and be admitted to the CCP. His speech, certainly controversial in terms of socialist doctrines, signified the legitimacy of the private sector and entrepreneurs in China mainly as a result of the rapid growth of China's non-state-owned and private economy. As of

2005, China had 24 million small and medium independent businesses which accounted for 75% of new jobs (Kshetri, 2007). Entrepreneurs have also become a viable and even desirable career choice (Moy *et al.*, 2003). Chen *et al.* (2006) indicated that Chinese private sector entrepreneurs, previously mainly from working class, have increasingly emerged in higher social classes and consisted of members who have greater access to political, social, and economic resources. Chen *et al.* further added that individuals have been motivated to become entrepreneurs primarily by their aspirations for personal achievements and/or wealth instead of by necessity in earlier years due to unemployment and job insecurity.

10.4. Cultural Factors

The traditional Chinese culture encompasses diverse, sometimes contrasting and even competing schools of thought, e.g., Buddhism, Confucianism, and Taoism. Confucianism, however, is unarguably the most influential school and provides foundations of the Chinese cultural traditions, Confucianism also provides moral, social, and behavioral norms of all individuals, which govern every aspect of human interactions and social relationships in society. While Confucianism was blamed for economic backwardness and lack of entrepreneurship in China (e.g., Weber, 1905), the success of overseas Chinese family businesses and rapid economic growth in China have brought Confucianism back into cultural explanations of economic success (e.g., Hofstede and Bond, 1988). Confucianism has understandably been praised for China's remarkable economic achievement (Fukuyama, 1995; Redding, 1990). Unique perspectives of oriental cultural values are provided in the Chinese Values Study (CVS) of 22 countries, which developed four factors: integration (social stability), Confucian dynamism, human heartedness, and moral discipline (Hofstede and Bond, 1988). In comparison with Hofstede's (1980) four dimensions of culture, Hofstede and Bond suggested that three of the factors identified in CVS, namely, moral discipline, integration, and human heartedness, are aligned with the power distance, individualism and masculinity dimensions. The non-matching CVS dimension (Confucian dynamism) was subsequently incorporated into the Hofstede instrument and referred to as "long-term orientation" (Hofstede, 1991). High Confucian dynamism characterizes individuals who tend to be more future oriented (persistence, status-ordered relationships, thrift, and a sense of shame), while low Confucian dynamism characterizes individuals who tend to be more past and present oriented (steadiness and stability; protection of face; respect for tradition, and reciprocation of greeting, favors and gifts). Confucianism has been widely regarded as a critical contributing factor for the rapid growth of private sector and entrepreneurship (Cheng and Rosett, 1991; Redding, 1990; Yu and Stough, 2006). Chinese traditional culture and inherent culturally prescribed aspirations fuel entrepreneurial activities and lead to the flourish of private entrepreneurship in China.

In contrast to the growing consensus that Confucian values promote entrepreneurship and small business development, Kirby and Fan (1995) compared 59 Chinese cultural values and over 90 individual entrepreneurial attributes and concluded that Confucian values basically tend not to support entrepreneurship, though some important entrepreneurial elements and attributes are aligned with or even embedded within the Chinese cultural values. Kirby and Fan maintained that Confucianism depreciates merchants because the ideal man in Confucian teaching is not a successful merchant or entrepreneur but a scholar bureaucrat or a wise emperor who is able to effectively govern a state. It is further suggested that the key value in Confucianism is harmony on order and Schumpeterian entrepreneurship would be disruptive to existing harmonious balance, be treated as a threat to social and interpersonal harmony, and be suppressed or at least discouraged (Kirby and Fan, 1995; Timmons *et al.*, 1997). Holt (1997) found that there are common entrepreneurial characteristics across cultures, specifically, the acceptance of uncertainty did not differ significantly between Chinese and U.S. entrepreneurs. He concluded that it may be private businesses rather than particular cultures that either foster such entrepreneurial characteristics or attract individuals who possess those attributes.

Away from discussions on Chinese cultural values in general, studies also focused on a particular cultural artifact, *guanxi*, and its effects on Chinese entrepreneurship and private sector. *Guanxi* is a network of personal relationships emerging from the fundamentals of Chinese culture, traditions and social organization (Anderson and Lee, 2008). Cheng and Rosett (1991) contended that cultural and family values as well as *guanxi* connections shape business culture and practices in China. Tsang (1999) suggested that *guanxi* networks processed by an organization and/or its members are part of the organization's human capital and concluded that a well-connected *guanxi* network is the necessary condition, but not sufficient, condition for successful private businesses in China. Carlisle and Flynn (2005) maintained that *guanxi* allows entrepreneurs to build up social capital and reduce transaction costs. Licht and Siegel (2006) suggested that entrepreneurs may partially overcome institutional deficiencies by depending on social networks, and Ahlstrom and Bruton (2001) indicated that *guanxi* is an important tool that firms need to navigate uncertain and fast changing Chinese institutional environment. The critical role of *guanxi* and relationship networks has given rise of networked entrepreneurship (Li and Matlay, 2006) and entrepreneurship by alliance (Krug and Mehta, 2004), both of which emphasized *guanxi* when formal property rights laws were ineffective and market institution remained relatively underdeveloped in China.

10.5. Institutional Factors

Entrepreneurial discovery and innovative processes are constrained by formal and informal institutions, rules and norms. Institutions provide guidance, allow for routines to develop and ultimately reduce the uncertainty of social interaction (North, 1990). Entrepreneurs particularly those in a transitional and emerging market economy, however, are destroyers of old and inefficient institutions and pioneers of new institutions, in addition to their more traditional roles in the Schumpeterian "creative destruction" process in the marketplace. In an emerging market economy, such as China, entrepreneurs often have to face more challenges and therefore be more versatile, compared to their counterparts in more mature market economies, in navigating in an imperfect market environment and at the same time in a restrictive and even hostile institutional setting. Unlike organized groups being crucial in pressuring or lobbying for institutional changes in more mature market economies (Davis and North, 1961), entrepreneurs have played a significant role in advocating, pushing, and leading institutional changes in transitional economies. Such entrepreneurs are referred to as institutional entrepreneurs in contrast to their counterparts in a more traditional sense (Li *et al.*, 2006; Yang, 2004, 2007).

China's entrepreneurship and private sector emerged from a hostile institutional environment characterized with socialist and ideological prejudice against private businesses. Peng (2000) characterized China's institutional environment as a combination of socialist legacy, dense culture and transitional economy. Built upon Oliver's (1991), Tsang (1996) explained four strategic responses of private enterprises, namely concealment, co-optation, influence, and escape in China's unique institutional environment and transition where their legitimacy is doubtful. Tsang maintained that the first two tactics, concealment and co-optation, are more likely to be used compared to the latter two strategies, in part due to their relative success. As one of the most commonly used strategies, concealment is adopted to cover up the private businesses' private identify by registering them as collective or pseudo-collective enterprises (Tsai, 2005). Tsang further explained that the registration of pseudo-collectives has to be done generally in agreement with local authorities and in exchange for management fees to the local authorities. In addition to cover-ups, private businesses may have to apply "co-optation" strategy to seek political protection and favors from local authorities and neutralize institutional opposition (Tsang, 1996). Private entrepreneurs have to cultivate *guanxi*, or even bribe officials, to maintain close connections with local governments and officials. The close tie and even collusion with local governments and authorities are characterized as entrepreneurship by alliance (Krug and Mehta, 2004) or networked entrepreneurship (Li and Matlay, 2006), both of which emphasize using Chinese culture, values, and social networks to complement if not substitute for institutions if they are underdeveloped or impeded.

Even though China's institutional transition and environment may inhibit the development of Chinese private entrepreneurship and small businesses, it may, at the same time, create unique opportunities for entrepreneurs. Yang (2004, 2007) introduced the concept of "institutional holes" in connection with Burt's (1995) "structural holes," and institutional holes represent institutional, regulatory, and organizational gaps where rules are often incomplete, ambiguous and subject to provisional interpretations and negotiations that may vary case by case. Yang proposed that institutional holes themselves represent entrepreneurship and profit opportunities, and identification and exploration of such opportunities are essentially entrepreneurial activities. Entrepreneurship or entrepreneurial activities, consequently, can grow out of an adverse institutional environment and can be enhanced by the inherent ambiguity and inconsistency around the institutional holes. Yang further added that it is risky, though equally rewarding, to maneuver around institutional holes and boundaries, which may change or reshape constantly due to revision, reinterpretation, and multiplication to the rules. Political connections with and protections from local authorities become critical for Chinese entrepreneurs to minimize political and administrative risks when they cross the line intentionally or unintentionally, and at the same time maximize profits, resulting from manipulation of incompleteness, ambiguity, and inconsistency of the institutional environment. Yang concluded that China's institutional environment in its transition is full of both rewards and penalties, and Chinese entrepreneurs attempt to achieve "dual entrepreneurship" of profitability and legitimacy simultaneously by exploiting institutional holes and by nurturing alliance with and seeking political protection from local authorities. The "institutional holes" approach, however, implies a short-term orientation in business operation of Chinese entrepreneurs, who strategically maneuver around and push institutional boundaries to explore and exploit profit opportunities. This is because the institutional holes tend to be fixed or expected to be fixed fairly quickly, and it would be difficult or unwise to establish long- or longer-term business operation and goals around such soon-will-disappear opportunities. Furthermore, a short-term orientation may also reduce the chances of "being caught" and reduce political risk, even though alliance with political authorities may have been established. The "institutional holes" approach also implies that when institutional holes become less available as China's institutional environment transition progresses, the alliance between entrepreneurs and local authorities may loosen up due to the needs for political protection may decline.

Different from the institutional arbitrator role of private sector entrepreneurs in Yang's (2004, 2007) "institutional holes" and "dual entrepreneurship" approaches, entrepreneurs can also sever as institutional advocators who help destroy institutional barriers and establish market institutions in the process of their business activities (Li *et al.*, 2006). Li *et al.* further explained that entrepreneurs generate externalities, which may result in or at least are conducive to institutional changes, through their entrepreneurial and profit-driven activities within their firms. Entrepreneurs represent grassroots forces who actively advocate, push and pursue institutional changes out of their own profit maximization self-interests (Ahlstrom *et al.*, 2008). Despite the sharp contract to the view of institutional entrepreneurs as rent-seekers who manipulate institutions, both types of institutional entrepreneurs need to possess "political nimbleness" and "interpersonal harmony" to be successful, in addition to profit opportunity alertness (Liao and Sohmen, 2001). Li and Matlay (2006) suggested that both "political nimbleness" and "interpersonal harmony" can be enhanced by a well-connected *guanxi* network in China, i.e., networked entrepreneurship.

10.6. Conclusions and Discussions

China's private sector has grown tremendously, from initial political opposition, to selective accommodation, and to enthusiastic encouragement. This chapter presents a theoretical account of both policy evolution and cultural and institutional determinants of China's private sector entrepreneurship. Like any transitional country, particularly those from centrally planning economies, China's entrepreneurs and their entrepreneurial activities are constrained by socialist legacy and underdeveloped market institutions. Unlike other transitional economies, Chinese culture and especially *guanxi* networks enable entrepreneurs to either as pioneers or champions advocate and persuade institutional changes or as rent-seekers or arbitrators to manipulate and take advantage of incomplete or ambiguous institutions. It is therefore concluded that the policy, cultural, and institutional factors are interdependent and they combined together have shaped the development and future direction of China's private sector entrepreneurship. It is also suggested that China's private sector entrepreneurs must possess skills beyond those of traditional entrepreneurs in more developed market-oriented economies. They have to be institutional arbitrators, economic exploiters, and cultural practitioners to maximize economic profits and at the same time minimize political or institutional risks.

References

Ahlstrom, D., and G. Bruton (2001). Learning from successful local private firms in China: Establishing legitimacy. *Academy of Management Executive* **15**(4): 72–83.

Ahlstrom, D. *et al.* (2008). Private firms in China: Building legitimacy in an emerging economy. *Journal of World Business* **43**: 385–399.

Anderson, A., and E. Lee (2008). From tradition to modern: Attitudes and applications of guanxi in Chinese entrepreneurship. *Journal of Small Business and Enterprise Development* **15**(4): 775–787.

Baumol, W. (1990). Entrepreneurship: Productive, unproductive, and destructive. *Journal of Political Economy,* **98**(5): 893–921.

Bian, Y., and Z. Zhang (2006). Explaining China's emerging private economy, in A. Tsui, Y. Bian, and L. Cheng (Eds.) *China's Domestic Private Firms.* Armonk, NY: M.E. Sharpe, pp. 25–39.

Burt, R. (1995). *Structural Holes: The Social Structure of Competition.* Cambridge, MA: Harvard University Press.

Carlisle, E., and D. Flynn (2005). Small business survival in China: Guanxi, legitimacy, and social capital. *Journal of Developmental Entrepreneurship* **10**(1): 79–96.

Chen, J. (2006). Development of Chinese small and medium-sized enterprises. *Journal of Small Business and Enterprise Development,* **13**(2): 140–147.

Chen, G. *et al.* (2006). Who are the Chinese private entrepreneurs? A study of entrepreneurial attributes and business governance. *Journal of Small Business and Enterprise Development* **13**(2): 148–160.

Cheng, L., and A. Rosett (1991). Contract with a Chinese face: Socially embedded factors in the transformation from hierarchy to market 1978–1989. *Journal of Chinese Law* **5**: 143–244.

Davis, L., and D. North (1971). *Institutional Change and American Economic Growth.* Cambridge, MA: Cambridge University Press.

Djankov, S. *et al.* (2006). Entrepreneurship in China and Russia compared. *Journal of the European Economic Association* **4**(2–3): 352–365.

Fukuyama, F. (1995). *Trust: The Social Virtues and the Creation of Prosperity.* London: Penguin.

Guiheux, G. (2006). The political "participation" of entrepreneurs: Challenge or opportunity for the Chinese communist party? *Social Research* **73**(1): 219–246.

Hebert, R., and A. Link (1988). *The Entrepreneur: Mainstream Views and Radical Critiques.* New York: Praeger.

Hofstede, G. (1980). *Culture's Consequences: International Differences in Work Related Values.* Beverly Hill, CA: Sage.

Hofstede, G. (1991). *Culture and Organisations.* New York: McGraw-Hill.

Hofstede, G., and M. H. Bond (1988). The Confucius connection: From cultural roots to economic growth. *Organizational Dynamics* 16(4): 5–21.

Holt, D. (1997). A comparative study of values among Chinese and U.S. entrepreneurs: Pragmatic convergence between contrasting cultures. *Journal of Business Venturing* 12: 483–505.

Hsu, C. (2006). Cadres, getihu, and good businesspeople: Making sense of entrepreneurs in early post-socialist China. *Urban Anthropology*, 35(1): 1–38.

Kirby, D., and Y. Fan (1995). Chinese cultural values and entrepreneurship: A preliminary consideration. *Journal of Enterprising Culture* 3(3): 245–260.

Kirzner, I. (1973). *Competition and Entrepreneurship*. Chicago: University of Chicago Press.

Kirzner, I. (1999). Creativity and/or alertness: A reconsideration of the Schumpeterian entrepreneur. *Review of Austrian Economics* 11: 5–17.

Krug, B., and J. Mehta (2004). Entrepreneurship by Alliance, in B. Krug (Ed.) *China's Rational Entrepreneurs: The Development of the New Private Business Sector*. New York: Routledge Curzon, pp. 50–71.

Kshetri, N. (2007). Institutional changes affecting entrepreneurship in China. *Journal of Developmental Entrepreneurship* 12(4): 415–432.

Li, D. (2006). A survey of the Economics Literature on China's Nonstate Enterprises. In A. Tsui, Y. Bian and L. Cheng (Eds.) *China's Domestic Private Firms*. Armonk, NY: M.E. Sharpe, pp. 128–146.

Li, D. *et al.* (2006). Institutional entrepreneurs. *American Economic Review* 96(2): 358–362.

Li, J., and H. Matlay (2006). Chinese entrepreneurship and small business development: An overview and research agenda. *Journal of Small Business and Enterprise Development* 13(2): 248–262.

Liao, D., and P. Sohmen (2001). The development of modern entrepreneurship in China. *Stanford Journal of East Asian Affairs* 1: 27–33.

Licht, A., and J. Siegel (2006). The Social Dimensions of Entrepreneurship. In N. Wadeson, B. Yeung, and A. Basu (Eds.) *The Oxford Handbook of Entrepreneurship*. New York: Oxford University Press, pp. 511–540.

Lin, Y. (2001). *Between Politics and Markets: Firms, Competition, and Institutional Change in Post-Mao China*. New York: Cambridge University Press.

Lin, Y., and Z. Zhang (1989). Backyard profit centers: The private assets of public agencies, in J. Oi and A. Walder (Eds.) *Property Rights and Economic Reform in China*. Stanford, CA: Stanford University Press, pp. 203–225.

Lu, D. (1994). *Entrepreneurship in Suppressed Markets*. New York: Garland Publishers.

Malik, R. (1997). *Chinese Entrepreneurs in the Economic Development of China*. Westport, CT: Praeger.

McMillan, J., and C. Woodruff (2002). The central role of entrepreneurs in transition economies. *Journal of Economic Perspectives* 16(3): 153–170.

Moy, J. *et al.* (2003). Perceptions of entrepreneurship as a career: Views of young people in Hong Kong. *Equal Opportunities International* 22(4): 16–40.

North, D. (1990). *Institutions, Institutional Change and Economic Performance*. Cambridge, MA: Cambridge University Press.

Oliver, C. (1991). Strategic responses to institutional processes. *Academy of Management Review* **16**(1): 145–179.

Peng, Y. (2004). Kinship networks and entrepreneurs in China's transitional economy. *American Journal of Sociology* **109**(5): 1045–1074.

Redding, G. (1990). *The Spirit of Chinese Capitalism*. Berlin: Walter de Gruyter.

Schumpeter, J. A. (1936). *The Theory of Economic Development: An Inquiry into Profits, Capital, Credit and the Business Cycle*. Cambridge, MA: Harvard University Press.

Tan, J. (1996). Regulatory environment and strategic orientations in a transitional economy. *Entrepreneurship: Theory and Practice* **21**: 31–46.

Timmons, J., L. Smollen and A. Dingee (1997). *New Venture Creation*. Homewood, IL: Irwin Publishing.

Tsai, K. (2005). Capitalists without a class: Political diversity among private entrepreneurs in China. *Comparative Political Studies* **38**(9): 1130–1158.

Tsang, W. (1996). In search of legitimacy: The private entrepreneur in China. *Entrepreneurship: Theory and Practice* **21**(1): 21–30.

Tsang, W. (1999). Can guanxi be a source of sustained competitive advantage for doing business in China? *Academy of Management Executive* **12**(2): 64–73.

Von Mises, L. (1959), *Human Action*. London: William Hodge.

Walder, A. (2006). China's Private Sector. In A. Tsui, Y. Bian, and L. Cheng (Eds.), *China's Domestic Private Firms*. Armonk, NY: M.E. Sharpe, pp. 311–326.

Yang, K. (2004). Institutional holes and entrepreneurship in China. *Sociological Review* **52**(3): 371–389.

Yang, K. (2007). *Entrepreneurship in China*. Burlington, VT: Ashgate.

Young, S. (1995). *Private Business and Economic Reform in China*. Armonk, NY: M.E. Sharpe.

Young, S. (1998). The Chinese private sectors in two decades of reform. *Journal of the Asia Pacific Economy* **31**: 80–103.

Yu, J., and R. Stough (2006). The determinants of entrepreneurship development in China. *International Journal of Management and Enterprise Development* **3**(1–2): 30–52.

Zhang, H. (1999). The rising of another bloc. In H. Zhang and L. Ming (Eds.) *Report on the Development of Chinese Private Enterprises*. Beijing: Shehui Kexue Wenxian Chubanshe, pp. 3–59.

Chapter 11

Culture Matters to Entrepreneurship Policies: Entrepreneurship Policies in the U.S. versus China

Ting Zhang

University of Baltimore

11.1. Introduction

Culture is defined as a shared public context (Geertz, 1973), or community-specific ideas about truth, goodness, beauty, efficiency, etc. (Shweder, 2000). As culture is community-specific values, the Chinese and the U.S. societies have many different cultural perspectives. Culture is shared: within a community, people share values and behavior. Although individuals have diverse values, behavior, and attitudes, the concept of "culture" captures the common characteristics shared by the individuals within a context. On one hand, culture is not constant, but changes (Inglehart, 1988); on the other hand, cultural differences persist (Kelly *et al.*, 1987).

Over the past decades, Chinese culture has changed with socio-economic changes, but the traditional Chinese culture elements still play an important role. This chapter compares the culture differences between China and the U.S. and argues that those differences result in and also require differences in entrepreneurship policies between the two countries. After introducing the concept of entrepreneurship and entrepreneurship policy, this chapter first compares the key cultural differences between China and the U.S. Then, this chapter analyzes the cultural impact on entrepreneurship policy differences in the two countries.

11.2. The Concept of Entrepreneurship and Entrepreneurship Policy

Although classical theorists Marshall (1930), Say (1845), Schumpeter (1961), Cantillon (1755), and Kirzner (1973) interpreted entrepreneurship in various ways, they basically agreed on the following aspects of the notion of entrepreneurship: innovation by exploring new technological possibilities, initiative taking, organizing, and reorganizing social and economic mechanisms, and somewhat risk bearing.

Since entrepreneurship is generally considered as a positive social capital catalyzing economic development, many analysts, such as Hart (2003), argue that entrepreneurship ought to be an explicit focus of policy design. Thus, entrepreneurship policy can be defined as the policy enhancing entrepreneurship and thus developing the economy in a society.

Entrepreneurship policy is an important source to foster entrepreneurship. At the individual level, individual psychology, including needs to achieve (McClelland, 1961), willingness to bear risk, desire for independence (Hagen, 1962), and job dissatisfaction (Lordkipanidze, 2002) all contribute to the supply of entrepreneurship. The environmental forces (or entrepreneurial milieu elements, shown in Figure 11.1) come from

(i) the private sector;
(ii) social aspects, including entrepreneurial culture; and
(iii) the public sector, such as macro policies, business policies, and public safety (Rural Development Council, 2001).

The entrepreneurship policy, as part of the public sector efforts, includes business policies, public policies, and macropolicies to enhance entrepreneurship.

A Global Entrepreneurship Monitor (GEM) survey found out that both the U.S. and China were among the countries with top scores for the effectives of their entrepreneurship policies and the scores for these two countries are very close (Fitzsimons, 2004). In total, 1,300 key informants, the

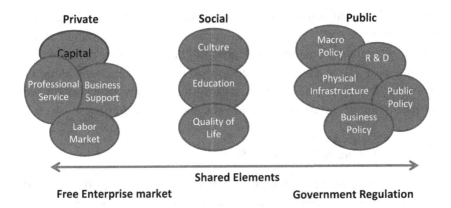

Figure 11.1.   Entrepreneurial milieu elements.

Source: Rural Development Council, 2001.

participating national experts, and entrepreneurs were asked for their opinions as to whether government policies and programs that aimed at supporting new and growing firms in their countries were effective. The responses used a five-point scale: *1:Completely False, 2: Somewhat False, 3: Neither True nor False, 4: Somewhat True, 5:Completely True.* The U.S. scored 3.36 and China scored 3.15 (Fitzsimons, 2004). However, due to different cultures, there exist huge differences in the entrepreneurship policies of the two countries.

11.3. Chinese Culture and the U.S. Culture

With different histories, Chinese and the U.S. culture differ in many dimensions. Chinese culture is rooted in the teachings of Confucius (Hofstede and Bond, 1988) and further shaped by the communist doctrine and socialistic socio-economic and political system (Lan, 1987). This background determines the core of collectiveness and social harmony in Chinese culture. Different from China, with a capitalistic business environment that evolved out of the English legal and political systems, the U.S. culture is characterized as being individualistic (Tan, 2002). China and the U.S. represent ideological opposites along the cultural spectrum, in spite of the current move towards capitalism in China (Tse *et al.*, 1994;

Dunne, 1995). This section briefly compares the two cultures in terms of the following aspects: collectiveness, power distance, uncertainty avoidance, and high/low context. Of course, neither of the two cultures is an extreme case. They are just located toward different directions along the power distance spectrum. Globalization further fusions the world cultures together, though certain culture elements and tendencies persist.

11.3.1. *Individualistic versus Collective*

According to Hofstede (1994), Chinese culture differs from the U.S. culture in terms of collectiveness and individualism. China has a typical collective culture, whereas the U.S. is classified with a typical individualistic culture. In China, people tend to focus on the collective group interest, social members try to be consistent with the mainstream value and behavior, and emphasizing too much of individual needs is not preferable. The collectiveness, on one hand, maintains social harmony, and on the other hand approaches social uniformity and thus kills differences. In contrary to the situation in China, the U.S. culture emphasizes individual achievements and rights. Individualistic culture results in pluralism but also in a certain level of social chaos.

11.3.2. *Power Distance*

Hofstede (1994) defines power distance as the extent to which less powerful parties expect and accept the inequity of power distribution. For the relationship between the government and people, power distance describes the extent to which people accept their subordinate positions to the government. According to this definition, China can be classified as a culture with a high power distance. In China, people accept and welcome legitimate authority and seldom express their disagreements against the authority that could be the government or bosses in a firm. The relationship in such institutions tends to be unequal and hierarchical.

Compared to Chinese culture, the U.S. tends to be classified with a low power distance, where the bosses and the subordinates tend to be more equal and independent. With a low power distance, people work closely and may consult each other, everyone tends to have a voice, and equality and pluralism tend to be emphasized.

11.3.3. Uncertainty Avoidance

Uncertainty avoidance relates to the extent to which societies tolerate ambiguity (Hofstede, 2001). A culture is characterized by high uncertainty avoidance when its members feel threatened by uncertain or unknown situations. People in a culture with high uncertainty avoidance tend to make events clearly predictable and thus have less leeway for negotiation; people in a culture with low uncertainty avoidance tend to have more opportunity to negotiate, but also face more uncertainties and ventures (Hofstede, 2001). China's high power distance on the one hand relates to high uncertainty avoidance, while in the U.S., it is almost the opposite. With absolute authority in a society, there is less opportunity for an individual to express disagreements in China. However, the U.S. also has aspects related to high uncertainty avoidance especially in its legal system. With various detailed Rule of Laws, people have less flexibility to negotiate beyond the law, though negotiation is possible almost everywhere in the pluralistic U.S. society, even in the court.

11.3.4. High Context versus Low Context

Hall (1981) describe a high-context culture as situations where most of the communication is either in the physical context or internalized in the person, and very little is in the coded, explicit, or transmitted part of the message. Accordingly, a low-context culture is the opposite. China is classified as a high-context culture while the U.S. is basically a low-context culture. People raised in high-context systems tend to expect more of others than the participants in low-context systems (Hall, 1981: p. 113). China, as a collective culture with a high degree of social harmony, has intensive group interactions with much shared knowledge; the Chinese generally tend to communicate less directly and less explicitly with each other, compared to Americans. With much shared information and high expectation among social members for obtained information, the Chinese communication tends to be more ambiguous, abstract, imprecise, and symbolic. Compared with China, in the U.S., a typical immigrant country with a big demographic diversity, it is more difficult for people to program information before real communication and thus, this kind of communication need to be more direct, explicit, precise, and specific. In comparison to high-context cultures, the low-context U.S. culture tends to offer as much information as they could during communication.

11.3.5. *Culture Matters*

Culture matters to almost every corner of people's life. Harrison and Huntington (2000) suggest that culture matters in social economic societies and culture influences social and economic development, including policy formation. Stevenson and Lundström (2001) further indicate that entrepreneurship policies are influenced by the social and economic context, including history, culture, industrial structure, the current state of entrepreneurial activity, etc. Culture is an important force to shape entrepreneurship policy.

11.4. Entrepreneurship Policy and Culture

Culture matters to each socio-economic activity, including those related to entrepreneurship policies. The differences in the U.S. and Chinese cultures therefore are associated with differences related to entrepreneurship policies. This section analyzes the cultural impact on entrepreneurship policies in terms of public–private relationship, leadership and authority, Rule of Laws, and the size of businesses.

11.4.1. *Relationship between government and businesses*

First, entrepreneurship policies in China and the U.S. differ in the relationship between the government and businesses. Although entrepreneurship has been nurtured for a long time in the U.S., the American government seems only to play a small role in the development of entrepreneurship. Entrepreneurship in the U.S. is formed mainly through the market by non-governmental sectors. The government efforts to encourage entrepreneurship are mainly from the Small Business Administration (SBA) that was established in 1953. Stevenson and Lundström (2001) indicate that the U.S. does not have an entrepreneurship policy *per se*, except the policy initiatives of the SBA. The SBA's mission is only to address imperfections in financial markets that erect barriers to the growth of start-ups and small or medium enterprises (SMEs). Other than the SBA, major efforts for entrepreneurship are from the National Commission on Entrepreneurship (NCOE), which basically lobbies for an entrepreneurship policy focused on the promotion of innovative entrepreneurship, venture capital for start-ups, more favorable tax treatment of employee stock options, and better intellectual property protection (Stevenson and Lundström, 2001). However, NCOE is a private-sector-led policy initiative.

Although recently the U.S. government has increasingly become a partner of American businesses, the U.S. government has not dominated, but only placed certain level of restrictions or provided incentives toward the entrepreneurial process. The restrictions or incentives include rules on prices and cost inequalities, competition restriction, paper work burden, and so forth. Even with this elevation of government's role in terms of entrepreneurship, the U.S. government is still only as important as a *partner*, not a controller or dominator for entrepreneurship development. As Golay (1960) described decades ago, American economy is an enterprise or market economy in which the role of the individual, not the government, in the production process is central.

Compared to the U.S. government, the Chinese government is much more involved in economic activities. According to Liu (2003), the entrepreneurial process in China is controlled by the government, not by the enterprises themselves or by the market. Liu (2003) described the Chinese economy essentially as a government economy: along with Chinese economic reform and open policy, the government has controlled less but still intervenes in some microeconomic activities in a redundant manner. Pearson (1991) also noted that decisions with important problems in China are not made by majority vote.

The dominance of Chinese government in entrepreneurial process is not only shown in central government but also in provincial and local government. Chinese entrepreneurship has a big entry barrier — local protection. Local protection allows the local government to control resource allocation and personnel promotion for enterprises. As a result, entrepreneurs in China need to have not only skills of innovation but also skills of bureaucracy. Long and Ng (2001) notes that Chinese entrepreneurs have to "keep one eye looking at the market and the other eye at the mayor", and the latter is actually more important. This situation could hinder market-driven entrepreneurial process and entrepreneurs' productivity.

This difference in the government's role in promotion of entrepreneurship reflects the cultural and economic backgrounds in the two countries. The U.S. is a culture with a low power distance, while China is a culture with a high power distance. As de Tocqueville (1994) indicates, the unique American history determined the emphasis of equality and freedom as the culture pursuit. As an immigrant country without much old hierarchical history and built by people from various backgrounds, the U.S. has a much smaller hierarchical legacy. To survive well in the new land, people fight side by side for their common goods. In such a background, the U.S. has a strong concept of equality, and social status is not emphasized as much as many other countries, such as France and China. The pursuit of equality and freedom determines that the U.S. government cannot be absolute authority in the society. American history has delineated America's low power distance.

Compared to the Chinese high-power-distance culture, the U.S. government is relatively less dominant over people. With the long history of Chinese feudalism system, which emphasized the absolute power of the emperor and which took advantage of Confucian hierarchical administration mode, Chinese people are used to and even feel legitimate and secure to maintain social hierarchy and an extreme power. The extreme power is the highest authority in China. With the high power distance, the Chinese government has more power, initiative, and responsibility in economic activities, including entrepreneurial process.

History is not the only factor resulting in the different relationship between the government and businesses, economic reason is also critical. The U.S. is a capitalistic society, implementing market economy for a long time. A market economy itself emphasizes the self-adjustment function for its economic cycles. The government in this case only plays a partner's role to enterprises. Only when market appears "failure", the government intervenes to ensure a health market environment for competition. Seven decades ago, China, at the other end of the culture spectrum, adopted communism political system and implemented a planned centralized economy. The planned economy naturally requires the government to take the lead for policy formation. Though, since 1978, China opened its policy and gradually approached the market economy, the legacy from the planned centralized economy and feudalism extreme power of the government is difficult to be cleared immediately.

11.4.2. *Importance of Leadership and Authority*

Leadership is important in the promotion of entrepreneurship, and who takes the lead matters. In the U.S., although the entrepreneurial milieu is mature, entrepreneurship development still faces numerous challenges. The policy initiatives, in most cases, are not emphasized only by few political elites in the government, such as the president. The American media does not only emphasize the entrepreneurship policy initiatives from the president. Entrepreneurship policy shown to the public is delivered by the government agency SBA, interest groups, other privately led sectors, or just grassroots voice, not the president.

Contrarily, in China, almost all important entrepreneurship policy initiatives are taken by the national leader, expressed through the media. Due to their history and cultural legacy, the Chinese tend to expect and accept the national leader's role of ideology orientation and trust the authority as legitimate. Thus, the words of national leaders or the elite carry much weight while average entrepreneurial individuals can barely participate in entrepreneurship policy discussion and formation. Many Chinese entrepreneurship policy researches, such as Gao (2002), attribute the development of entrepreneurship in China into two major factors. The first one is from the leadership of Deng Xiaoping, the Chinese national leader at that time and the so-called General Designer of Chinese Reform and Opening. According to Gao (2002), since Deng Xiaoping pointed out that China would become a market economy when he visited South China in 1992, entrepreneurship was encouraged nationwide. It seems that Chinese entrepreneurship policy does not depend much on government legislation, or entrepreneurship milieu, but more on national leader's words. Leadership in China, on one hand, seems extremely contributive to Chinese entrepreneurship development; on the other hand, this situation reflects the absolute social authority of China's national leaders.

This emphasis of leadership in national policymaking relates to the culture. In China, the high power distance and high uncertainty avoidance make the social authority extremely powerful. Their words can be more important than universal laws and their comments and suggestions are accepted as people's guide of behavior. Until the late 1970s, Mao Tsedong, the national leader who led Chinese people to build and develop Communist China, was still considered as the soul leader or nationwide idol in people's heart. His words were once printed in books and pamphlets and recited by most Chinese as a guide to behavior for about two decades. This situation is rarely seen in a culture with low power distance and low uncertainty avoidance, where almost everyone tends to believe they have equally important opinions. This strong role of the top leadership results from and also reinforces the Chinese high power distance.

The American society is considered as pluralistic since, in principle, every social member's voice can be counted. Pluralism can motivate the growth of entrepreneurial milieu by encouraging diversity and creating unique business opportunities, though sometimes conflicting stakeholders' interests can slow down policy decision process. Chinese tradition does not allow total pluralism yet, but the recent economic development in China and globalization are changing Chinese culture and make China closer to pluralistic cultures. This situation strengthens Chinese entrepreneurial milieu and will eventually be reflected in entrepreneurship policies.

11.4.3. *Rule of Law*

Entrepreneurship policy itself relates to the rule of law. Without a certain rule of law to ensure innovative individual's benefit and motivate them to establish enterprises, there would not be any entrepreneurship. As indicated earlier, entrepreneurship includes risk taking. In a market fraught with uncertainty, initiating a new business is extremely risky. In the absence of good monetary policies to equip individuals with the necessary capital and without a good fiscal and other macropolicy system to enhance enterprises' profits, few people would be attracted to take the risk and initiate an enterprise. As a mature market compared to China, the U.S. has had many monetary and fiscal policies and Rule of Laws to motivate entrepreneurship and to protect fair competition. However, sometimes the oversophisticated regulations undermine the entrepreneurship. Lopez (1999) suggests that the total economic burden for regulatory compliance on the federal level alone is $700 billion annually, or $7,000 per household, according to the National Association of Business Economists. It seems that American entrepreneurs are confronting too many laws and regulations, including wage laws, environmental regulations, rules for health and safety, and legions of other burdensome regulations, from zoning laws to occupational licensing to record-keeping requirements. All these complicated Rule of Laws could stifle entrepreneurial growth.

Contrary to the U.S., China seems to lack a sufficient Rule of Laws for a good entrepreneurial milieu. Gao (2002) notes that while major financing institutions in GEM countries, like the U.S., include informal private investment, venture capital, and a growing enterprise market, in China, informal investment is the dominant financing source for new ventures. Without the necessary Rule of Laws to ensure a secure and credible capital market, new Chinese ventures can only predominantly rely on informal investment. The high-context culture also contributes to the internal trust between group members for informal investment.

However, owing to the lack of a credit system, even informal investments encounter many problems. Lacking in credit mechanisms and business rules, and without monitoring and punishment mechanisms for bankruptcies, China has not built a healthy and mature banking system to support entrepreneurial capital. This situation leads to a lack of necessary options to access capital, which further limits entrepreneurial behavior. Liu (2003) suggests that the Rule of Laws will be needed to further supplement and consummate China's new responsibilities, especially after China's entry to the World Trade organization. Also, Accenture (2004a) and Long and Ng (2001) indicate that Chinese business executives tend to behave more like bureaucrats rather than entrepreneurs. Lacking necessary transparent universal Rule of Laws to ensure a market with fair competition, entrepreneurs have to reserve their innovation, and instead, spend more energy on bureaucracy to protect their businesses. This situation is a big barrier preventing the development of Chinese entrepreneurship.

The different systems of Rule of Laws in China and the U.S. have cultural roots. The U.S. is a low-context culture, where rules tend to be explained clearly. With huge racial, ethnic, historical, and other social diversities among people, explicitly interpreted sophisticated laws are necessary. China, on the contrary, is a relatively homogeneous society with *Han* culture as absolutely dominant culture. This situation allows for efficient high-context communication. The high-context culture regulates the society via moral ethics in many cases, which discourages establishing sophisticated laws. The immature market economy of China is partially reflected by the incompleteness of Rule of Laws in the market.

11.4.4. *Small Business or Large Business?*

As mentioned earlier, in the U.S., government efforts to encourage entrepreneurship are delivered under SME policy initiatives through SBA. Even from the name of the only government agency in charge of entrepreneurship policy, SBA (*Small* Business Association), it is obvious that small business is the focus for the promotion of U.S. entrepreneurship.

However, in China, its government focuses on developing large- or medium-sized enterprises (LMEs) instead of small businesses. At the Fifteenth Congress of the Chinese Communist Party (CCP) in September 1997, the central government approved the reform program known as *zhuada fangxiao* ("grasp the big, enliven the small") (Smith, 2000). This program is intended to promote LMEs. In addition, the CCP is developing a number of enterprise groups. Even when Iqbal and Urata (2002) explain the recent development of SMEs in China, they mention that the SMEs' recent grow is due to the benefit from the withdrawal of state control. The government's support for SMEs is relatively limited to allowing for their freedom, but SMEs are not as lucky as LMEs to obtain government funding support.

Stevenson and Lundström (2001) classify "Niche" Entrepreneurship Policy into two types:

• Type I focuses on social inclusion. The selected target groups represent minority in the society as business owners, including women, youth, ethnic minorities, the unemployed, etc. The objective is to promote entrepreneurship for those minority groups.
• Type II is a "techno-entrepreneurship policy", focusing on wealth creation and innovation. The target is people with the highest potential for starting high-growth potential firms, including scientific researchers, inventors, university graduates, and people with technology experience. The objective is to generate high-growth potential businesses based on R&D, technology or knowledge inputs.

The U.S. entrepreneurship policy through SBA belongs to Type I, and Chinese entrepreneurship policy is classified as Type II. Chinese entrepreneurship policy focuses on promoting high-tech firms. Many technological innovation-promoting programs have been set up, such as the Spark Program, the National New Product Program, and the "Torch" Program. The projects of R&D and intermediary testing account for 73% of all the projects; innovation fund support concentrates on the information technology industry (30%), the bio-pharmacy industry (18%), and the new-materials industry (15%) (Gao, 2002).

The discrepancy in the total entrepreneurship policy between China and the U.S. again relates to their culture differences and socio-economic background. The U.S. is a relatively individualistic culture, where individual's rights and benefits are emphasized, including citizens from minority groups. In addition, because the U.S. economy is mainly market driven, large businesses tend to benefit naturally in the market due to scale of economy. Therefore, entrepreneurship policy, as an adjusting factor to bridge market imperfection, tends to emphasize more on small businesses and individuals' benefits. Increasing social inclusion becomes extremely important in such an individualistic pluralistic and market-driven society. Rules encouraging minority entrepreneurs and limiting large enterprises are major part of its entrepreneurship (Stevenson and Lundström, 2001). In China, a society of collective culture, group benefits are emphasized more than that of individuals. The social goal is to make the whole society develop well. There may be many moments for individuals and minority groups to sacrifice to ensure the achievements of the big goal of the society as a whole. Therefore, the Chinese entrepreneurship policy focuses on LMEs and enlivens the small enterprises.

Socio-economically, the U.S. is a capitalism society with a long tradition of encouraging market competition. To improve the quality of the market economy and maintain certain level of competition, enhancing the social inclusion and promoting market pluralism is necessary. For China, a country at the nascent stage of market economy, the first thing is to increase the social wealth in general. Therefore China picks the type II entrepreneurship policy approach to promoting efficiency of economy instead of focusing on social equity.

11.5. Conclusion

Cultural and social context matters to entrepreneurship policies in both China and the U.S. The cultural and socio-economic differences shape the differences in entrepreneurship polices between these two countries. For China, the high power distance results in the dominance of governments in business and entrepreneurship policy initiatives from the national leader. The high context culture and its collectiveness brings about the lack of explicitly written laws for entrepreneurship development in the market economy, and the collectiveness of Chinese culture results in the policy focus on LMEs, not the small businesses. Contrary to China, in the U.S., the low power distance and the reliance on market results in the smaller role of the government or national leader for promoting entrepreneurship. The immigrant culture makes the U.S. a low context culture and requires detailed written laws to regulate entrepreneurial activities. In addition, individualism makes small businesses extremely important, and national entrepreneurship policy focuses on benefiting SMEs. Other social elements, including economic context and historical backgrounds, also help shape the entrepreneurship policies in the two cultures. Although culture is not the only element directly influencing the formation of entrepreneurship policy, it matters in the whole socio-economic environment and influences entrepreneurship policies both directly and indirectly throughout the socio-economic settings.

Globalization expedited by international trade and the Internet is transforming the global culture and this change is inevitably penetrating to entrepreneurship policies. A further development in market economy calls for entrepreneurship with the global market mechanism. The interaction between culture and socio-economic perspectives calls for better entrepreneurship policy to serve the economy and culture better. On one hand, the traditional Chinese culture would still persist with legacy effects and with fundamental differences from American culture, on the other hand, the globalizing and market-orienting will transform China's entrepreneurship policy to somewhat mirror developed economies' experience. This makes comparing China's entrepreneurship policy experience to developed economies' meaningful. China's entrepreneurship policy therefore needs to integrate Western style entrepreneurial milieu and China's unique culture perspectives. Instead of just following developed economies' entrepreneurship development path, respecting China's culture legacy is important.

References

Accenture (2004a). Barriers to entrepreneurship in China. Available at http://www.accenture.com/xd/xd.asp?it=enweb&xd=ideas\entrepreneurship\china\barriers.xml. Accessed November 10, 2004.

Accenture (2004b). Encouraging findings in China. Available at http://www.accenture.com/xd/xd.asp?it=enweb&xd=ideas\entrepreneurship\china\encouraging.xml. Accessed November 10, 2004.

Cantillon, R. (1755). *Essai sur la nature de commerce en general*. H. Higgs (Ed.) London: Macmillan, 1931.

Dunne, M. J. (1995). Scaling the wall of China. *Management Review* **84**(8): 13–14.

Fitzsimons, P. (2004). Entrepreneurship and government policy: An international perspective. Delivered at *Knowledge Clusters and Entrepreneurship in Regional Economic*

Development conference, Humphrey Institute of Public Affairs, University of Minnesota, Minneapolis, USA.

Gao, J. (2002). Structural change, environment and policies of entrepreneurial firms in China, in H. J. Pleitner, T. Volery and W. Weber (Eds.) *Paging of the World — KMU Before High-Altitude Flight or Crash? Radical change into the World — Does SMEs Want Soar or Crash?* St. Gallen, Swiss: KMU-HSG.

Geertz, C. (1973). Thick description: Toward an interpretive theory of culture, in *The Interpretation of Cultures*. New York: Basic Books.

Golay, F. H. (1860). Entrepreneurship and economic development in the Philippines. *Far Eastern Survey* **29**: 81–86.

Hagen, E. (1962). *On the Theory of Economic Change: How Economic Growth Begins.* Homewood, IL: Dorsey.

Hall, E. T. (1981). *Beyond Culture.* New York: Doubleday.

Hofstede, G. (1980). *Culture's Consequences.* Beverly Hills, CA: Sage.

Hofstede G., and M. H. Bond (1988). Confucius and economic growth: New insights into culture consequences. *Organizational Dynamics* **16**(1): 118–131.

Hofstede, G. (1994). *Cultures and Organizations — Intercultural Cooperation and its importance for survival.* London: HarperCollins Business.

Hofstede, G. (2001). *Culture's Consequences; Comparing Values, Behaviors, Institutions and Organizations Across Nations.* 2nd edn. Thousand Oaks: Sage.

Hornsby, J. S., D. F. Kuratko and D. W. Naffziger (1998). Public policy and private enterprise: A study of small business owner perceptions. United States Association for Small Business and Entrepreneurship. Clearwater, Florida: January 15–18, 1998.

Inglehart, R. (1988). The renaissance of political culture. *American Political Science Review* **82**: 1203–1230.

Iqbal, F., and S. Urata. (2002). Small firm dynamism in East Asia: An introductory overview. *Small Business Economics* **18**: 1–12.

Kelly L., A. Whatley and R. Worthley (1987). Assessing the effects of culture on managerial attitudes: A three-culture test. *Journal of International Business Study* **18**(1): 17–31.

Kirzner, I. M. (1973). *Competition & Entrepreneurship.* Chicago: University of Chicago Press.

Lan, X. L. (1987). The guiding principles of values adjusting the relationship between fairness and efficiency. *Brightness Daily* May 11: p. 3.

Liu, Y. (2003). Development of private entrepreneurship in China: Process, problems and countermeasures, in M.-J. Atwater and I. Fujimatsu (Eds.) *Entrepreneurship in Asia: Playbook for Prosperity* (*Proceedings of the Entrepreneurship in Asia Expert Workshop*, July 8–10, 2002, Hong Kong), Washington, D.C.: The Mansfield Center for Pacific Affairs.

Lo, D. (1997). Re-appraising China's state-owned industrial enterprises. Department of Economics, School of Oriental and African Studies Working Paper No. 67.

Long, G., and M. K. Ng (2001). The political economy of Intrap-provincial disparities in post-reform China: A case study of Jiangsu province. *Geoforum* **32**: 215–234. UK: Elsevier.

Lopez, N. (1999). Barriers to entrepreneurship: How government undermines economic opportunity. *Quick Study*, 1999. Lewisville, TX: Institute for Policy Innovation.

Lordkipanidze, M. (2002). Enhancing entrepreneurship in rural tourism for sustainable regional development: The case of Söderslätt region, Sweden. *IIIEE Reports* 10.

Marshall, A. (1930). *Principles of Economics*. London: Macmillan and Co.

McClelland, D. (1961). *The Achieving Society*. New Jersey: Van Nostrand.

Pearson, M. (1991). *Joint Ventures in the People's Republic of China: The Control of Foreign Investment under Socialism*. Princeton, NJ: Princeton University Press.

Rural Development Council (2001). Entrepreneurship in rural America. *Culture & Entrepreneurship*. [Online]. Available at: http://www.wvrdc.state.wv.us/chapter3.pdf. Accessed July 29, 2002.

Say, J. B. (1845). *A Treatise on Political Economy*. 4th edn. Translated by C. R. Prinsep. Philadelphia: Grigg & Elliot.

Schumpeter, J. A. (1961). *The Theory of Economic Development*. 2nd edn. New York: Oxford University Press.

Shweder, R. A. (2000). Moral maps, first world conceits, and the new evangelists, in L. E. Harrison and S. P. Huntington (Eds.) *Culture Matters: How Values Shape Human Progress*. New York: Basic Books.

Smith, R. (2000). Should China be promoting large-scale enterprises and enterprise groups? *World Development* **28**(4): 721–737.

Stevenson, L., and A. Lundström (2001). Patterns and trends in entrepreneurship/AME policy and practice in ten economies. *Entrepreneurship Policy for the Future Series*. Vol. 3. Sweden: Swedish Foundation for Small Business Research.

Tan, B. L. B. (2002). Researching managerial values: A cross-cultural comparison. *Journal of Business Research* **55**: 815–821.

de Tocqueville, A. (1994). *Democracy in America*. Vol. II. New York: Everyman's Library.

Tse, D. K., J. Francis and J. Walls (1994). Cultural differences in conducting intra- and intercultural negotiations: Sino–Canadian comparison. *Journal of International Business Study* 537–555.

Wang, Y., and Y. Yao (2002). Market reforms, technological capabilities and the performance of small enterprises in China. *Small Business Economics* **18**: 197–211.

Part VI
Case Studies

Chapter 12

Beyond Small Business and Private Enterprises in China: Global and Spatial Perspectives

Xinyue Ye* and Mark Leipnik[†]
*Bowling Green State University
†Sam Houston State University

12.1. Introduction

The failure of state socialism prompted the launch of economic reforms in 1978, and since then, China has been undergoing a profound and miraculous process of market economy development, diversification, and rapid expansion and proliferation of private enterprises (Wei and Ye, 2009). However, with China's changing institutional environment, intensifying competition from other developing economies, and a world-wide economic recession, small business has been facing challenges. Since the late 1980s, small business has gone through two major rounds of restructuring (from family enterprises to shareholding cooperatives to shareholding joint-stock enterprises). This process has included four major types of strategic response: institutional change, technological advancement, industrial diversification, and spatial restructuring (Wei, Li and Wang, 2007).
With respect to spatial restructuring, firms have gone through localization and delocalization. Location choices reflect the dichotomy between globalizing cities (Shanghai, Shenzhen, Chung-King, etc.) with external transportation links and interior cities (Urumqi, Lhasa, etc.) which are more inaccessible and usually farther from the coast. Chung-King is the exception that proves the importance of transportation links to the global

economy. Since the Three Gorges dam locks came into operation on the Yangtze River, Chung-king is an internal city with low-cost global transportation links. The formation of new firms and clusters has been accompanied by mergers, acquisitions, and the emergence of multiregional enterprises (MREs), some of which have relocated their headquarters and specialized functions to metropolitan areas.

China has been the fastest growing major economy in the world for the past three decades, with an average annual GDP growth rate above 10%. While some of the underlying statistics reflect inflated values for joint-stock companies and the most recent growth may be closer to 6% than 10%, by all measures the growth of China's economy has been phenomenal and one must look to the 19th century to find analogous growth in any other economy (in that case the economy of the U.S. after the civil war) (Holz, 2006). China has quickly emerged as the world's manufacturing/ assembly center and in fact the dominant manufacturer in the world for many categories of products like shoes, toys, and consumer electronics. However, there are various layers and dimensions to the transition. Careful and probing research on China can reveal a complex landscape with various regional models and areas that are exceptions to these models (e.g., Ye and Wei, 2005; Wei and Ye, 2009).

The three well-known models of regional development in China are: the Sunan model, the Pearl River Delta (PRD) model, and the Wenzhou model. These three models have generated considerable scholarly interest (Fan, 1995; Lin, 1997; Oi, 1999; Marton, 2000; Wei and Ye, 2004; Lu and Wei, 2007; Wei and Ye, 2009).

This research deepens the existing literature on the local response to globalization (Cox, 1997; Scott, 1998). Research on small business in China drew substantial international attention in the early 1990s (Nolan and Dong, 1989; Y. L. Liu, 1992; Parris, 1993), and interest has been renewed in recent years (Ma and Cui, 2002; Wei and Ye, 2009). The authors argue for a spatial (geographical) perspective in the study of small business in China. At the same time, we investigate the role of institutions and human capital in local economic development. The authors will also look to models from various parts of the world, including the European Economic Community, the U.S. and Canada, South Asia (India, Bangladesh), Vietnam, and Singapore, for examples of methods being used to promote small business. This material is also coming from a geographic perspective, since the desire for wealth and entrepreneurial motives may be universal, national and regional realities can influence the choice and success of methods to promote small business. In the latter part of this chapter, we will utilize a more localized focus by making a detailed examination of the Wenzhou Model in local economic development in Zhejiang. The diverse experiences of the authors as well as our years' of experience as economic consultants, environmental consultants, urban planners, and in particular fieldwork starting from early 1990s in Zhejiang working with small business and private enterprises have been essential to our understanding of the complexity of this dynamic topic.

12.2. Global Perspective

A number of governments and institutions around the world have adopted the solution of providing the capital that small businesses need to start up or to trade through establishment of programs for providing small loans at lower interest rates or with fewer strings attached than those that would be available from private banks. Singapore has an active program called Enterprise One to foster small businesses using loans that are available to both Singaporeans and citizens of other countries that open new businesses in Singapore. Firms may borrow up to S$15 million (Singapore Dollars) for equipment, S$250,000 for working capital and there are also microloans of up to S$50,000 are available. Firms may import equipment without tariff charges, bring in experts without having to pay local income taxes, and repatriate profits without high taxes. All these benefits are gone after a few years. But they may help investors choose to locate in Singapore in preference to places in Asia with lower labor costs.

In the U.S., the Small Business Administration has a program of federally guaranteed loans that carry low interest rates. These loans have 10-year

Entrepreneurship and Economic Growth in China

maturities on start-up capital and 25-year maturities on plant and equipment. They are for amounts from $25,000 to $500,000. There is an almost endless series of special provisions and programs, such as tax incentives for investment in areas that are economically blighted; preferences for firms that are minority owned, women owned, or owned by military veterans; and in areas impacted by natural disaster. There are also special programs for loans to firms involved in export-oriented activities (these can be larger in value). But the firms must be "small" to qualify. It is a truism in the U.S. that all people are "middle class", that all farms are "family owned" and that all businesses (or at least the ones politicians say they are trying to promote) are "small". The criteria for what constitutes small as far as the SBA is concerned is contained in a 61-page document full of formulas, charts, and exceptions, but basically the SBA considers $7 million in total receipts or a workforce of 100 of fewer employees to be "small" (SBA, 2009) . This leads many growing firms to spin off subsidiaries, set up front companies, and lay off employees subsequently rehired as independent contractors to fit inside the procrustean bed of the "small" definition.

A technology incubator is a sort of collective organization, usually a nonprofit organization sponsored by a regional government with participation of a university. They have the role of connecting inventors, academics, venture capitalists, and government agencies with grant money to foster and promote the development of new technologies. They also provide a roof over the heads of inventors, a place to have meetings, direct communications, etc. The Houston Advanced Research Center in the Woodlands, Texas, is an example of such an incubator (HARC, 2009). An example of technology developed and commercialized there includes pulsed laser-based LIDAR terrain mapping hardware and software to create digital elevation models rapidly and accurately. There are technology incubators in many countries generally associated with universities in larger cities such as the Macquarie University Technology Centre and The Australian Technology Park in Melbourne located in a former railroad yard and workshop area (ATP, 2009). A complication with the feasibility of technology incubators is the ownership of the inventions that are commercialized. Much of the effort involved in these incubators involves getting the mix between guaranteeing the interests of all parties to future profits balanced against the open exchange of ideas and cross-fertilization between business, academia, and government. Nevertheless, as China strengthens its universities and existing research establishments controlled by government ministries look to commercialize and perhaps find a new source of funds, the technology incubator may be a concept that will prove valuable to developing small technology oriented firms in the future.

Venture capital refers to money available from typically wealthy investors that can be made available to promising firms to help them develop and expand. There are firms around the world that specialize in serving as conduits for investment in independent firms by holders of wealth. Usually the investor obtains an ownership stake such as a block of preferred stock, a significant stake (perhaps a 51% controlling interest), or at least a seat on the board of the start-up firm. Many of the innovative firms in Silicon Valley and in the area around Boston were driven by the activities of venture capital firms. In Canada, venture capital firms have been very active. Between 1996 and 2007, venture capital investors financed 2,175 technology companies in Canada. 1,740 of those were operating in Canada in 2008. In addition, prior to 1996, venture capital financed 15 companies that are still operating and have sales larger than $ 50 million in 2008. On an average, these 1,755 companies have sales of $10.5 million and directly employ 47 persons. They are a mix of small and medium companies. In aggregate, they generate sales of $18.3 billion. They employ 63,955 people in Canada and 17,760 abroad. In addition, they generate 83,549 indirect jobs in Canada for a total of 147,504 employees supported by firms financed by venture capital (CVCA, 2009).

The risk of fraud is only one limitation of venture capital in the Chinese context, another is that wealthy individuals are probably that way as a result of their own trading and business activities and would prefer to invest their capital in their own businesses. Also, overseas Chinese may be reluctant to invest in Chinese businesses by way of an intermediary. They are more likely to invest directly in the purchase of plant and equipment, install a salaried managed that is a relative or is well trusted and open their own firm in China.

One of the most exciting innovations in the development of small businesses has been micro-loans. For decades, it was felt that large loans from organizations like the World Bank or International Monetary Fund or direct investment by large multinational firms was the best way to foster economic growth in developing countries. But these programs often left behind the disenfranchised millions living in rural areas in abject poverty and built up government ministries and a few trophy projects such as bridges without surface roads leading to them or dams without a power grid or consumer or industrial demand for the soon rusting turbines. A refreshing grass roots alternative to big programs and big loans is the concept of micro-loans. This idea came out of the developing world. This idea has been so successful that its principle originator and proponent Mr. Muhammad Yunus (and the Grameen Bank of Bangladesh, which he established) received the 2006 Nobel Peace Prize for his contributions to mankind. Micro-loans are small short-term loans made directly to local people to start small businesses or acquire needed tools. An example of a real world micro-loan would be one made for $100 (or 100,000 rupees) to buy a hand cart to move produce to a market. The idea behind the micro-loan is that for the subsistence farmer with a few mango trees, the difference between a barefoot barter existence and having money and participating in the local economy, is a cart with which to move and then sell his crop of mangoes in the nearby village. The cart might only cost the equivalent of $100, but this is $100 more than he has ever held in his hand. If the mango farmer could get a loan for the $100, he could start to make money and can pay back the loan over a short time and even pay a little interest. In the context of a rural village in Bangladesh, India, or Africa, where the farmer and several billion other people like him live, the only available loans are for the expenses of marriage or funerals available from local usurers. Local usurers who frequently use violence to collect small loans with 100% per year or more interest rates are hardly a good option for a farmer to buy a push cart. This situation was appreciated by Mr. Yunus, who developed a program to loan local men and women (particularly women, who could buy the sewing machines to do home-based piece work). The results have far exceeded the expectations of the hard-eyed economists from international development programs (Grameen, 2009).

While large-scale projects (often funded by loans or direct investment) are needed to build a dam like Three Gorges, or a semiconductor factory, a loan that allows a pedi-cab driver to purchase a natural gas–fueled taxi, a loan that allows a toy maker to go from gluing hair on dolls to injection molding the heads as well, a loan that allows a fruit vendor (who got the cart using an early loan now fully paid back) to get a cell phone so he can text customers with his location and daily varying wares… these sorts of small loans can have a cumulatively transforming impact on an economy (Sullivan, 2007). Micro-loans have worked very well in the Indian sub-continent, less well in Africa. In the Chinese context, the issue of what entity makes and collects the loans could be an issue. Grass roots local activists working through non-profit foundations funded by philanthropists have been the model elsewhere. The system of state-directed capitalism with communist party involvement that is present in most areas of China might not lend itself to the micro-loan concept. Nevertheless, the concept's outstanding success in some of the poorest countries such as the perennially overpopulated and debt-ridden Bangladesh indicated that it is worthy of consideration in China.

One area where established large businesses have an advantage over small and start-up businesses is the available expertise and human capital they can deploy. In order to rectify this deficiency in the U.S., an agency of the U.S. Department of Commerce named the Small Business Administration has been established. This organization helps educate small business owners in accounting and taxation rules, government contacting, sponsors classes in marketing and promotion, trains the staff of small businesses in international trade practices and use of common business software applications, provides loans, and after disasters, provides recovery loans to small businesses. Similar organizations exist in Canada, Australia, and in E.U. member countries. The European Commission in its Council of Trade and Industry has an Education for Entrepreneurship program that teaches principles of promotion, marketing, accounting and export trade to small and medium enterprise owners and managers (European Commission, 2006).

In order to foster small business growth, special programs have been put in place in many European countries and in North America to encourage the purchase of goods and services from "small" businesses. These incentives can take the form of designation of certain services that must be purchased from small firms (such as janitorial, painting, or landscaping services). These are usually services that can easily be rendered by small firms and in which they might have a positive advantage (due to being local or having low overhead costs). Thus maintaining lawns and plantings does not take much capital and having local expertise is probably an advantage. Conversely, one would not imagine that a small business would be designated to manufacture a fighter jet. But surprisingly, it is likely that some fighter jet components are likely to be built by small businesses since the system of set asides and incentives is quite pervasive in many developed countries. One odd aspect of such programs involves the definition of what constitutes a "small business". In point of fact many "small" businesses can be pretty large. In the U.S., a firm with up to 500 employees can be considered small under some circumstances for purposes of government programs (SBA, 2009).

A number of nations around the world have disadvantaged minorities. In order to encourage the development of small businesses by members of these minorities, special government programs have been put in place in the U.S., Canada, and Australia to give preferential treatment to members of these minorities (CASMC, 2009). Thus Native Americans get preferences in Canada; Original Australians get preference in Australia, and African Americans, Hispanics, Women, and Native Americans all get preferences in the U.S. There is even a minority Business Development Agency within the U.S. Department of Commerce (MBDA, 2009). Asians get no preferences whatsoever in the U.S. (or Australia or Canada) despite historical patterns of discrimination against them, since Asians (including Chinese) in the U.S. are far wealthier on average than the dominant majority group. In the U.S., these programs to promote minority-owned small businesses typically take the form of the requirement that all government purchases by U.S. Federal and State governments have to include submission and evaluation of bids from minority-owned firms.

The U.S. Federal government goes further and requires that a proportion of all government purchases come from minority-owned small businesses. But the main method for steering work to minority-owned small businesses is the greater ease with which products and services can be purchased from minority-owned small businesses without going through cumbersome federal procurement contracting rules and procedures. To use a specific example, a Federal agency wishing to purchase janitorial services would have to distribute and evaluate hundreds of bids to purchase services from a non-minority-owned firm. This process would take many months and considerable trouble. Alternatively, the same agency could call a Native American-owned firm and have them subcontract the work out to the firm, that would have been the original preferred choice after an exhaustive open bidding process. The Native American-owned firm can take 5% "off the top" of the contract for serving as a "prime contractor". From the point of view of the government agency contracting bureaucrat, the intermediary has performed a huge service since the company they wanted to hire is on the job in a week rather than six months, while the minority-owned business has also benefited. Of course, the potential for corruption in such a system is large, with many companies setting up *Potemkin* front companies that on paper are minority (or women) owned. The wives of politicians are well known to add to their husband's income through this route, and the claim of membership in a disadvantaged minority is sometimes rather dubious, as in the case of the 1/8 Cherokee Indian who is nevertheless on the list as the proprietor of a Native American-owned business.

In the Chinese context, there are many minorities in China (at least 80 million Uigurs, Tibetans, Miao, Mongols, Koreans, etc.). The option of developing minority purchasing incentives or set asides may be an attractive way of spreading wealth and encouraging entrepreneurship in these minority communities. At present, it seems that the pattern is typically of Han Chinese moving to these minority areas and, with their superior communications skills, etc., monopolizing available opportunities for government contracts and openings for new businesses.

One method of fostering small business is to encourage immigrants with capital and expertise to settle in a given country and set up a firm there. In the U.S., Canada, and Australia, this approach has encouraged the immigration of hundreds of thousands of hardworking people from many countries, who have invested money in their adopted home country, usually in purchase and expansion of existing businesses. There are specific requirements for obtaining such immigrant visas from each country. Canada, which is the second largest in area of the world's nations, with only 33 million residents, has the most liberal rules (CIC, 2009). The U.S. has long been a Mecca for immigrants but it has made its rules increasingly restrictive. Currently, an immigrant family must invest $1 million and open a business that employs 10 persons who are American citizens in order to get an investor visa. This has led many immigrants to open gasoline stations with attached convenience stores and motels. In particular, immigrants from the Indian subcontinent have taken this route with frequent success. The Patels from the Indian state of Gujarat specialize in opening motels in small towns (a motel in a large city would involve an investment in excess of $1 million plus higher wages for the employees) (Daily Wealth, 2006). The Khans and other Sufi Muslim followers of the Aga Khan in Pakistan have specialized in gasoline stations (they feel that the motel business is likely to involve the promotion of immorality) and many do not sell alcohol at their stores despite the large loss of potential profits.

While China is historically a source of immigrants and not a magnet for them, internal migrations within China have helped populate many coastal areas with the initiators of small businesses. It is possible that China might adopt programs that encouraged members of its huge diaspora to return to China and open businesses there using their contacts, language skills, and capital acquired overseas. Incentives to get Chinese business people to consider retiring in China or purchasing a second home in China might also be considered. Costa Rica has found that encouraging retirees to settle there has also fostered the development of many businesses. The methods it uses include exemption from taxes on foreign assets and pensions and liberal import rules on personal goods and import of things like home appliances and cars, which are cheaper and more available in the immigrant's home country (Infocostarica, 2009).

The Internet has been a remarkable stimulus to the development of many small businesses. Examples of this phenomenon include the many artisans with unique handmade items that have become visible by creating a web site. As long as their products can come up on the first 25–50 responses to a Google or Bing search they have a chance to sell their products to a worldwide clientele. The development of secure pay options like PayPal, the widespread use of credit cards for online purchases, and the proliferation of high-resolution digital cameras and tools for viewing products on the Internet all make this mode of commerce feasible. Also the development of worldwide rapid package delivery services is key to success. Thus especially for small handicrafts or jewelry makers, where the product is light but valuable, the economics of using the web to reach consumers and package delivery firms to dispatch purchases is very attractive. While it is more common to purchase products over the Internet within one's own country, the development of banking firms that can take payment in one currency from customers using a credit card for products offered in another country has facilitated these transactions across borders. Thus among other items one of the authors (Leipnik) has purchased over the Internet was a pair of Spanish castanets and a fan from a small Spanish firm specializing in flamenco dancing–related products and a ostrich leg skin replacement watch band from a small German firm that only sells watch bands. Of course it is easier for Euro-zone–based companies to adopt this method of reaching consumers since most purchases would be with Euro currency. In order to develop this mode of selling, a number of developments would need to be effectuated in China. These include better package delivery services, creation of secure means to pay for products with a mechanism to settle disputes and return merchandise for refunds, legal safeguards to punish those engaging in Internet fraud, more widespread use of credit cards, more internet connectivity, etc.

Another related small business–dominated web-based activity is exemplified by the Internet auction site eBay (Gomes-Casseres, 2001). While most eBay sellers are itinerant, many people have made successful small businesses effectively recycling the overabundance of material goods in many modern societies. eBay is particularly suitable for resale of antiques and collectibles. With the longest permanent history of civilization on the planet, China has a vast stock of antiquities and handicrafts. Internet auction sites are a very effective means to connect small sellers specializing in a particular product with collectors. Of course, eBay can also be an effective means of recycling products that are no longer needed by their original purchases, but still have utility. eBay-like mechanisms are particularly attractive to the small business that is being conducted part time. Of course, easy access to package delivery services is important. eBay has spawned an industry of people who aid sellers in learning the processes and holding and dispatching merchandise for shipment. A one-second eBay search can turn up a treasure trove of items. For example, a search for "Antique Burmese Jade Pendants" had 8050 responses. Of course many if not most of these are not exactly for that type of item, they are fakes, poor copies, not high-quality jade, not antique, not Burmese, not pendants, etc. But the eBay site is still an amazing method to link sellers and buyers. Examples of eBay sellers run the gamut from someone who only sells a single item such as a used baby carriage to large firms trying to tap into the eBay market. eBay is popular in the U.S., Canada, and Great Britain, but popularity outside this region is more limited. In particular, recent commentators have suggested that eBay has "lost" the potential market in China, but perhaps indigenous firms will be able to use its model to help promote small businesses (Chen, Zhang, Yuan and Huang, 2007).

While eBay has garnered the online auction market, sites like *Craig's List* has come to dominate small business commerce in areas such as specialized services and products. This is particularly true for specialized personal services, *Feng shui* masters, astrologers, acupuncturists, carpenters, landscapers, plumbers, masseuses, health and fitness advisers, and many similar personal services conducted by small (typical one person) businesses have found Craig's List as the way to connect to customers. The downside is that as much as 15% of listings are sexual in character and there are examples of crimes committed via taking advantage of the anonymity of the Internet. Usually the sellers are the criminals, but in recent cases, the providers of sexual services have themselves fallen victim to predators that used *Craig's List* to make contact with them. A more common Internet scam would be selling non-existent cats and dogs, which after purchase require extra fees for "shots" or documents to get the animals through West African customs. Thus an attractive "cat" listed as available for "free" by a "missionary" in Cameroon, West Africa, became a "dog" on follow-up emails. This example points to the existence of widespread fraud involving certain areas of the world. At present, China does not have the reputation for Internet fraud as, for example, West Africa, the Ukraine, Moldavia, or Russia does. But once a reputation has been acquired for being a focus of fraud, it is hard to shake. The fact that most communications received by Internet users that come from Nigeria are fraudulent means that legitimate firms in that country carry a heavy stigma that perhaps will never be shaken.

12.3. Entrepreneurship and Local Capitalism in China

Scholars have been studying the process of development and globalization in the former socialist bloc countries of the COMECON (Council for Mutual Economic Assistance). These and other centrally planned economies such as the former USSR, Poland, Hungary, Angola, Cuba, etc.

There have been intense debates over the consequences of reforms (and collapse and partial rejuvenation of Socialist regimes), especially whether reform has intensified regional inequalities and what are the most appropriate policies to take for future advancement (e.g., Petrakos, 2001; Bradshaw and Vartapetov, 2003; Anderson, 2005; Vu, 2008). The process has been anything but smooth, with some countries such as Hungary, Poland, and The Czech Republic, and the Baltic States fairing reasonably well; Romania, Bulgaria, Albania, and other former Soviet Republics often stagnating or declining as in the case of Georgia; and outright reversals to a more socialist model as in the Ukraine and Moldova (which are poorer now by any real measure than even in the chaotic days of the early 1990s). There are also models of Stakhonovite solidity and stolidity like Belarus, North Korea and to a lesser extent Cuba. The country that perhaps comes closest to China's path away from state socialism is actually its neighbor Vietnam (Vietnamese Ministry of Foreign Affairs, 2010).

In order to understand the process of the transition of economic institutions in China, one must understand that the reform process in China has been a gradual, experimental, and evolutionary one. This approach is premised upon the fact that Chinese institutions, especially the post-socialist state and the enterprises it owns, are transitional in nature. This perspective is essential to understanding the policy changes and transitional problems facing China and Chinese small businesses today (Wei and Ye, 2009). The traditional heavy industrial areas (dominated by industries such as steel, petrochemicals, and armaments) favored by socialist centralized planning and dominated by state-owned enterprises (SOEs) have fallen behind in economic growth, while coastal localities with effective local governments and entrepreneurial populations that are better positioned for marketing and globalization have emerged as the biggest winners of economic reforms.

Since the late 1970s, China has been undergoing economic reforms that have been introducing market mechanisms and opening up trade to the outside world. Scholars have been intensely debating the nature, trajectory, and impacts of the reform (e.g., Fan, 1995; Weng, 1998; Wei, 1999; Lu and Wang, 2002; Wang and Zhang, 2003; Ye and Wei, 2005; Fan 2006). China's reforms can be understood as a triple transition process of decentralization, marketization, and globalization, giving rise to three dominant agents of regional development — the state, the locality, and the trans-national investor (Wei, 1999; Wei and Fan, 2000). China's "open door" policy and the process of globalization have made China more integrated with the global economy, and foreign investment has become a major source of capital formation. Decentralization and marketization have transformed the Chinese state from a rigid, centralized socialist institution into a flexible, decentralized, and growth-oriented institution. The role of the state has simultaneously been reduced, although many SOEs remain and some are surprisingly nimble. The role of the state has changed from one of planning and the allocation of economic resources directly, to one where the state manages overarching policies, promotes infrastructure development, and adjusts the operation of markets (World Bank, 1992). One area where China still is struggling is in the control of gangster activity and the equal application of the rule of law and the enforceability of contracts. This area is one where small businesses often suffer because they lack the financial and political pull to deal with issues such as extortion, corrupt local and customs officials, acquisition of land and facilities, and enforcement of terms of contracts.

China's reforms have given birth to a new diversity in organizational forms, a wide variety of property rights and ownership arrangements, and local/state corporatism. Reforms have empowered local provinces and institutions in seeking growth and development. Consequently, globalization, the state, and localities have become the three dominant forces underlying regional development in China. Those geographically defined regions and places favored by any or all of these forces tend to grow faster than other areas.

By conducting detailed research at finer scales, recent efforts have revealed complex patterns and mechanisms of regional development in municipalities, counties and at province levels in China (e.g., Lu and Wei, 2007). Overwhelming evidence has demonstrated that core–periphery and urban–rural inequalities have been rising within and between provinces (Weng, 1998; Wei and Ye, 2004). Given the importance of the fastest growing regions as models for regional development, research has also addressed the trajectories and mechanisms underlying the rise of "winning regions" (e.g., Lin, 1997; Shen, 2002). Three models of regional development embedded inside diverse local institutions in "winning regions" have been identified. These include the externally driven foreign private investment–dominated Pearl River Delta model of development in Guangdong Province, the local state-led Sunan model exemplified by Southern Jiangsu Province, which is based on the development of township- and village-level controlled enterprises, and the Wenzhou model in Zhejiang Province, which is centered on the development of indigenous private enterprises including many small businesses. These varied models of regional development underscore the fact that developmental regimes and institutional frameworks vary not only between nations but also between regions and localities within a given nation (at least one as large, diverse and populous as China).

12.4. Small Business and Economic Growth in Zhejiang Province

Zhejiang is a coastal province spearheading China's phenomenal growth and is known for its Wenzhou model of development (Wei and Ye, 2004). As a laboratory for radical reforms based on privatization, the trajectory of development in Wenzhou, where bottom-up reforms were first initiated, has had tremendous impacts on regional development in Zhejiang and influence throughout many other areas of China. While multiple mechanisms — the state, the locality, and the global investor are shaping regional development in China (Wei, 1999), the configuration of these mechanisms varies between regions and at differing geographical scales. As will be examined in detail, the Wenzhou Model is heavily embedded in local institutions, which play a significant role because most producers are small, market-oriented, and often located in semi-rural areas.

As the smallest land province in China, Zhejiang was traditionally divided into a Southwest portion (Wenzhou, Jinhua, Quzhou, Taizhou, and Lishui Counties) and Northeast portion (Hangzhou, Ningbo, Jiaxing, Huzhou, Shaoxing, and Zhoushan Counties). Northeast Zhejiang is part of the historical trading center of the Yangtze Delta and the prosperous Taihu region. The area is flat, well served by waterways, port access, and rail lines, and is more developed and heavy industry-oriented. It is also where some of the earliest traces of civilization in China are found. Southwest Zhejiang, on the other hand, is more mountainous and less developed, except for a few places like the coastal area around Wenzhou.

Zhejiang is known for being oriented toward commerce and education and for the high quality of its handcrafted products. The province traditionally had a hierarchy of numerous market towns that connected the major trading cities with the rural countryside often by canals and other waterborne transportation modalities (Forster, 1998). Its handicrafts such as Hangzhou embroidery and the so-called *three sculptures* (Dongyang Wooden Sculpture, Qingtian Stone Sculpture, and Boxwood Sculpture) and paper products such as painted paper parasols and fans, as well as bamboo and grass products, were the basis of commercial trading during the Ming and Qing Dynasties. These institutions and capabilities made Zhejiang one of the most developed regions in Imperial China. Over the years, Zhejiang has developed a tradition of active entrepreneurship and commercial activities. Place-based business networks, especially those based in Ningbo and Wenzhou, two now booming port cities, have expanded across China and extended abroad. The strong presence, cooperation, and pro-business attitude of local officials and the institutions they represent in Wenzhou are atypical in most other regions of China.

In the 1950s and 1960s, Mao Tse Tung invested heavily in China's strategic interior, but due to its coastal location and lack of natural resources such as coal or iron suitable for heavy industry, few SOEs were built in Zhejiang. This forced Zhejiang to develop its own indigenous small enterprises, and even underground private enterprises. With the policy of rural industrialization in the early 1970s, some TVEs were established, which laid the foundation for post-Mao period development. During Mao's era, Zhejiang's economy stagnated, and its average annual growth rate of per capita GDP was 3.5%, slower than the national average. Zhejiang's enterprises were small, and many were collectively owned.

Since the reforms of 1978, Zhejiang has been undergoing dramatic growth and transformation. It is one of the fastest growing provinces in China by all measures. From 1978 to 2004, the growth rate of per capita GDP in Zhejiang was 12.4%, much higher than the national average (9%). In 2004, the provincial GDP grew to 1.12 trillion yuan, and with only 3.5% of China's population, Zhejiang produced 8.2% of China's GDP (SSB 2005; ZSB 2005). Zhejiang's economic miracle took place without a natural resource base except for a propitious location. This demonstrates the importance of location factors in the global economy.

During this process of growth and development, there was little central government support and lagging development of new transportation networks and nodes, such as rail, road, airport, canal, or port facilities, and infrastructure. The basis for Zhejiang's development was its leading role in marketization and the development of private enterprises. The contribution of SOEs to industrial output was 61.3% in 1978, significantly lower than the national average, which declined to only 6.8% in 1998, and 5.3% in 2002. Newer data would likely show the trend continuing, as the size of the provincial economy continues to grow with relatively little growth in the existing SOEs and few if any new SOEs being initiated. Therefore we can state that Zhejiang's economy is based on relatively small scale, private enterprises. The booming private enterprises have contributed significantly to the growth of Zhejiang. Zhejiang has also become increasingly integrated with the global economy. In 2004, Zhejiang's exports amounted to U.S. \$58.1 billion, ranked fourth in the nation out of 33 province-level divisions, and FDI (Foreign Direct Investment) was U.S. \$4.98 billion, with major investment coming from Hong Kong, the U.S., Taiwan, Japan, and the UK.

12.5. Regional Development in Wenzhou Municipality

Zhejiang is known in China for its development of private enterprises, originating from the Wenzhou model of development. Regional development in Zhejiang is characterized by the emergence of coastal Counties with a strong private sector, especially a southeast cluster centered on Wenzhou and Taizhou. To further understand the processes at work, we will examine the Zhejiang "miracle" via a bottom-up strategy of a detailed investigation of the development of Wenzhou County/Municipality.

Located in southeastern Zhejiang, Wenzhou was one of the national centers of commerce, handicraft production, and international trade, especially during the Southern Song Dynasty (AD 1138–1276). This dynasty is regarded as the most prosperous and refined period in Chinese history (at least until the present era) and famed for its painting, egg shell porcelain, and the invention of compasses, gunpowder, and the concept of the restaurant, among other significant developments. As a dominant coastal trading port, Wenzhou was known for craft production and light industry and traded extensively and directly with Southeast Asia and Japan, and indirectly with India and ports as far as Arabia and Africa. Under the alien Yuan (Mongol) and Qing (Manchurian) dynasties, it lost its luster and under the period of the Republic of China (1912–1949). Wenzhou was first sidelined since it was not a treaty port such as Shanghai and then it was beset by Japanese occupation (1938–1945). Under the Maoist government, it was treated as a backwater and risk. As a coastal city vulnerable to attack by the Nationalists and their American and British allies, it was considered strategically vulnerable and likely to be a source of infiltration of dangerous ideas and potential escape route for fleeing "unreliable elements".

On the other hand, the lack of dominating State enterprises provided Wenzhou with a more welcoming environment for the initiation of reforms and the development of private enterprises. A survey of 35 enterprises in Ruian in 2002 found that half of the private enterprises were established in the 1980s, when the State's preferred development strategy focused on SOEs and TVEs. By 1998, the share of SOE output in the industrial sector dropped to 3.87%. In 2001, light industry accounted for 63% of output, much higher than Zhejiang as a whole (56%) or Guangdong (53%). Major industrial products include footwear, clothing, auto parts, metal cigarette lighters (China is the largest consumer of cigarettes in the world), eyeglass frames, plastic products, such as toys, packaging materials, and printing.

The packaging and printing industries are mutually supportive and serve the needs of many of the small local factories. Many of Wenzhou's townships engage in specialized production. Thus there may be a town that only produces stuffed animals or dolls or toy cars perhaps for a single world famous brand. Known for "small commodities, large markets," the Wenzhou Model represents a successful trajectory of regional development centered on small scale, family-based and extended family-based, manufacturing-oriented private enterprises, with distribution networks linking producers and consumers all over the country and extending directly from nearby ports to global markets (Wei *et al.*, 2007).

The Wenzhou model has been conceptualized as development/urbanization from below (Nolan and Dong, 1989; Liu, 1992; Ma and Cui, 2002). While acknowledging the significance of development from below, we maintain the rise of Wenzhou is attributable to the synergy of multiple forces of globalization, proximity to other nation states, and local factors. The essence of the Wenzhou model is the geographically embedded "thick" local institutions and intertwined networks, which are historically rooted and geographically based. The local culture emphasizes pragmatism and financial achievements. This entrepreneurial spirit is well reflected by the Yongjia School of thought. Yongjia is the Soong Dynasty name for Wenzhou and the school of thought embodied by its name implies an unceasing drive to obtain wealth through travel, trade, and entrepreneurship.

People from Wenzhou have flocked to all over China and world to prosper and seek wealth through opening new small businesses. Zhong Pengrong, a prominent Chinese economist in Beijing is quoted by a March 12, 2007, *Los Angeles Times* newspaper article on Wenzhou's entrepreneurial spirit by staff writer Don Lee as stating:

> "Wherever there is business opportunity, there are Wenzhou people,… '(they are) a people of four thousand spirits' — they walk through a thousand rivers and mountains, speak a thousand words to promote their goods, dare to solve problems in a thousand ways and endure a thousand hardships".

Small enterprises have traditionally formed the backbone of the Wenzhou economy, rooted in entrepreneurship and rural markets throughout the municipality. Our survey found that half of the enterprises had output less than 2 million Yuan. Extended families typically form the main production units, relying on social networks for acquiring capital, raw materials, and information, as well as for production and marketing. Most investment comes from private sources (presumably much of it from expatriates with family and village connections), and our survey found that only 28.6% of enterprises listed bank loans as the major source of financing of enterprise development. Such place-based networks are intensely interwoven, with a foundation of mutual trust and culture rather than written contract, and maintained by mutual exchanges and more or less equal power relations.

Moreover, municipal and county governments in Wenzhou are locally embedded and are pro-business. They promote local businesses by protecting private enterprises and improving the business environment. The

Wenzhou government has been shaped not only by national policies, but more importantly, by local geographies and institutions. The underground economy was never totally eliminated during Mao's era, largely because local governments were often sympathetic to the tradition of local capitalism and handicraft manufacture and small trading. The local institutions of business creation and networks have created a strong presence of business owners in government and business people with strong and long-standing connections to a sympathetic locale cadre of apparatchiks and officials. In this region, businessmen (most business people are men) not only influence public policy but are often government officials themselves. Local governments have implemented a series of reform policies, typically one or many steps ahead of other places in China. They achieved this partially by creatively labeling private enterprise as *"Socialism with Chinese Characteristics"*. Among the milestones in this process was the designation of Wenzhou as an open coastal city in 1984, the establishment of the Wenzhou Reform Policy Experiment Zone in 1987, and implementation of the first local regulation promoting the development of private enterprises in China in 1987. In the 1990s, Wenzhou's government shifted its focus to the improvement of the business environment, emphasizing goals of improvement in product quality, education, and infrastructure. Since the mid-1990s, Wenzhou has been making efforts to support the scale and diversify the scope of enterprises by encouraging spatial agglomeration and networks and the development of conglomerates, and further improving the production efficiency and quality management in local firms.

Lastly, globalization also plays an important role in the development of Wenzhou. Historically, millions of Wenzhounese have migrated overseas to abandon the constrained life there and seek economic opportunities. This immigration was facilitated by the seaport and a local mindset of risk taking and wealth creation. The case of Jin, a Wenzhou native now doing business in Erinhot, Inner Mongolia exemplifies the *Yongjia* spirit:

> Jin was just 23 when he arrived in 1993 with little more than two large sacks stuffed with hairpins and trinkets to peddle to Chinese, Mongolian and Russian tourists. "My parents told us, 'Go out and explore," says the

brush-cut Jin, whose four brothers and sisters are scattered in Italy making and selling apparel. "The farther you can reach, the stronger you get." Jin is similar to hundreds of entrepreneurs from the southeastern Chinese city (of Wenzhou) 1,200 miles away that have flocked to Erinhot, Inner Mongolia, opening retail stores and developing hotels and apartments, even a $1-million nightclub featuring topless Mongolian dancers. (Lee, 2007).

Undaunted by treacherous terrain, harsh climate, unfriendly local people, and difficult immigration regulations, Wenzhou natives are spreading Chinese commerce not only in Mongolia but across the globe. They are mining molybdenum in North Korea, acquiring cow leather from African tribes (for shoes to be made in Wenzhou), selling plastic wash-tubs made in Wenzhou in market places throughout the globe, selling shoes (made in Wenzhou) in Iraq, Russia, and Ukraine, and exporting Arctic shrimp and turbot from Iceland back to China. Almost 2 million people from Wenzhou, (out of a metropolitan population of 7.5 million), have left their homes over the years in search of riches. The migration goes back at least a century but has accelerated in the last 30 years. Now the expatriate community is returning to invest and build local networks and they have connected Wenzhou to the global market place and provided capital, expertise, information, and equipment for Wenzhou's businesses. Wenzhounese associations are among the most active Chinese associations abroad, and local governments also actively nurture and promote global–local networks. Although Wenzhou companies have been more focused in the domestic market recently, they have increasingly imported modern equipment and promoted international trade. From 1998 to 2002, exports grew by an average 39% per year to reach U.S.$2.65 billion. Footwear and clothing, major sectors of Wenzhou's economy, are the main export items, accounting for over half of the total exports in 2002. By 2002, Wenzhou traded with 170 countries and all regions in China. Those networks connect Wenzhou to the global economy and provide capital and markets for Wenzhou's products. Wenzhou has become one of the leaders in institutional innovation and among the richest places in China. Although dominated by small sole proprietor enterprises and personal networks, a group of private firms have emerged as the largest private enterprises in

China. The operation of the largest firms has also become multiregional, often benefiting from the intense competition of local governments for external capital.

Although the booming Wenzhou has challenged traditional rich areas in the north and changed the traditional core (northeast)–periphery (southwest) structure, inequalities within Wenzhou have risen drastically. The coast–interior divide has been intensified because of the development of coastal Wenzhou, spearheaded by private enterprises, which has also contributed significantly to the rise of the coast–interior divide in Zhejiang.

Within Wenzhou, a new pattern of uneven regional development between the core and the periphery has emerged. Before reform, Wenzhou was already spatially more clustered than Zhejiang as measured by Moran's I[1] (Zhejiang: 0.17 versus Wenzhou: 0.27), reflecting the existence of the gap between Wenzhou City and the rest of the municipality. Such a spatial pattern reflected the general pattern of spatial inequality between the city and the countryside, as found in other provinces like Jiangsu (Wei and Fan, 2000). This pattern of spatial inequality has been changing. While Wenzhou City remains the place with the highest per capita GDP, Yueqing, and Ruian, two county-level cities, and the neighboring Wenzhou City have been catching up, due to the rapid growth of new private enterprises, while Wenzhou proper has a higher proportion of the slower growing established SOEs.

The rise of Yueqing and Ruian, both among the National Top 100 County level cities in terms of growth, is worthy of particular attention. Yueqing, with 1.16 million people, is a prototype of the Wenzhou model. Yueqing houses two of the largest private enterprises in China: CHINT and Delixi, both consumer electronics manufacturers. Yueqing is also the largest garment production base in south Zhejiang with 425 manufacturers, and 15

---

[1]Moran's I is a measure of spatial autocorrelation developed by Patrick A.P. Moran. Negative (positive) values indicate negative (positive) spatial autocorrelation. Values range from −1 (indicating perfect dispersion) to +1 (perfect correlation). A zero value indicate a random spatial pattern.

of which had annual sales over 100 million Yuan. In 2002, the output of casual wear and business suits reached 32 million pieces, yielding 11.08 billion Yuan in sales. The county has also developed auto and motorcycle parts manufacturers, supported by extensive external networks.

South of Wenzhou is Ruian, another coastal county-level city with 1.18 million people. Over 60,000 Ruian people live in more than 60 countries and regions in the world, and they connect Ruian to global markets. Ruian has five main industries: an electronics industry, an automobile and motorcycle parts industry, a knitting and shoe-making industry, a specialty chemical industry, and a plastic products industry.

However, the poorest counties in the province remain poor. Most of the towns and villages in mountainous Wencheng and Taishun still struggle to improve their economies. Their gaps with the richer counties have been rising, quantitatively leading to a sharp rise of coefficients of variation and divergent location quotients and qualitatively leading to stagnating aspirations, out-migration and growing dissatisfaction that may manifest itself in corruption and potentially in social unrest. Dongtou is another area of poverty, an "island" of relative backwardness isolated within the prosperous Wenzhou. Consequently, two "Wenzhous" have emerged: one coastal and rich, mainly Wenzhou, Ruian, and Yueqing, and another composed of interior, mountainous areas, which are poor and backward. There is no sign of decreasing inequality between these two groups, in fact the reverse as the rich get richer and the poor remain impoverished.

12.6. Conclusion

This book chapter has investigated the patterns of small business development in China. This focus has concentrated in three model areas of rapid development, one of whom the Wenzhou region has been driven primarily by privately owned small businesses fostered by local government, owned by local families with personal connections of a local diasporas of immigrants who serve as a nexus to the global economy and source of investment capital, trade outlets and expertise. Despite the success of the Wenzhou model in several coastal cities in Zhejiang Province economic inequalities have increased. Wei and Ye (2009) argues that both location and non-state enterprises play significant roles in the uneven regional development observed in Zhejiang. They notice that a broader spatial cluster across municipality borders has emerged. More counties, instead of central cities with more significant presence of state-owned enterprises, are surrounded by poor areas, indicating widening inequality among rural areas.

Small businesses face many challenges in the global economy or even in the fast-paced economy of other growing regions in the country. These challenges include lack of expertise in technology such as the Internet, poor local access to landline and/or cell phone communications limited credit card order processing infrastructure, larger competitors who many advantages such as easier access to investment capital and regulatory issues such as licensing and tax issues. However, in many societies, small businesses have been the incubators and originators of new ideas and the engines for job creation. For example, it was in a garage in Santa Clara county California that Hewlett-Packard originated, Microsoft, Oracle, and Nokia (which made rubber boots originally) all started out as small firms. The world's leading computer mapping firm ESRI is still a sole proprietorship still entirely owned by its founder, Jack Dangermond, from 1969 and headquarters in the small California town where his father raised orange trees. Conversely, the then technology giant Xerox essentially gave away the idea for the graphic user interface, its short-sighted salaried bureaucrats deeming it impractical in the early 1980s, and the originally small business, Apple Computer, developed it into the way most of mankind interacts with their computers, cell phones, and other electronic devices (Lecyurer, 2007). Small businesses are often owned by persons outside the nomenclatura, not by apparatchiks or oligarchs or wealthy land owners but by members of the proletariat, by women, and by racial and ethnic minorities. Therefore, it is important to foster the development of small businesses. The following section discusses a variety of methods used in a variety of nations that can be employed to help small businesses prosper. While these ideas do not themselves have a geographically limited applicability, their character varies from one region and one country to another. Thus micro-loans are an innovation that is associated with the Indian sub-continent, while small business loans are associated with North.

The development of private enterprises is the major reason for the rise and uneven development in Zhejiang as well as across China particularly between the coastal periphery and interior. During the reforms since 1978, the Wenzhou model, the Pearl River Delta model, and the Sunan model have been widely recognized as the three major models of regional development in China. Each has developed under different institutional environments and has diverse mechanisms, details, and local variations. Unlike the externally driven Pearl River Delta model and the TVE-centered Sunan model, Wenzhou, with a dense population and an isolated location due to mountains, yet with easy access via its ports to global markets, has led China in the development of private enterprises. The development of Wenzhou is closely related to the rise of private enterprises and the importance of entrepreneurs, and is facilitated by pro-business local government and global forces (particularly expatriates). We have found that private enterprise development is also uneven within Wenzhou Municipality. While Wenzhou City, and Yueqing and Ruian, have moved ahead with private enterprises, the rest of Wenzhou has fallen behind, leading to a rising coast–interior income and opportunity divide within the municipality. This divide mirrors the larger divide between haves and have-nots that is perhaps the biggest social and economic challenge in 21st century China.

References

Anderson, E. (2005). Openness and inequality in developing countries. *World Development* **33**: 1045–1063.

ATP (2009). Australian Technology Park Home page. Available at: http://www.atp.com.au/.

Bradshaw, M. J., and K. Vartapetov (2003). A new perspective on regional inequalities in Russia. *Eurasian Geography and Economics* **44**: 403–429.

CASMC (2009). Canadian Association for Small Minority Communities. Available at: http://www.camsc.ca/engine/web/news/read/2009/pr_20090331.html

CIC (2009). Citizenship and Immigration Canada. Available at: http://www.cic.gc.ca/EnGLIsh/immigrate/. business/index.asp

Chen, J., Zhang, C., Y. F. Yuan and Huang, L. H. (2007). Understanding the emerging C2C electronic market in China: An experience-seeking social marketplace. *Electronic Markets* 17(2): 86–100.

CVCA (2009). Canadian Venture Capital Association Impact Study. Available at: http://www. cvca.ca/files/Downloads/CVCA_VC_Impact_Study_Jan_2009_Final_English.pdf.

Daily Wealth. (2006). How the Patels conquered America. Available at: http://www. dailywealth.com/archive/2006/may/2006_may_22.asp

European Commission (2006). Entrepreneurship training for small business. Available at: http://ec.europa.eu/enterprise/policies/sme/files/support_measures/training_ education/doc/oslo_agenda_final_en.pdf

Fan, C. C. (1995). Of belts and ladders: State policy and uneven regional development in post-Mao China. *Annals of the Association of American Geographers* 85: 421–449.

Fan, C. C. (2006). China's eleventh five-year plan (2006–2010). *Eurasian Geography and Economics* 47: 708–723.

Forster, K. (1998). *Zhejiang in Reform*. Sydney: Wild Peony.

Gomes-Casseres, B. (2001). History of eBay. Available at: http://www.cs.brandeis.edu/~ magnus/ief248a/eBay/history.html.

Grameen. (2009). A short history of Grameen Bank. Available at: http://www.grameen- info.org/index.php?option=com_content&task=view&id=19&Itemid=114.

HARC (2009). Houston Advanced Research Center Homepage. Available at: http://www.harc.edu/df

Holz. C. (2006). Do official statistics exaggerate China's growth. *Review of Income and Wealth Series* 52(1).

Lecyurer, C. (2007). *Making Silicon Valley: Innovation and Growth of High Tech*. Cambridge, MA: MIT Press.

Lin, G. C. S. (1997). *Red Capitalism in South China*. Vancouver: UBC Press.

Liu, Y. L. (1992). Reform from below. *China Quarterly* 130: 293–316.

Lu, M., and E. Wang (2002). Forging ahead and falling behind: Changing regional inequalities in post-reform China. *Growth and Change* 33: 42–71.

Lu, L. C., and Y. H. D. Wei (2007). Domesticating globalization, new economic spaces, and regional polarization in Guangdong Province, China. *Tijdschrift voor Economische en Sociale Geografie* 98: 225–244.

Ma, L. J. C., and G. H. Cui (2002). Economic transition at the local level. *Eurasian Geography and Economics* 43: 79–103.

MBDA (Minority Business Development Administration) (2009). Available at: http://www.mbda.gov/

Nolan, P., and F. R. Dong (Eds.) (1989). *Market Forces in China*. London: Zed Books.

Petrakos, G. (2001). Patterns of regional inequality in transition economies. *European Planning Studies* 9: 359–383.

Parris, K (1993). Local initiative and national reform: The Wenzhou model of development. *The China Quarterly*, 134: 242–263.

SBA (2009). Small Business Administration Size Standards. Available at: http://www. sba.gov/idc/groups/public/documents/sba_homepage/size_standards_methodology.p

Shen, J. F. (2002). Urban and regional development in post-reform China. *Progress in Planning* 57: 91–140.

SSB (State Statistical Bureau) (2005). *Zhongguo Tongji Nianjian* (Statistical Yearbook of China). Beijing: China Statistics Press.

Sullivan, N. (2007). *You Can Hear Me Now: How Micro-loans and Cell Phones are Connecting the World's Poor to the Global Economy.* Jossey-Bass Books. San Francisco: Jossey-Bass.

Vietnamese Ministry of Foreign Affairs (2010). A review of Vietnam's economic transformation. Available at: http://www.mofa.gov.vn/en/tt_baochi/nr041126171753/ns050308085459#U1V1AMnQsPq2.

Vu, K. (2008). Economic reform and growth performance: China and Vietnam in comparison. Dissertation at National University of Singapore.

Wang, D. G., and L. Zhang (2003). Knowledge disparity and regional inequality in post-reform China. *Post-Communist Economies* **15**: 383–399.

Wei, Y. H. D. (2007). Regional development in China: Transitional institutions, embedded globalization, and hybrid economies. *Eurasian Geography and Economics* **48**: 16–36.

Wei, Y. H. D., and C. C. Fan (2000). Regional inequality in China: A case study of Jiangsu Province. *Professional Geographer* **52**: 455–469.

Wei, Y. H. D., W. M. Li and C. B. Wang (2007). Restructuring industrial districts, scaling up regional development: A study of the Wenzhou model, China. *Economic Geography* **83**: 421–444.

Wei, Y. H. D., and X. Y. Ye (2004). Regional inequality in China: A case study of Zhejiang Province. *Tijdschrift voor Economische en Sociale Geografie* **95**: 44–60.

Wei, Y. H. D., and X. Y. Ye (2009). Beyond convergence: Space, scale, and regional inequality in China. *Tijdschrift voor Economische en Sociale Geografie* **100**: 59–80.

Weng, Q. (1998). Local impacts of the post-Mao development strategy. *International Journal of Urban and Regional Research* **22**: pp. 425–442.

Ye, X. Y., and Y. H. D. Wei (2005). Geospatial analysis of regional development in China. *Eurasian Geography and Economics* **46**: 445–464.

Lee, K. (2007). Available at http://www.indonesiamatters.com/711/discrimination-against-chinese/.

Zhejiang Statistical Bureau (2005). *Zhejiang Tongji Nianjian* (Zhejiang Statistical Yearbook). Beijing: China Statistics Press.

Chapter 13

Linking Government Procurement to Long-term Government Performance: A Theoretical Instrument with Tentative Solution for China

Roger R. Stough* and Junbo Yu[†]
*George Mason University
†Jilin University

13.1. Introduction

The surface of Communist Party of China (CPC)'s new guideline for China's development strategy, namely, the Scientific Outlook of Development, is inevitably reshaping the structure of government performance assessment system in China. Though a local economy's growth record will still stand as the top principle when its governor's achievement is considered by superior authorities, boosting the prefecture's overall performance in additional terms such as innovation capability, environmental sustainability, and social harmony becomes indispensable.

With the expansion of the targets of governance, the restraint on Chinese government's revenue naturally crunches, even though the tax revenue for both the central government and local government increased dramatically in recent years. Moreover, taxpayers are requiring more from their tax-Yuans. Not only do tax payers expect that increased services will be provided, they also expect their money to be dispensed fairly, through open competition, and with disadvantaged business inclusion and the health, safety, and welfare of the public in mind. At all times, the

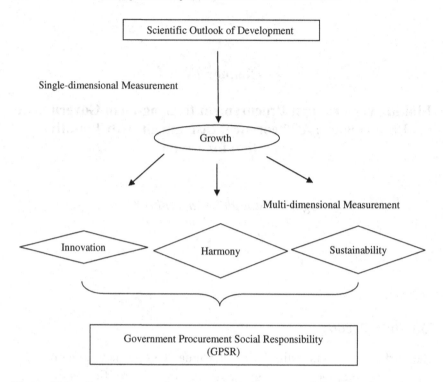

Figure 13.1. Government performance appraisal system and the role of government procurement in China.

tax-Yuan is to be ethically expended to maximize the efficiency and effectiveness of government for the benefit of society as a whole. At this point, the bottom-up consciousness of the right as a taxpayer among most Chinese citizens will increasingly strengthen the inspection on government's expenditure strategy in addition to the top-down pressure from the aforementioned multi-dimensioned government appraisal system (see Figure 13.1).

The promulgation of Government Procurement Law (GPL) on June 29, 2002, apparently demonstrated the determination of Chinese government to establish a comprehensive system of government procurement, which centers on "openness", "transparency", and "fair competition". However, the efforts of posing government procurement under the rule of law cannot replace the importance of a sound procurement policy, which not only serves to obtain those desirable items but also aims to optimize the effect of the purchase on the whole economy (Baumol, 1947). If such is the case, where can we identify the linkage between government procurement and the concerns of both the Scientific Outlook of Development and the vast taxpayers, so as to construct such a policy? And, accordingly, is there any practical model which can be adapted to the situation of China to put this policy into effective?

This research merely seeks to formulate a certain aspect of China's government procurement policy and its underlying theoretical rationale. Furthermore, a best practice in terms of the execution of similar policies is presented with a case study. Following a summarization of the merits of the best practice, a discussion on the feasibility of applying the previous practical model to China is conducted. An outline of the whole research is provided in the end as a conclusion.

13.2. Economic Development, Entrepreneurship, and Public Policy

"Creative destruction" is the term economists use to describe the ultimate engine of economic development in a market economy. According to the Austrian School, firms compete to create new technology, new products, and new uses for old products. The first successful innovator grows rapidly and takes customers away from rivals that failed to innovate, ultimately destroying those firms; hence, the term "creative destruction". Creative destruction was first proposed in 1911 by Joseph Schumpeter as an explanation for the rapid technological advances of the early 20th century. Theories of the "knowledge-based economy", "endogenous growth", and many other descriptions of the "new economy" are all variants of this idea (Ács *et al.*, 2001).

Echoing Schumpeter's observation that entrepreneurship is the fundamental momentum persistently enabling the process of creative destruction, a vast of recent empirics in industrialized and developing countries prove that structural economic changes are still mostly initiated and propelled by entrepreneurship development, which directly leads to intensified globalization and technical change (Audretsch and Sanders, 2007).

Not surprisingly, economic development in the "creative destruction" sense, which is characterized by continuous innovation and the rapidly upgrading of industrial structure, may find itself easily compatible with the essence of development strategy in China, a globalizing country on her expressway to industrialization and modernization: creativity, sustainability, and harmony. While China starts to approach to the frontier of economic development, the transformation of her single-dimensioned development measurement (GDP growth rate) to a cluster of composite indicators is actually a timely response to the nation's upgraded comparative advantage, restrained natural resources, and increased social tensions caused by income disparity as well as the lagged social security system. Historical experiences of the developed countries at the same stage accordingly suggest Chinese government to adopt an entrepreneurship-favoring policy as a solution.

Much confusion exists about the proper definition of entrepreneurship. Some observers use the term to refer to all small businesses; others, to all new business. In practice, however, many well-established businesses engage in highly successful entrepreneurship. The term, then, refers not to an enterprise's size or age but to a certain kind of activity. At the heart of that activity is innovation: what Peter Drucker defines as "the effort to create purposeful, focused change in an enterprise's economic or social potential." Since the focal issue of our discussion is the design and effect of public policy, which primarily relate to the overcome of market failure, in this chapter, we shed more light on the subset of small- and medium-sized enterprises (SMEs) that innovate and are therefore entrepreneurial in nature.

Innovative SMEs are critical to the improvement of innovative capability of any market economy. This is not only because most revolutionary new ideas have been, and are likely to continue to be, provided preponderantly by independent innovators from SMEs, but also due to the fact that radical innovation and adjustment, which can only happen in SMEs, are irreplaceable in terms of the formation of a healthy, competitive market structure for innovation (Baumol, 2002). Meanwhile, dramatic technical changes and industry restructuring driven by continuous innovation above will squeeze out those enterprises that keep relying on higher energy and environment costs and in turn improve the sustainability of the economy by attracting new entrants with resource-saving and environment-friendly technologies to attack those incumbents. Preferential policies for SMEs development can therefore enlarge the population of potential entrants of our economy. Furthermore, in accordance with the empirics of developed economies, where over two-thirds of the new jobs have been generated by firms employing fewer than 20 persons, over 70% of the new jobs in China have been created by private SMEs in China since the mid-1990s (Wang, 2004). Apparently, job creation tends to be a more active, sustainable solution for increasing social harmony in addition to those current policies related to second distribution.

In brief, the foregoing analysis with respect to the consistency between entrepreneurship, SMEs development, and three-principle measurement indicators of China's Scientific Outlook of Development, has provided a ground work to identify a proper joint for public policy and the given development strategy. Then, what is the current situation and potential challenges of exploiting on this joint in China's extant government procurement system?

13.3. Government Procurement: Preference or Fair Competition

Despite the fact that government agencies are the largest purchaser of goods and services in China (An and Liu, 2006), and the relative importance of government procurement to SMEs profitability, industry restructuring and market repositioning (Baumol, 1947; Rasheed, 2004), limited research has systematically examined the connections among government procurement, entrepreneurship and economic development strategy in China.

In most of the cases, government procurement officials issue requests for bids and/or proposals with product or service specifications that are unique to each contractual event, thus each contract event can be taken as a firm's entry or re-entry into a market, or at least, a repositioning within the industry's subgroup. In each procurement opportunity, decision-making is influenced by the existence of competitive barriers to new or repositioning entrants and the competitive advantages of incumbency. Therefore, rules and policies devised to regulate government procurement behavior will naturally affect the availability of entrepreneurial opportunity, particularly, in terms of the liability they conveyed to promote or suppress market entry. In short, the greater the magnitude of government procurement, the more significant influence it could have on the prevention or adoption of an innovation, assuming a certain combination of associated policies.

In addition, as we have noted in Section 13.2, government procurement is especially responsible for supporting SMEs development since they are facing more substantial financial and capital barriers due to the market failure. Consequently, government procurement policies and legislation have been established and continuously improved in developed countries to limit disparity and discrimination for the purpose of fostering entrepreneurship. For instance, legislations in the U.S. define some procurement areas as "small business set-asides", where procurements are solely applicable to small business, as a preferential policy; Apart from U.S., the Small Business Administration (SBA) specially devises an appeal procedure for those possibly infringed small businesses, which have been bypassed for a higher bid, namely, the Certificate of Competing (COC).

However, preferential policies for small business development in government procurement are increasingly controversial, which is usually ascribed to their violation on the fair competition principle. As a result, again taking U.S. as an example, small business development policy has experienced a typical S-shaped paradigmatic life cycle: from the proactive inception of the U.S. Department of Commerce and the SBA to the less favorable administrative, judicial and legislative rulings of the late 1990s.

Although the evident contribution of SMEs to macroeconomy has already been widely recognized by policy makers in China, and the Standing Committee of the National People's Congress promulgated a SMEs Promotion Law at the very same session that the GPL was adopted, it is curious that a provision granting preferential treatment to SMEs contained in the draft GPL did not find its way into the final law (Gebhardt and

Mueller, 2002). Furthermore, a substantial amount of SMEs would have been barred from government procurement due to the GPL's Article 24: the GPL only allows a group of suppliers to jointly engage in government procurement when each individual supplier separately meets the qualifications stipulated by the GPL. Therefore, SMEs that individually do not qualify as suppliers because they do not possess all the necessary equipment or expertise have no chance of compensating this by forming a consortium.

How does one explain the indifference to SMEs in the GPL of China? Subsequent analysis may interpret it more sensationally rather than an immediate complaint on the oversight of the policy makers: First, the concern on the principle of fair competition. Lessons from developed countries showed that too many preferential policies tend to undermine the competitive environment of the government procurement market, thus spoiling a certain group of SMEs. What is more, preferential policies may induce higher transaction cost, monitoring cost, and stronger rent-seeking liability, which in turn significantly reduce the social benefits yielded by the policies. Second, although government procurement was not part of China's obligations when she entered the World Trade Organization (WTO), China promised to begin negotiations for accession to the WTO Agreement of Government Procurement (GPA) as soon as possible. However, there have been growing suspicions and criticism on China's delay to fulfill this promise, which mostly can be attributed to market protectionism. A preferential statement for domestic SMEs in GPL will inevitably run counter to the principle of non-discrimination that is fundamental to GPA and deteriorate the international atmosphere for the right started reform of government procurement system. Last but not least, some recently promulgated government procurement rules of several local governments, i.e., Guangdong government, present that China's Ministry of Finance (MOF) is apparently encouraging its local divisions to issue experimental preferential policies for SMEs development so as to accumulate associated experiences.

In sum, a severe challenge confronting Chinese government is that on one hand, the prospect of using preferential policies to support SMEs through government procurement is obscure, particularly when China is short of associated practical experiences; on the other hand, domestic concern about the principle of fair competition and the international call for the government to shake up its rules that favor domestic goods and services will continuously reduce the space for preferential policies. In result, policy makers in China will soon start to pursuit a "moderate" way for sponsoring entrepreneurship development by government purchase.

In the mid-1980s, the Government Procurement Outreach Center (GPOC) appeared in the U.S. as a supplementary facility aiming at assisting firms in winning government purchasing contracts. Instead of distributing those reserved shares of government procurement to preferred small business, a GPOC is normally public funded to provide detailed information and personal instruction to companies, thereby increasing their chances of successfully selling their product or service to government agencies and to government prime contractors in the private sector. In this case, previous government payment to the set-aside product and service rendered by certain group of small businesses has been transformed to investment on qualifying those really competitive and ambitious companies, and their increased probability to get more contracts in the long run.

As a supplement to the existing economic and business development activities, more and more GPOCs later began to mesh with other economic development efforts at the local, state, and national levels in U.S. In Section 13.4, we will survey a best practice of such evolved centers with the expectation to construct a meaningful reference for China's government procurement policy.

13.4. Procurement Technical Assistance Program of Mason Enterprise Center

The statewide Procurement Technical Assistance Program (PTAP), located in Fairfax, Virginia, is an excellent example of how a GPOC can be successfully used in fostering entrepreneurship and propelling economic development. When the recent economic restructuring forced by the advent of the Knowledge Economy hit Northern Virginia, business and community leaders set out to find a way to update their industries and create new jobs. That is where PTAP has been surfaced as a part of the solution.

13.4.1. *History*

The Procurement Technical Assistance (PTA) Cooperative Agreement Program was established by the U.S. Congress in 1985 in the Department of Defense (DoD) Authorization Act. The program is supported by the DoD to assist state and local governments and other private non-profit entities in establishing or maintaining PTA activities in order to provide technical assistance and information to small businesses interested in selling their goods and services to the DoD. In 1991, the PTA program was extended to offer the same assistance to firms wishing to market not only DoD but any Federal agency.

The PTA centers are funded by the DoD Defense Logistics Agency (DLA) and also by local or state funding. The program runs on a nationwide basis with approximately 100 centers located in different states.

The PTAP at the Mason Enterprise Center (MEC), one of the nationwide PTA centers located in Fairfax, Virginia, has been successfully synthesized with other business development programs in the MEC so as to overcome a most critical challenge for every PTA center: the sustainable availability of personnel and knowledge to help small business efficiently. As is easy to be perceived, government agencies are not designed to execute business development/ assistance programs, hence their successful investment on associated programs normally depend on the existence of a qualified, non-profit agency, whose human resource and network has been accordingly specialized and developed to communicate with small business and instruct them on selected topics [CITE]. Administered by George Mason University's (GMU) School of Public Policy (SPP), MEC is a university-based economic development knowledge center focusing the energy, skills, and intellectual capital of GMU on entrepreneurship creation, business enterprise development, and economic expansion. Specializing in the areas of small business start-up and incubation, government contracting services, international business development, capitalization, training and consulting, entrepreneurship, and teleworking, the MEC offers a cluster of programs, services, and resources related to small business development and assistance from which the PTAP could benefit ever since its inception in 2001.

13.4.2. *Mission*

In a nutshell, PTAP's mission is to help businesses tap into the world's largest market for goods and services, the U.S. Government. Uncle Sam purchases about $316.4 billion in goods and services each year, with about 53% of that total awarded on a competitive basis. By assisting local businesses in preparing bids, the PTAP staff makes sure they get their fair share of the federal pie.

The first step of the PTAP's assistance in is client orientation. When a business owner or manager makes contact with the MEC and gets involved in the PTAP, he or she is scheduled for an orientation session where an overview of government contracting is given. Bid consultants also gather as much information as possible about what the client currently sells, and what the client is capable of producing, but may not currently be doing so.

Following this informational meeting, a market research project is undertaken. There are now over 2,800 buying entities in the federal government, and many of these purchase different items, and use different systems. Trained staff are appointed to investigate this huge federal market to pinpoint the most likely purchasers of the client's products or services, and what it takes to get on the proper Bidders Mailing Lists.

After a marketing plan is developed for the client, it is usually only a matter of time before he or she receives a bid solicitation packet. The bid consultants will walk the clients through the processes by explaining each step in completing the bid. In fact, the consultants will do just about everything except put the price on the bid, which is up to the business owner or manager's exclusive information about his firm.

13.4.3. *Services*

When clients request PTAP's services, they are asked to come to the PTAP's local representative/satellite office. At that time, they are introduced to the federal procurement process by attending a brief orientation program conducted by the staff. The Bid Consultant will arrange to visit the business facility in order to fully understand what the business does. After the orientation program, the client is asked to be as specific as possible about the services they desire. Parameters such as geographic limitations and extent of business capabilities are explored.

Once the capabilities and products or services are decided, the business is assigned a Standard Industrial Classification Code (S.I.C.) and Federal Supply Classification Code (F.S.C.). When the codes are assigned and a match is made with the business and the procurement activity, the bidder is issued the Bidders Mailing List Application SF 129 and attachments necessary for getting on the Bidders Mailing Lists. It is also at this stage that the client is shown how to use the *Commerce Business Daily and* how it is used on their behalf by the PTAP staff. In the PTAP office, a posting area for bid opportunities is maintained. All clients are supplied with the application to get on the Small Business Administration Procurement Automated Source System (PASS) list.

Once a business is introduced to the process of government procurement, the PTAP staff will assist them in reading, preparing, and submitting bids. The Bid Consultant provides any of the following information which may be required for a bid preparation or contract compliance:

(1) Specifications
(2) Regulations
(3) Past procurement history
(4) Copies of drawings from aperture cards
(5) Qualified vendor information
(6) Competition hit list (if requested), and
(7) Prime contracting information

In this stage of the procurement process, the Bid Consultant explains the federal system of stock numbering, item description, and nomenclature; how to use past procurement histories; and the difference between contracting and solicitation methods.

As long as the client has been awarded a contract, the Program will launch to assist in preparing for any inspections that may be required. For instance, the MEC quality assurance specialists may visit the business facility and show them how to conform to government requirements. Such specialists are also qualified to:

- Interpret quality clauses and specifications to ensure that the businesses meet the requirements.
- Assist in the set-up and maintenance of a calibration system that is acceptable to government standards.
- Interpret quality assurance specifications for a business to follow proper procedures for certifying employees
- Ensure that the business conforms to packaging requirements.
- Assist businesses with various report forms such as First Article Test Reports, Certificates of Conformance, and Material Inspection and Receiving Report.

After a business has completed the contract successfully, the PTAP is ready to assist them with the next bid. It is an ongoing process of notifying clients of solicitations and assisting them with any bids on which they need our help.

13.4.4. *Clients*

This past year PTAP served approximately 500 local clients who market both products and services. Clients include machine shops, construction firms, janitorial services, manufacturers, education and training firms, and software designing firms. If a product or service is purchased in the private sector, it is highly possible that someone in the federal government will also be purchasing it.

13.4.5. *Success*

Since its inception, the PTAP has established a very successful track record. It has assisted businesses in winning over $24 million in contracts, but more importantly, the Program has helped to create or retain over 2,400 jobs in Virginia. In fact, for every $1 spent on the PTAP, it has returned $6 to the region, and that is a return on investment any business could be proud of. The PTAP also serve as a recruitment tool to bring new industry to Virginia by assisting those new businesses in selling to government buyers.

13.5. PTAP-MEC Satellites

The most recent phase of development for the PTAP has been in the Satellite Program. Since the PTAP has been so successful, many other communities have called to ask for help in establishing their own centers, making PTAP-MEC a state authority on government contract procurement.

The Satellite Program was developed to assist other communities, on a fee basis, in setting up their own centers as branches of the PTAP. Local branches of PTAP will be established to fit the unique needs and economic characteristics of each member community. Each branch will be equipped to provide the same types and levels of services to local clients that the PTAP provides to businesses in Northern Virginia.

A sponsoring group in the interested community contacts the PTAP-MEC, expressing interest in the possibility of establishing a satellite unit. A PTAP representative meets with the sponsoring group at the headquarters, or in the interested community, to explore the feasibility of establishing a unit. Issues such as need, funding, staff requirements, and location are discussed at this time. At the end of this exploratory period, a decision is made to: (1) drop or postpone the idea or (2) move toward culmination of a contract. Following this procedure, the PTAP has been expanded to the whole Virginia state, with two additional regional branches located in Charlottesville and Hampton.

13.5.1. *Merits of the PTAP-MEC Practice*

Some intuitive merits of the PTAP-MEC practice include but are not limited to:

(1) A success in strengthening fair competition by assisting disadvantaged yet ambitious small business to enter the government procurement market. This model is also illuminating in terms of circumventing GPA's nondiscrimination requirements by efficiently improving domestic SMEs' competitiveness.

(2) Positive externality and knowledge spillover among PTAP and other business development programs operated by MEC. Besides PTAP, MEC also hosts Virginia's Small Business Development Center (SBDC), an international business development accelerator, a high-tech business incubator (Fairfax Innovation Center), and the Mentor-Protégé Program sponsored by DoD. Although these programs are not devised to substitute each other, they all share some fundamental characteristics of their customers, i.e., small size and the infancy of life cycle. Therefore, the management team in PTAP as well as its customers can easily benefit from those relevant knowledge, information and partnership all along floating inside MEC.

(3) In addition to the previous merit, customers of PTAP will constantly find that they are also eligible for services and products of other programs, or vice versa. For instance, a training course on government procurement policies of the federal government may become the common interest of customers involved in SBDC and Mentor-Protégé Program. In this situation, the economy of scale becomes exploitable. While the cost of such activities could be reduced due to the overlap of interest, public investment to associated programs can be saved for updated and broader services to small businesses.

13.5.2. *Assisting SMEs to Bid for Government Procurement in China*

The case study of PTAP-MEC provides at least two inspirations for the improvement of China's current government procurement policy. First, instead of running into a direct conflict with the principle of fair competition and the criticism on domestic protectionism, public-funded organizations function similarly as GPOC may become a "moderate" yet very efficient alternative to assist SMEs' competition on government contract. Therefore, in the long run, government procurement can foster competitive and capable entrepreneurship instead of encouraging SMEs' sluggish dependence on the government' rescue. Government procurement is ultimately able to contribute on the Scientific Outlook of Development via a healthy promotion of entrepreneurship.

Second, in a practical sense, government-supported business development agencies, which are widely existent in China, have formed a solid and promising platform to undertake the country's own GPOC program. Since 1987, operated by the Torch Program of the Ministry of Science and Technology (MoST), the central government of China has invested enormous amount of money to build up over 435 business incubators (Yu and Cheng, 2005). Originally, these purely state-owned business incubators were devised to improve China's innovation capability by accelerating the growth of high-tech SMEs with their Innovation Fund from the government budget and their widely stretched network among government agencies, research institutes, large enterprises, and financial institutions (see Figure 13.2). In addition, after the mid-1990s, business incubators funded by local governments, universities, and international investors first became legalized and then expanded quickly, while their customers consist of small businesses from mixed industries.

As is easy to tell, China's second largest business program among all the nations has established a groundwork with great potential and feasibility to exploit on the PTAP-MEC model. This idea is particularly applicable in an experimental sense in light of the financial and political bond between business incubators and the government, and the human resources, management skills and experiences accumulated inside those business incubators through 20 years or so of business development practice.

In accordance with the incremental reform logic of China, a marginal investment can enable the operation of limited GPOCs in selected

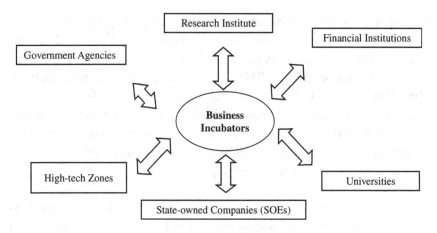

Figure 13.2.   Networks of business incubators in China.

best-practiced business incubators. For those high-tech oriented business incubators, government procurement assistance should start with instructions focusing on the requirements of government or principle contractors' technology procurement or subcontract activity. Critical lessons regarding two issues can be gained from preceding experiments: how to build the coordination and compensation mechanism between the MoF and the MoST; how to embed a GPOC in the business incubator so as to benefit it with the spillover effect, and positive externality of the incubator's entrepreneurial surroundings. As long as a successful, matured solution to these two questions above can be formed, GPOC can be applied economically through the extant business incubator system to wider territories in the spatial sense or in the industrial sense.

13.6. Conclusion

This research pursuits a practical solution for maximizing the utility of government procurement so as to fulfill Chin's recently surfaced Scientific Outlook of Development. After a literature review and theoretical analysis to relevant economic development theories and modern growth empirics, entrepreneurship is identified as a desirable joint between an ideal government purchase policy and the composite development indicators. However, the negative influences of imposing preferential policies to foster entrepreneurship, which were found in developed countries, the domestic and international concerns against policy discrimination all suggest Chinese government to proceed cautiously on the road of supporting SMEs with preferential policies. In contrast, business development activities that are sponsored by government investment to assist SMEs to become more aggressive and qualified competitors in government procurement market, appear to be more flexible and efficient. This assumption is further demonstrated and confirmed by a case study to the PTAP-MEC practice in the U.S. An additional feasibility analysis indicates that China's government procurement assistance program could be applicable assuming the proper exploitation on the nation's comparatively well developed business incubators.

References

Ács, Z. *et al.* (2001). Entrepreneurship, globlization and public policy. *Journal of International Development* **7**: 235–251.

An, B., and Z. Liu (2006). China annuls last government-planned procurement meeting. *Xinhua News*. Beijing: p. 16.

Audretsch, D., and M. Sanders (2007). Globlization and the rise of the entrepreneurial economy. *Jena Economic Research Papers* 1–45.

Baumol, W. (2002). *The Free-Market Innovation Machine: Analyzing the Growth Miracle of Capitalism*. Princeton: Princeton University Press.

Baumol, W. J. (1947). Notes on the theory of government procurement. *Economica* (February): 1–18.

Gebhardt, I., and M. Mueller (2002). China's new government procurement law: A major step towards establishing a comprehensive system? *China Law & Practice*. July: 1–5.

Rasheed, H. S. (2004). Capital access barriers to government procurement performance: Moderating effects of ethnictiy, gender and education. *Journal of Developmental Entrepreneurship* **9**(2): 109–128.

Wang, Y. (2004). Financing difficulties and structural characteristics of SMEs in China. *China and the World Economy* **12**(2): 34–49.

Yu, J. B., and S. M. Cheng (2005). *The Government's Role in Business Incubators Development*. In *The 2005 50th World Conference of the International Council of Small Business,* Washington D.C.

Index